Great Wine
Made Simple

Great Wine
Made Simple

Straight Talk from a Master Sommelier

Andrea Immer Robinson

Broadway Books

New York

BROADWAY

GREAT WINE MADE SIMPLE. Copyright © 2005 by Andrea Immer Robinson.
All rights reserved. No part of this book may be reproduced or transmitted in any form or by any means,
electronic or mechanical, including photocopying, recording, or by any information storage and
retrieval system, without written permission from the publisher.
For information, address Broadway Books, a division of Random House.

PRINTED IN THE UNITED STATES OF AMERICA

BROADWAY BOOKS and its logo, a letter B bisected on the diagonal, are trademarks of
Random House, Inc.

Visit our Web site at www.broadwaybooks.com
Visit the author's Web site at www.andreaimmer.com

First published in 2000

Library of Congress Cataloging-in-Publication Data

Robinson, Andrea Immer.
Great wine made simple : straight talk from a master sommelier /
Andrea Immer Robinson.—Rev. ed.
        p.   cm.
Includes index.
I. Wine and wine making. I. Title.

TP548.I46 2005
641.2'2—dc22
2005042068

ISBN 0-7679-0478-8

3 5 7 9 10 8 6 4

To the loves of my life, John, Lucas, and Jesse

ACKNOWLEDGMENTS

"It's a different world" is something we think and hear a lot these days. In the revised *Great Wine Made Simple*, we'll explore and taste what's different and new in the wine world. A lot has changed, and yet tradition powers on, keeping us connected to the land and to our history, which has been washed in wine since ancient times.

But it's a different world in other ways, too. Windows on the World, the place that did so much to shape American wine service and education and my own career, is now a memory both of beautiful times and of friends and family members lost and deeply missed every single day. To Tony Marden of Ladder 165 Brooklyn, thank you for finding and saving a keepsake photograph of my Windows times and for seeking me out to send it. I will never forget how thrilled you were to learn that the girl in the picture taken years ago at Windows on the World was not there on September 11. I think of the work and sacrifices of you and those in your firefighting family every day, with immense gratitude.

In my world there is a new family. It is amazing to live in a house with two of the most extraordinary men on earth. To my husband, John, thank you for love, passion, creativity, and integrity that I never dreamed possible in one man, plus something I never thought I'd have—a daughter. I get the joy of looking forward to a lifetime of aspiring to earn your gifts and of watching you teach and share them with our children. To Lucas, our pride and joy and the best big brother in the world, thank you for the privilege of being your mom. To our parents, Sharon and David McKinster and Mildred and Garner Robinson; and to the Niemeyers, Whittiers, Steinmetz-Firras, and Yeatses, thank you for being part of the birth of this new family. Here's to many years of toasting our milestones together.

To my dear friend Cindy Renzi, if I could offer just one sip of Champagne for each helping hand and creative idea of the last year alone, I'd do it—because you'd end up with a lifetime supply of your favorite wine. And you deserve every drop!

To the professionals and friends who've guided and inspired me so much over the years—Kevin Zraly, my Court of Master Sommeliers colleagues, Dorothy Hamilton and the French Culinary Institute team—thank you for your friendship and for modeling the very best of the hospitality profession.

Thanks to Steve Rubin, Jennifer Josephy, Rebecca Holland, and Umi Kenyon of Broadway Books; John MacDonald, Charles Segars, Susie Romano, Stephanie Eno-Bianco, and the Fine Living Network team; Gordon Elliott, Sandy Green, and the Follow Productions crew; and Greg Duppler and the Target team, for helping me pursue a dream to share with millions of people a simple approach to wine.

To Kimberly Johnson and John McJunkin, thanks for bringing the spirit of this book to the cover; and to Napa Valley's Truchard family, thank you for letting us use your gorgeous vineyard to show everyone who picks up this book where heaven on earth is.

And to the waiters, vinters, wine students, and just wine lovers who've shared your thoughts, questions, enthusiasm, and expertise as I've continued to explore this deeply historic, personal, and inspiring topic, thanks for helping to bring it to life for others in this revised edition. These pages are for you and because of you.

CONTENTS

Wine by the Glass

An Immersion Course

For anyone who has ever picked up a book to try to learn about wine, *Great Wine Made Simple* will be like nothing you've ever read before. That's because I don't teach wine "by the book." I teach wine the easy way: by showing how different styles taste and how to understand the label. In teaching countless consumers and restaurant waiters, I have found my method to be the fastest, most powerful way imaginable to overcome all the everyday wine-buying handicaps. You'll never again have to fear:

Pricey bottles that don't deliver

Snobby wine waiters

Foreign languages

Wine lists the size of *War and Peace*

Cryptic labels

Forget "Wine Knowledge"

Most wine books, even the most basic, try to teach the technical facts about wine—things like labeling laws, soil types, and industry jargon. Memorize these, the theory goes, and you will be able to buy and enjoy wine easily, applying your so-called wine knowledge at the wine shop, a restaurant, or in your own home.

For most people, reading and trying to memorize wine facts is boring and pointless. And after teaching hundreds of waiters and thousands of restaurant customers, I know that it almost never works. We all have high hopes when we buy these books, but as anyone who's ever read one of these titles knows, most of that academic stuff proves pretty useless when it comes to choosing a bottle in a store or restaurant. ("I think a wine made from Gamay grapes grown in granite soil and made by carbonic maceration would be perfect for tonight's dinner, don't you?")

Worse, the memorization approach is no fun. Who ever fell in love with wine by reading a textbook? I am convinced that scholarly books are the reason legions of open-minded readers, drowning in jargon but still helpless in wine stores and restaurants, fall out of love with wine.

Great Wine Made Simple is completely different. It had to be. As a sommelier, it is my job and my joy to share the shorthand, the tips, and the answers that make choosing wine convenient, not confusing. Although so-called wine experts might have you believe otherwise, the truth about wine is that you do not have to memorize the minutiae of grape growing and fermentation to buy and enjoy a bottle of wine, any more than you need to know the ingredients and techniques involved to savor a Caesar salad. I will spare you the agonizing initiation rites and let you in on the allure of wine right away, from an insider's point of view.

After reading *Great Wine Made Simple*, the biggest barrier between you and enjoying a good glass of wine will be the cork. In these pages I will show you how to:

- know what taste and style to expect from 90 percent of the quality wines sold in stores and restaurants, just by looking at the label or wine list entry;

- know how to ask for, and get, the kind of wine you want when shopping or dining out;

- branch out of your wine rut (there's a whole world beyond Chardonnay and Merlot) and confidently choose new styles to try;

- get pleasure and great value from wine every time you buy and drink it, whether you spend a little or a lot.

Who's Afraid of the Sommelier?

You know him. The middle-aged man with the superior sneer and the ash-tray-on-a-chain around his neck. As his telephone-book wine list hits your table, your spirits hit bottom, because you know that the only thing you can count on him for is attitude. No wonder most Americans' approach to wine in restaurants is "a glass of white Zinfandel, please."

The sommelier's function descends from the role of the traditional English butler, among whose duties was looking after m'lord's cellar, and somehow a snooty outlook became part of the job. These days, however, sommeliers no longer seek to inspire fear. A new breed of young American sommeliers, passionate about wine and dedicated to ensuring a relaxed, flavorful wine experience for every customer, has redefined the term by breaking with tradition and chucking the attitude baggage.

Still, the stereotype remains fixed in the minds of wary diners. More than a decade ago, when I became the first woman cellarmaster at Windows on the World in New York City, my first approach to a table would sometimes startle my guests. They would try to recover and say something polite like, "We expected you to be . . . *taller*." (They really meant *older*, and a man.) And of course, they also expected that any conversation with me—the "wine expert"—would be impossible, or excruciating, or both—you know, the wine-language barrier. (In reality, I use all sorts of technical terms like *delicious*.) They assumed that I only drank amazing wines with unpronounceable names and extraordinary prices. (I do *serve* a lot of these wines, but I *drink* the best deals I can get, just like you do.) And they feared that I would instantly pass judgment on their value as a person based upon what they chose to drink. (Actually, I just want you to have a wine you like at a price you're comfortable paying.)

The new generation of sommeliers has totally rewritten the restaurant wine-buying transaction in major ways. No more uppity sommelier means no more guests having to battle for their budget and their dignity. The diner can regard the sommelier with trust rather than trepidation. We emphasize value for the money rather than crazy markups. We push the envelope, with cutting-edge wines and extensive wine-by-the-glass programs, and our customers have responded. All of this is extremely liberating for the wine-buying diner, who should never have been made to feel shackled in the first place. Nowadays, Europeans readily acknowledge that for the best restaurant wine lists and the best wine service, America wins hands down. May the *tastevin* (that silver tasting-cup-on-a-chain) rest in peace.

Taste Your Way to Expertise

You're not alone if, when you look at a wine list, all you really see are lots and lots of prices. As we say in the restaurant business, most diners read the wine list from right to left, or price first. Don't feel self-conscious. In my experience, wine buyers of every budget focus on price and value. And it's not because they're cheap. People often choose wine by the price because it has a clear meaning while the rest of the label information may not. But price and quality are rarely proportional, meaning you cannot assume that a twenty-dollar bottle is twice as good as a ten-dollar one. The good thing about price tags is that they help you narrow the field.

And then there are the ratings. Often you will see wines rated on a one-hundred-point scale. But ratings from even the most talented and experienced critics can be problematic, for two key reasons. First, preferences are individual; the wine rating reflects the personal tastes of the critic, and you may not be on the same wavelength. Of course, a skilled critic's top-rated wine *is* likely to impress a high proportion of wine drinkers. And that becomes the second problem: Top scores regularly put wines out of reach of the very buyers they are supposed to serve. The demand and price shoot up for the super-scoring wines, and then you either can't find them or can't afford them.

Once you look beyond the ratings and choose your price range, you've got other questions: What will this wine taste like? Will it be good? All but the gamblers among us want this information before the bottle is bought. I'm going to teach you how to quickly and simply figure out everything you need to know about a bottle just by reading the label or menu listing.

We'll do it the easy way—by tasting. My method is literally wine by immersion, the way all wine professionals, even the authors of those academic wine books, began their education. Tasting is also what professionals return to, again and again, to master the juice (partly because it's the fastest way to learn and partly because we just like to do it). In fact, with the tastings in the first two chapters alone, here is what we will accomplish:

1. You will learn what the major wine styles are and which ones you like best.

2. You will learn the lingo needed to ask for them or to pick them out yourself in stores and restaurants, and to help make sense of those cryptic back-label descriptions.

3. You will learn—or remember—that wine is actually fun (this is the best part).

Tasting is the only way to learn. My restaurant guests tell me all the time that they know what wines they like when they taste them. The trick is in understanding the style, and knowing how to ask for it and get it again: I'd like a Chardonnay with lots of buttery, toasty oak and gobs of creamy, tropical fruit flavors. If you don't know what it means, you may feel silly offering that kind of description in a wine store or restaurant.

But those words really are in the glass, and my easy-to-follow tasting lessons will show you how to recognize and interpret them. All you need in order to answer the question, How do I know if this wine is for me? is a simple, intuitive taste and style vocabulary that gets you what you like in a wine. If the words *chocolaty* and *crunchy* mean something to you, so can words like *oaky* and *fruity*. All you need is a frame of reference.

Introducing the Wine Buyer's Toolbox

This is usually the point where my wine students say, quite miserably: But to me, wine just tastes like wine. And that's when I tell them to relax. This is *Andrea's* world of wine, where the list of wine lingo is short and sweet. In the first three chapters, we'll learn (through tasting) a short list of terms that I call the Wine Buyer's Toolbox. They are simple terms that you can immediately put into action when shopping or dining out.

These terms will enable you to make your buying decisions, *with just the label or wine list as your guide*. This is what makes my approach so powerful. Simply put: Every word in the Wine Buyer's Toolbox has an obvious link to the bottle label—either by the word itself, or by a simple label cue that tips you off to the style. In fact, the label is loaded with easy clues for the buyer, including things like *body*—light, medium, or full; *crispness* (acidity)—tangy, or soft and smooth; and *oaky*, or not. No more guessing whether you'll like a wine, because the package tells you not just the price and the color, but *everything* you need to know about the style of the wine inside. The toolbox also helps you get your point across when buying, because it focuses on the key words that will give you common ground with sommeliers, wine merchants, restaurant waiters, and most anyone else from whom you might buy wine.

THE WINE BUYER'S TOOLBOX

Don't worry if you don't know what any of these words mean, and by all means don't try to memorize this list. In Chapters 1, 2, and 3, we'll be doing the tastings that will stock your toolbox with the following terms. Once you know this basic terminology (and you will), you can confidently select and buy wines that you'll enjoy.

Body Styles	The Big Six Grapes	Flavor Words
Light-bodied	Riesling	Dry
Medium-bodied	Sauvignon Blanc	Crisp
Full-bodied	Chardonnay	Oaky
	Pinot Noir	Tannic
	Merlot/Cabernet Sauvignon	
	Syrah/Shiraz	

Further along, if you like, we can stock your toolbox with the more mysterious back-label terms, such as grassy, buttery, and floral. They're a little tough for most tasters, because their meaning is vague and varies from one person to the next, just the way "too salty" bacon or "hot and spicy" barbecue sauce is a matter of individual taste. But, whether your passion is pottery or baseball or wine, learning some of the specialized lingo is part of the pleasure. With our tasting lessons, you will also gain a frame of reference for the more exotic wine words, and chances are it will make your wine life a lot more enjoyable.

The Wine Buyer's Toolbox is a foundation—what you need in order to arrive at a comfort zone with labels and wine styles, and to buy wine confidently. But there is more to it than just buying with dignity and precision. This book is about the fun of wine, about enjoying all its scents and tastes and possibilities, without big bucks and boring book-learning. That is what I hope to share with you. It is my job, every day, and it is a labor of love, because wine is my passion.

My love affair with wine began in college, when I took my first wine-tasting class at a little Dallas restaurant called The Grape. At the conclusion of each session, I would go to the wine shop, buy the same wines we had tasted in class, then go back to campus and repeat the tasting with my dorm-mates. A whole new world had opened up for me. I had drunk wine before, of course, but it was absolutely a revelation to comparatively taste several wines side by side. That is what you will be doing, with the tasting lessons in this book, so let's prepare a bit. The process of tasting is one of the neatest parts of learning about wine, so read the next few pages with care. The steps may seem detailed at first, but after a while, they'll become second nature.

Learning to Taste

I know you know how to drink. I am going to teach you how to taste. It isn't just about what you experience on your tongue. Wine stirs *all* of your senses: seeing, smelling, touching, tasting—and even hearing—as you clink glasses for the toast. (It also stirs your sense of excitement!) Let's walk through the steps of tasting a glass of wine. You should follow each of these steps in the tastings we'll do.

Take a Look

Pick up the glass. Wine is beautiful, and shimmers with beautiful colors. It just wouldn't be the same in a Dixie cup. Tip the glass away from you and look at the wine against a white background, such as a napkin or a piece of paper. Color reveals two basic things:

Is the wine in good condition? White wines darken and turn brown as they age. Red wines lighten and turn brown as *they* age. Why? Cut an apple in half and expose the flesh to air. It turns brown. That is oxidation, and the same thing happens to wine. Most wines are made to be consumed young and fresh—within one to three years of the vintage, or year, on the label. A lot of brown in the wine is a tip-off that the wine may have prematurely oxidized, which usually occurs with poor storage or a faulty cork seal that allowed air into the bottle. An oxidized wine loses a lot of its fruit flavor, freshness, and scent. For young wines in good condition, here is the color range you are looking for:

White	Red
Pale yellow-green	Dark pinkish-red
Straw yellow	Ruby red
Yellow/gold	Inky, dark purple

Is the wine light, medium, or full? As a general rule, the darker the color, the fuller-bodied the wine. When you have a few different wines poured side by side for tasting and comparing, stand up and look down

PINK PINOT TO CRIMSON CABERNET

The Color Difference in Red Wines

The juice of red wine grapes is the same as that of white wine grapes—clear. Red wine gets its color when winemakers steep the grape skins with the juice. They call this part of winemaking maceration, "skin contact." The juice soaks up color pigment from the skins, coloring the wine red.

The amount of color pigment in the skin varies depending on the kind of grape. For example, Pinot Noir has thinner skins, with less color pigment, than Cabernet Sauvignon, and thus is usually lighter in color. Another reason for the color difference in some wines is the amount of time the grape skins soak with the juice—a short time gives just a little color, a long time gives lots of color. White Zinfandel, for example, has just a blush of color (short skin contact), while red Zinfandel can be very dark in color (long skin contact).

into the tops of the glasses. You will see the color differences of each style, typically getting deeper in the fuller-bodied wines.

Swirl the Wine Around in the Glass

Swirling is your ticket to the real taste of the wine, because the alcohol in the wine vaporizes when you swirl. Those airborne vapors carry the scents of the wine to your nose. And the nose lets you savor all of the wine's flavor. The tongue can perceive four different tastes: sweet, salty, sour, and bitter. But the nose is capable of isolating literally thousands of different scents. It's no contest. Although the nose is the winner, the tongue is still certainly vital to the tasting process. It senses temperature—think of the hot and cold thrill of a hot fudge sundae—and it perceives texture—gooey fudge, creamy ice cream. But it is the nose that lets us savor *flavors*—chocolate and vanilla. If you have a head cold, your sundae will be hot and cold, gooey and creamy, and sweet, but you won't taste the flavor of chocolate or vanilla. You don't have to wait until you have a cold to test this phenomenon. The next time you are digging into a sundae, pinch your nose closed and take a bite.

Taste is perceived on the tongue, but *flavor* comes from scent. Scents travel through your nose and the back of your throat to the olfactory bulb, the nerve center for smell. It shoots a message to the brain and the brain fires back: Chocolate! Big Mac! Garlic bread, and so on if the flavor is familiar. Or if you're trying something new, it might say, What is that?

So swirling isn't a trick to help you look cool at cocktail parties. You have to swirl to get the real scent and flavor of the wine. It takes practice at first, but it will become second nature before you know it.

Smell the Wine

Put your nose near the rim of the glass and take in the scent. Periodically swirl again so the alcohol vapors keep rising. What do you smell? If the words *white wine* and *red wine* come to mind, you're right on. You will identify more specific wine smells such as Chardonnay or Chianti after you have experienced them a few times by doing the tastings in this book. Any other scents that you notice are good to use as a reference point, but don't worry if you can't precisely identify them.

So much of the pleasure that we get from wine comes from just smelling it. The diversity of scents in different wines is utterly exciting to me. The anticipation builds, the mouth waters. You know the feeling—chocolate chip cookies are much more seductive when you can smell them baking before you eat one. So be sure you really take the time to breathe in the wine's aroma in your tasting.

You will quickly discover that scent triggers powerful responses. Over time, as you continue to sample different wines, you may find that certain wines evoke powerful memories, that a scent or taste can spark a recollection of something that may have nothing to do with wine. I have smelled wines that reminded me of my grandmother's rhubarb jam, the Tropical Blend tanning oil that my girlfriends and I wore during summers in high school, and the Sloppy Joe sandwiches my mother used to whip up for us kids when she and my dad were going out on a Saturday night (well, yes, that last wine *was* a little questionable).

Taste the Wine

Take a mouthful and hold it there for a moment or two. Professional tasters swish or swirl the wine around in our mouths quite a bit. Not particularly elegant, but it reveals a lot:

- Body and texture The richness and body of a full red wine, the bubbles of a sparkler, and so on are some of the things you can feel.

"WHAT ABOUT THE LEGS?"

I'm sure you've seen people swirl their wineglass, peer at it, and say "Good legs." Yes, wine has "legs," but they are neither good nor bad. They are the streams of wine that run down the sides of the glass after you swirl it (some people call them tears). Thick, slow-moving legs can indicate fuller body; fast-streaming legs suggest lighter body. But they are not a sign of quality, good or bad. So don't worry about "good legs" when you're tasting. That may apply to your date, but not your wine.

- Taste *Sweetness*, if any, is sensed mainly on the tip of the tongue; *bitterness*, a subtle element in certain wines (usually red), is mainly sensed at the back of the tongue; *acidity* is perceived mostly on the sides of the tongue. It feels a bit tingly, and makes your mouth water.

- Flavor The heat in your mouth helps send the wine's aromas to your smell center, letting you distinguish, for example, the style and flavors of the Riesling grape versus the Chardonnay grape.

- Balance This is your overall impression of the wine. Do all the components—body, texture, flavors, sweetness, bitterness, and acidity—seem in harmony? Do they seem pleasant? That's balance. It is the same way you evaluate a culinary creation—for example, is there the right amount of pepper in the steak au poivre? Enough butter, but not too much, in the mashed potatoes?

- Quality Did all your senses sit up and take notice? Does the wine's flavor linger pleasantly in your mouth? Do you like the wine? How much? Did you think "That's nice," or did your senses shout "Wow!"?

A Note on My Tasting Notes

In each of the tastings in this book I will be suggesting which wines to buy and giving you notes on tasting and comparing them. If you have read wine descriptions in other books or on bottle labels, my wine notes may not be what you expect—namely, they are fairly short and to the point. My strategy is not to use specific and subjective wine descriptors unless we have already defined and sampled those styles together in one of the tasting lessons. So you will notice that, as the chapters progress, I will add a little more detail to the wine notes. I like to work this way because I have found that, like anything else, it's best to absorb information in gradual doses—the "walk before you run" theory. And I want every wine note to be clear and helpful when you read it.

You Can Do It!

Feeling a little skeptical? Worried you don't have what it takes? Remember, the subject is wine, not rocket science. And it's *me* you're talking to. My method works for anybody. I have tested the principles on thousands of restaurant guests, from investment bankers to travel agents to high-tech gurus. And I have trained literally hundreds of chefs, waiters, bartenders, and sommeliers around the country, in everything from suburban family steakhouses serving no-name "house wine," to pinnacles of fine dining like Windows on the World in New York City. The light goes on every time.

CHAPTER ONE

The Big Six Wine Grapes

Where do you look to start learning about wine? The label. Given that it contains everything you need to know to confidently choose a bottle, I think it is some of the most important real estate in the entire wine world. In this chapter, I'll show you how to navigate it easily.

What you find on the label of most quality wine sold in this country is the name of the grape variety used to make it. Wines labeled with the grape are called "varietal wines." They are most common in the United States and in Southern Hemisphere wine countries (such as Australia and Chile). You have seen many of the popular ones—Chardonnay, Merlot, and so on—so it is a familiar place to begin our tasting lessons.

The "Power Elite" of the Wine World— The Big Six Wine Grapes

There are hundreds of wine grapes, but we're going to focus on just a handful of them, the white and red grape types that I call the Big Six. The white grapes are **Riesling** (REES-*ling*, not RISE-*ling*), **Sauvignon Blanc** (*Sow-veen-yone* BLAHNC), and **Chardonnay** (*Shahr-duh*-NAY). The reds are **Pinot Noir** (PEE-*no* NWAHR), the partner grapes **Merlot** (*Murr*-LOW or *Mare*-LOW, your choice) and **Cabernet Sauvignon** (*Cab-uhr*-NAY *Sow-veen*-YONE), and **Syrah** (aka Shiraz).

What's so big about the Big Six? They are the guts, literally, of about 80 percent of the quality wine sold in this country. Learn what these wines taste like in just one easy tasting lesson, and you will have mastered most of your wine world. The Big Six are everywhere, from Napa to Nuriootpa (an Australian wine region), because they can be grown successfully in almost every winemaking country in the world. They are good—*consistently* good. And often great. And they offer something for everyone in terms of style.

In short, these grapes are to wine drinkers what "please" and "thank you" are to a toddler's vocabulary. The sooner you get them down, the better off you will be for the rest of your wine-buying and -drinking life.

What If the Grape Name Is Not on the Label?

The Big Six have you covered there, too. One of the biggest things about the Big Six is that they really get around, turning up all over the world in some of the greatest, most famous nonvarietal wines. There are two main categories of these:

Regional wines These are named not for the grapes used to make them but for the region where the grapes are grown. These *regional,* or *appellation,* wines are most common in traditional European wine countries—France, Italy, and Spain. The idea is that regional factors like climate and soil are what make each wine's style distinctive. Once you taste them, it is easy to see the logic, which applies to other products as well: Dijon mustard (named for its hometown in France), the famously sweet Maui onions from Hawaii, and the famous cheese from the French region of Roquefort, to name a few.

Brand-name wines These are simply made-up names or trademarked names, and they range from the most basic of wines to the very top of the quality chain. Most people have heard of at least a few of them—Manischewitz, Mateus, Blue Nun, Opus One, and Sassicaia are some examples.

Now look at the most famous of these categories, the regional wines—Champagne, Bordeaux, Chablis, and Burgundy—and the top brand-name wines—Opus One and Sassicaia, for example. All are based on the Big Six. Once you know the grape identity behind the famous names, you'll have no problem deciding which to buy, because you will know the wine's style based on your Big Six tasting.

Screw-Cap "Chablis" and Jug "Burgundy"

These may sound like famous regional wines, but they're not. They are from the category of wines known as *generics*. Generic wines are usually jug or bulk wines packaged and sold under a classic European wine name, such as Rhine (from Germany) or Chablis and Burgundy (from France). Generics aren't made in the named region, but they do trade on the region's fame, making this category confusing for consumers. Many large American wineries use generic wine names. It's a sore point with European wineries, which are not allowed to use generic names in order to protect the quality image of the real wines from those famous European regions.

Tasting the Big Six

Tasting the Big Six grapes has two purposes. First, you get to know what the wines made from these important grapes taste like. When you taste the Big Six grapes side by side, you will see they are quite distinctive from one another, just as a pear tastes different from an apple. While it is true that a varietal wine will vary from one region and winery to the next—wine would be quite boring otherwise—the signature character of the varietal is still there, in the same way that chicken is recognizable whether it's the Kiev, chow mein, or barbecue version.

Second, you get to experience body, whether light, medium, or full. Body is the first, and most important, term in the Wine Buyer's Toolbox and it's interesting that this crucial wine-tasting term has nothing at all to do with taste. "Body" is a *textural* sensation, the feeling of weight, richness, and thickness in the mouth. As I tell the waiters I teach, this is one of the most important points about wine. In fact, I require new hires to understand body before their very first wine class on their very first day of training. And to help them grasp the concept, I use something my mentor Kevin Zraly taught me—milk. That's right, milk. You should do this comparison, too, because it is the perfect way to learn the meaning of body.

Skim milk—Watery, runny, feels kind of skimpy on your tongue and the taste goes away fast—is light-bodied.

Whole milk—thicker, richer, coats your mouth a bit, and the flavor lingers longer—is medium-bodied.

Heavy cream—dense, thick, really clings to the inside of your mouth, and the flavor hangs on—is full-bodied.

The difference in body is obvious both in the taste and to the eye—you can *see* how the texture thickens and the color deepens, and that the fuller-bodied liquid clings longer to the side of the glass.

I ask every consumer and waiter I teach to learn about wine and to talk about wine in terms of body, whether light, medium, or full. It's very easy to understand, because it's one of the few wine terms that has the same meaning to every taster. People quickly grasp differences in body, weight, and intensity in reference to wine, because they have experience in those differences. For example, they know that sole is *lighter* than salmon, although both are fish, silk is *lighter* than wool, and prime rib is *fuller* than chicken breast.

Also, I have found that body is a very comfortable realm for most people when it comes to talking about wine. Other descriptive terms are subjective and open to interpretation. I may think a certain Chardonnay tastes like an apple, but you may think it tastes like a pear, or just "white wine." If I describe a Cabernet Sauvignon as tasting like blackcurrants, I am likely to confuse 99 percent of my fellow tasters because so few Americans actually know what blackcurrants taste like.

How does body factor in to your Big Six tasting? Throughout the retail stores, hotels, and restaurants I consult to, and on my Web site's food-and-wine-pairing database, I work with thousands of different wines. But for me, this simple chart is the bottom line when it comes to teaching waiters and retailers. You will want to refer to it when you are tasting the Big Six:

Body Style	White	Red
LIGHT	Riesling	Pinot Noir
MEDIUM	Sauvignon Blanc	Merlot/Cabernet Sauvignon
FULL	Chardonnay	Syrah/Shiraz

That's all there is to it. It takes, at most, five minutes for me to teach a new waiter or bartender what he or she needs to know about wine in order to sell it: the Big Six grapes, their body style, and how to pronounce the names. As far as I'm concerned, that's enough wine knowledge to handle most wining and dining situations.

The Big Six

There are two options for doing this tasting.

Option 1 Taste all the Big Six grapes at once. This is great fun to do with a group of people—I demonstrate the entire tasting live with a group of wine lovers on my *Complete Wine Course* DVD. To simplify things, you will probably want to make it BYOB *and* G. In other words, give wine-buying assignments from my list of suggestions, and have your fellow tasters bring extra glasses, too.

I lean toward this option. It's enough to keep your attention span without being overwhelming. In fact, I do this exact tasting with waiters and consumers all the time. I usually do the test with beginners, but truthfully, the wine sophisticates love it just as much.

I estimate that on average I present this tasting to several thousand people every year, from beginners to experienced tasters. The reaction is always the same: *Now* I get it. Tasting the wines all together gives you the big picture—the whole spectrum of light, medium, and full body, and the flavors of the Big Six grapes—all at once. There is nothing like comparison to cement the differences in your mind.

Keep in mind: Opening six bottles of wine does not mean you have to finish them all. A tasting portion is about one to one and a half ounces, and six ounces of wine is about the amount you'd find in one glass in a restaurant. (See Chapter 10 for how to preserve wine leftovers.) If you do this tasting with a group, there probably won't be much to worry about.

Option 2 Taste the white grapes in the Big Six in one sitting, and do the reds another time. This will work fine, too. Either way, whenever possible, it is great to taste with someone else so you can share impressions and costs. Besides, wine is meant to be shared. It isn't sold in single-serving sizes except on airplanes (and don't even get me started on that subject).

Professional tasters use a spittoon, but any opaque cup will do. (I use a big plastic Yankee Stadium souvenir cup.) I do most of my professional tasting during the business day, so I really have to spit. Spitting doesn't mean you don't like the wine; it simply allows you to taste more wines, or to go back and forth comparing several. I always find that tasters who are new to the idea of spitting find it a bit awkward at first—it took me a while to get used to it, too. But I do not spit when I'm tasting or drinking for pleasure: so, as long as you're not driving, don't feel pressured to spit.

Tasting Set-Up: The Steps

Step 1. *Buy your wines.*

Choose one from each of the grape lists below. Decide on a price range, and stick with it for each wine choice so that you don't have major quality differences among the wines. This makes it easier to focus on the varietal styles. Chill the white wines in the refrigerator, or an ice-and-water–filled bin or bucket.

WHITES

GRAPE	RIESLING	SAUVIGNON BLANC	CHARDONNAY

PRICE RANGE: EVERYDAY	**CALIFORNIA**
	J. Lohr "Bay Mist"
	Kendall-Jackson Vintner's
	  Reserve
	Bonny Doon "Pacific Rim"
	Beringer Johannisberg
	  Riesling
	
	WASHINGTON
	Hogue Cellars
	Chateau Ste. Michelle
	  Johannisberg Riesling
	Columbia Winery
	Columbia Crest
	
	GERMANY
	Selbach "Fish Label"
	Lingenfelder "Bird Label"
	Louis Guntrum "Royal Blue"
	Blue Fish
		CALIFORNIA
		Dry Creek Fumé Blanc
		RH Phillips
		Sterling
		Morgan
		Simi
		
		WASHINGTON
		Columbia Crest
		Covey Run Fumé Blanc
		
		CHILE
		Casa Lapostolle
		Veramonte
		
		NEW ZEALAND
		Nobilo
		Brancott
		Villa Maria
		Kim Crawford
			CALIFORNIA
			St. Francis
			Gallo of Sonoma
			Estancia "Pinnacles"
			Kendall-Jackson Vintner's
			  Reserve
			RH Phillips
			Rodney Strong
			Clos du Bois
			Hess Select
			
			AUSTRALIA
			Lindemans Bin 65
			Rosemount Diamond Label
			Jacob's Creek
			Wolf Blass
			Penfolds Koonunga Hill
			
			CHILE
			Veramonte
			Casa Lapostolle

PRICE RANGE: MODERATE	**ALSACE, FRANCE** Trimbach Hugel Lucien Albrecht **GERMANY** Robert Weil Estate Burklin-Wolf Estate Selbach-Oster Estate Von Kesselstatt Kabinett Gunderloch Estate Strub Spatlese	**CALIFORNIA** St. Supéry Ferrari-Carano Fumé Blanc Frog's Leap Joseph Phelps Hanna Honig Robert Mondavi Fumé Blanc **LOIRE VALLEY, FRANCE** Sancerre, Jolivet Sancerre, Michel Redde Sancerre, Domaine Thomas Sancerre, Château de Sancerre Sancerre, Crochet	**CALIFORNIA** Beringer Napa Valley Robert Mondavi Napa Gallo Laguna Ranch Kunde Estate Acacia Calera Central Coast Chateau St. Jean Edna Valley Franciscan Cambria **AUSTRALIA** Devil's Lair Rosemount Show Reserve Coldstream Hills

WHITES		
RIESLING	**SAUVIGNON BLANC**	**CHARDONNAY**

ALSACE, FRANCE
Weinbach
Trimbach "Cuvee Frederic
  Emile"
Zind-Humbrecht
 	
AUSTRALIA
Grosset "Polish Hill"
Pike's
 	
GERMANY
Dr. Loosen Spätlese
Egon Muller-Kabinet
J.J. Prüm Spätlese
 	
AUSTRIA
Prager
Nigl
Pichler
	BORDEAUX, FRANCE
	Château Smith
	Haute Lafitte
	Pavillon
	Blanc de Château Margaux
	
	LOIRE VALLEY, FRANCE
	Pouilly-Fumé Pur Saug,
	  Dagueneau
	
	CALIFORNIA
	Robert Mondavi Reserve
	Selene
	Cakebread Cellars
	Matanzas Creek
	Duckhorn
	Rochioli
	
	NEW ZEALAND
	Seresin
	Cloudy Bay
	Brancott Reserve
	Goldwater "Dog Point"
		AUSTRALIA
		Leeuwin Estate
		Penfolds Yattarna
		
		CALIFORNIA
		Matanzas Creek
		Staglin Family
		Stonestreet
		Shafer Red Shoulder Ranch
		Chalone
		Talbott
		Robert Mondavi Reserve
		Beringer Private Reserve
		Chateau Montelena
		Far Niente
		Grgich Hills
		Trefethen Estate

GRAPE / *PRICE RANGE: SPLURGE*

REDS		
PINOT NOIR	**MERLOT/CABERNET SAUVIGNON**	**SYRAH/SHIRAZ**

CALIFORNIA
Beringer Founder's Estate
Clos du Bois
Kendall-Jackson Vintner's
  Reserve
Sebastiani
Pepperwood Grove
Meridian
Robert Mondavi Private
  Selection
Five Rivers Ranch
Echelon
Twin Fin
 	
OREGON
Willamette Valley Vineyards
Firesteed
	CALIFORNIA
	Meridian
	Two Tone Farm
	Gallo of Sonoma
	Wente Estate
	Fetzer Valley Oaks
	Louis Martini
	Canyon Road
	Estancia
	Ravenswood Vintner's Blend
	Sterling Vintner's Collection
	
	CHILE
	Los Vascos
	Casa Lapostolle
	Veramonte
	
	WASHINGTON
	Columbia Crest
	Covey Run
	Hedges
		AUSTRALIA
		Rosemount Diamond Label
		Château Tahbilk
		Jacob's Creek Reserve
		Wyndham
		Lindemans Reserve
		Buckeleys
		Wolf Blass
		Alice White
		The Little Penguin
		Yellow Tail
		
		CALIFORNIA
		Cline
		BV Coastal Estates
		Echelon
		
		WASHINGTON
		Columbia Crest Two Vines
		Hogue

GRAPE / *PRICE RANGE: EVERYDAY*

The Big Six Wine Grapes

GRAPE	PINOT NOIR	MERLOT/CABERNET SAUVIGNON	SYRAH/SHIRAZ

REDS

PRICE RANGE: MODERATE

PINOT NOIR	MERLOT/CABERNET SAUVIGNON	SYRAH/SHIRAZ
CALIFORNIA Buena Vista Carneros Calera Central Coast Estancia Pinnacles Truchard La Crema Cambria MacMurray Ranch Morgan Byron Dehlinger **OREGON** King Estate Sokol Blosser Benton-Lane WillaKenzie Ponzi	**CALIFORNIA** Markham Franciscan St. Francis Robert Mondavi Napa Sterling Napa Kunde Estate Clos du Val Joseph Phelps Napa Simi Chateau St. Jean J. Lohr Hilltop Beringer Knights Valley **CHILE** Casa Lapostolle Cuvée Alexandre Cocha y Toro Terrunyo **WASHINGTON** Chateau Ste. Michelle Columbia Winery	**AUSTRALIA** Brokenwood D'Arenberg The Footbolt Penfolds Kalimna Wynn's "Michael" Pike's **CALIFORNIA** Andrew Murray Truchard Jade Mountain Qupé Edmunds St. John Alban **WASHINGTON** Columbia Winery Chateau Ste. Michelle McCrea

PRICE RANGE: SPLURGE

PINOT NOIR	MERLOT/CABERNET SAUVIGNON	SYRAH/SHIRAZ
CALIFORNIA Domaine Carneros Etude Iron Horse Robert Mondavi Napa Marimar Torres Chalone Au Bon Climat Talley Williams-Selyem **OREGON** Domaine Drouhin Oregon Ken Wright Ponzi Reserve Panther Creek	**CALIFORNIA** Beringer Bancroft Ranch Arrowood Pride Mountain Frog's Leap Shafer Chalk Hill Robert Mondavi Reserve Grgich Hills Gallo Estate Beringer Private Reserve Mt. Veeder Far Niente Flora Springs Chateau Montelena Cakebread Cellars Merryvale Miner Family Staglin Family	**AUSTRALIA** Brokenwood Penfolds RWT Clarendon Hills Rosemount Balmoral Eileen Hardy Jasper Hill Henschke Jim Barry **CALIFORNIA** Lewis Jade Mountain "Paras" Frog's Leap **WASHINGTON** Betz Januik L'Ecole No. 41 Dunham Cellars Delille

Step 2: Set up your glasses.

Number the glasses from one to six (or one to three if you're using Option 2) with small pieces of paper or a napkin underneath. To keep track of which wine is which, I use placemats with numbered circles and put the glasses on the circles, then pour the wines accordingly (my printable placemats are available on my *Complete Wine Course* DVD). It is also handy to label each circle with the grape name (e.g., Riesling on circle #1) for quick reference.

Step 3: Open the wines and pour them in number order in the numbered glasses.

As previously mentioned, a good tasting portion is about one ounce. After you have sampled them all, you can always go back for more of your favorite.

Step 4: Taste the wines in number order.

The White Grapes

Glass #1, Riesling First, ditch your snobbery about Riesling. A lot of people hear Riesling and they think "sweet" and "no thanks." My theory is that as soon as people spot the traditional long, thin bottle, they have flashbacks to Liebfraumilch. But about the only thing great Riesling has in common with Liebfraumilch is its traditional home base—Germany. Other great Rieslings come from Alsace in France, New York, California, Australia, New Zealand, Oregon, Washington, and Austria.

Take a look. The color is pale yellow-green. Swirl and smell—take it in. Your mouth is watering now, because that is Riesling. Tasting it is just a confirmation of what you smell—this is mouthwatering, refreshing white wine. It is light-bodied but loaded with tangy, fruity flavor. Remember, it's *REES-ling* (although *RIES-ling* is a common mistake, so don't sweat it). If you're pronouncing it correctly, you have to smile when you say it. And in case you couldn't tell, I love Riesling.

Any of the wines I have recommended will give you a great Riesling experience, yet they are all a little different from one another. You wouldn't expect the tomato sauces of eight different chefs to taste identical. In the same way, the various growing regions and winemakers put their own "stamp" on the wine, but you still get excellent Riesling character. Here, in a nutshell, is how they differ:

Germany: the lightest-bodied of all

Austria and Alsace, France: the tangiest flavor

California and Washington: the strongest flavor

Glass #2, Sauvignon Blanc Sauvignon Blanc is one of my favorite everyday wines. Great ones are still available for under ten dollars, which is something you can't say about too many wine styles. It is delicious and versatile enough to go with many of the foods people eat regularly—vegetarian, Mexican, salads, sushi, and the like. The general style of Sauvignon Blanc is medium-bodied.

Pick up the glass and take a look—straw yellow, often a little darker than the Riesling. Swirl and smell. It packs a powerful punch. This is one distinctive grape. Go back and smell the Riesling again, and note the contrast. It is unmistakable. Now taste, and you will see it's fuller-bodied than the Riesling, and feels a bit heavier and richer in your mouth. And that distinctive flavor. Bookmark it in your brain, because that exotically pungent taste is Sauvignon Blanc.

After sampling the Sauvignon Blanc grape, my students often say, "It's drier." Let's don't go there—yet. "Dry" is one of the more dicey tasting terms, because tasters interpret it in several different ways, and that leads to confusion. For now, just focus on the flavor and style characteristics of Sauvignon Blanc and let yourself identify just that. If you were tasting a lime or an apple, you wouldn't say "dry," you'd say "lime-y" or "apple-y."

I have recommended Sauvignon Blancs from many different places—California, Washington State, France (the Loire Valley and Bordeaux), Chile, and New Zealand. If you decide you like this grape and wish to explore it, make a plan to try a range of the recommended wines over time. I think you will be delighted at the quality and enjoyment you get for the price.

Glass #3, Chardonnay This darling of wine drinkers reigns as Most Popular, hands down. And you'll see why when you taste it, but first pick up the glass and take a look. The color is yellow-gold, the darkest yet. Now swirl and smell. Did somebody turn up the volume? Absolutely. From the scent alone, you can probably sense that this wine is more full-bodied than the Sauvignon Blanc. Quite different, though, and perhaps quite familiar to you. Chardonnay is the top-selling white varietal wine in this country. Take a taste and feel the difference in body. It is the richest and heaviest white grape of the Big Six, and a high percentage of white wine drinkers prefer this full-bodied style.

The Red Grapes

Glass #4, Pinot Noir Pinot Noir is my favorite red grape. The reason is very simple: It has red wine flavor with white wine texture. It's soft and not heavy. In fact, to me, the texture is one of the greatest virtues of Pinot Noir (also called Pinot for short). It feels like silk in your mouth, and it's the lightest-bodied of the red grapes in the Big Six.

You can see this just by looking. Pick up the glass and tilt it against a white place-mat or napkin—you can see through it, can't you? It is obviously lighter-colored, and more translucent, than the other reds you've poured. That is a natural characteristic of the Pinot Noir grape—less color pigment than Merlot, Cabernet Sauvignon, and Syrah. The fragrance and flavor are subtle but seductive, luring you back to the glass.

Glass #5, Merlot or Cabernet Sauvignon Although everyone's talking Shiraz these days, Merlot and Cabernet Sauvignon remain the top-selling red varietal wines by far. I believe that is because both grapes grow well all over the world and in the hands of a skilled winemaker give excellent quality and consistency at every price level, from budget to splurge.

Pick up the glass and take a look. It's quite dark, almost inky—that is typical of Cabernet and Merlot, dark and medium- to full-bodied. Swirl the glass and smell it. The scent confirms what you expected. It is stronger and more intense than Pinot Noir. It also smells delicious. Cabernet Sauvignon's scent and flavor profile, in particular, are truly the paradigm for most of the world's top-quality red wines. That's probably why so many varietal Merlots are made to have a taste and texture similar to Cabernet.

Taste the wine. It really seizes your senses of smell, taste, and touch. You feel the almost velvety texture and the intensity of this wine in your mouth. And that intensity lingers in the aftertaste, which some tasters love. For others, it is overpowering—more intensity than they care for. It is totally a matter of personal taste.

Glass #6, Syrah/Shiraz Although Syrah (the French) is the classic, majestic rendition, it was the one-of-a-kind Aussie version, usually labeled *Shiraz*, that made this grape the major wine market phenomenon of the last decade, earning it a rightful spot in the Big Six (thanks to my husband, John, for pointing this out). The easy-to-remember grape name on the label, easy prices, and vibrant flavor clinched one of the best deals in wine, and now Shiraz is on a growth streak in every major wine-drinking country.

Depending on the vineyard source and winery style, Syrah/Shiraz occasionally weighs in lighter than Merlot and Cabernet. As a rule, though, it is full-bodied and quite dark and purple when young. Look at the legs: even they are stained with color. The scent and flavor are big and saturated, too: **red wine!**

You have met the power elite of the wine world, the Big Six wine grapes, and I'd be willing to bet you found their quality and style differences impressive. You may have liked every one of them, or perhaps one stood head and shoulders above the rest. Whatever your feelings now, you'll also find that the opinions you've developed about these grapes up to now will change over time. This is as normal as it is for your food preferences to evolve over time. When I was a kid, I hated mushrooms and olives; now I couldn't live without them.

Aside from knowing your favorites, the greatest thing about knowing the Big Six is that when you shop for wine or look at a wine list, you now know their body styles as well as the main flavor differences. *That* is buying power.

Practice, Practice!

Feel free to repeat the Big Six tasting as often as you like. It's a lot of fun, and you'll always learn something new. I do this tasting for my waiters several times a year, and even the most wine-savvy among them always come back for a brush-up. Every professional knows that the best way to learn a lot about wine is also the most pleasant: Taste everything you can get your hands on.

CHAPTER TWO

"What Does It Taste Like?"

Putting Flavors into Words

For many people, wine lingo might as well be a foreign language. Confusion with the language on French and Italian wine labels is understandable, but my wine students tell me they often have just as much trouble with a lot of the wine words in English. You have amassed a lifetime of experience tasting and describing foods, so saying "It's cheesy" or "It's hot and spicy" mean something. But most of us didn't grow up in a wine-drinking household, so we're not used to saying "It's oaky" or "It's tannic," and a little catch-up is in order.

Stocking the Wine Buyer's Toolbox: The Power Tools of Wine

I have a quick solution to the label problem, and you have probably already guessed it—a corkscrew. We have tasted and learned about the body styles of wine—light, medium, and full. With the tasting lessons in this chapter, I will show you how to get a grip on the other really useful wine words in the Wine Buyer's Toolbox. These big wine adjectives, used over and over again regardless of which region the wine comes from, or the grape used to make it, are **dry**, **crisp**, **oaky**, and **tannic**. We will explore each through tasting, but here is a short introduction.

Dry

In the everyday world of wine drinkers, "dry" is truly misunderstood, and it's a wine word that I find very frustrating. I still have vivid flashbacks to those nights working the floor at Windows on the World selling wine. I'd be cruising through the dining room, pulling corks, making recommendations, pointing out the Brooklyn Bridge from our quarter-mile-high perch, and then it would happen. An eager guest pondering the possibilities among Chardonnays, Merlots, Cabernets, Chiantis, and all the rest would ask, "Which one is the driest?" The customer would look up at me from the wine list innocently, expectantly, an unwitting conspirator in that dastardly mind game Stump the Sommelier. And I would have to answer, "They are *all* dry."

Since the word is going to come up again and again as we explore the world of wine, it's best to define it and include it in the Wine Buyer's Toolbox. I have to admit at this point that we in the beverage industry have only ourselves to blame for all this confusion, having used "dry" every which way, none of which make sense since we're talking about liquids. Just look at the possibilities. For each of the words below, the meaning of "dry" is completely different:

> Dry wine: completely without sweetness (but not without fruitiness—we'll explore this below)

> Dry beer: slightly higher alcohol and "smoother," according to beer marketers

> Dry Champagne ("sec" in French): slightly sweet Champagne

You can see why the word *dry* frustrates me. I thought about banishing the "d" word, but I recognize that it is deeply entrenched in the vocabulary of the wine world. Everyone, from amateur to professional, tosses the word around. So the only solution is to define it.

"DRY" VS. "SWEET" "Dry" in wine terms means without residual (leftover) sugar. Winemakers refer to sugar in wine (which makes it taste sweet) as "residual sugar" because, in the winemaking process, fermentation usually turns all the sugar in ripe grapes into alcohol. Thus most of the big-selling wine styles are, technically, dry. Wines *with* residual sugar are usually made that way deliberately, to achieve a specific style. Some popular sweet wines include:

Slightly sweet style (off-dry): white Zinfandel or German Riesling Kabinett

Medium-sweet style: Italian Moscato d'Asti or German Spätlese and Auslese

Very sweet style: dessert wines like Port or Sauternes

Unless you are looking in the dessert wine section of a wine list or wine shop, most of the wines that you see for sale in stores and restaurants are dry. That includes the popular varietal (named for the grape) wines that we have been tasting and talking about, as well as the best-selling European wines with regional names such as French Bordeaux and Burgundy, Italian Chianti, and so on.

Lack of residual sugar is the winemaker's definition of dry, but it also applies to the taster. From the taster's point of view, dry is simply the opposite of sweet. For your tongue to taste sweetness in a wine, sugar must be present. In a dry wine, there is no perceptible sugar, and thus no sweetness. The easiest way to see this is by comparing the first two wines we'll be trying in the tasting at the end of the chapter—a dry wine and its opposite, a sweet wine.

How sweet the wine is depends on two things:

1. **How ripe the grapes are at harvest.** *Normally ripe* grapes usually make a dry wine, because all the sugar in the grapes converts to alcohol during fermentation.

Overripe grapes have been left on the vine longer than normal before harvesting (you may see "late harvest" on the label—turn to page 29 for an example) to gain more sugar. These extra-sugary grapes can make a slightly sweet to very sweet wine, since not all the sugar converts to alcohol during fermentation. Some of it gets left over in the wine as residual sugar, which tastes sweet.

Raisined (dried) grapes make the sweetest wines of all, because nearly all the water in the grapes evaporates, leaving almost pure sugar (think how much sweeter a raisin tastes versus a table grape). Sometimes this is accomplished by laying the grapes out on mats or hanging them up to dry,

FEELING FRUITY

In the last half-dozen years or so, a new word has crept into the self-doubt–ridden wine buyers' lexicon: *fruity*. And as I have discovered working in restaurants, fruity means different things to different people. "Fruity" is often a cover for "sweet," used by those who are too self-conscious to be comfortable asking for wine styles with a little sweetness.

But "fruity" can also mean "ripe-tasting," "soft," or "approachable." Over the last decade, Americans have developed a renewed interest in wine-drinking and in discovering new wine regions and styles. But since the typical time-starved millennium wine drinker can't be bothered with cellaring wine or studying it, their taste is for here-and-now, easy-drinking, accessible wine styles. "Fruity" has become a catch-all term for these. But all quality wines have the taste of fruit. If not, what's the point? You might as well drink soda or beer. Since wine is made from grapes, the fruit character of those grapes is certainly something every skilled winemaker hopes to showcase in the finished product. What throws people off is how much this fruit character can vary from wine to wine, although I am not sure why this seems so strange. Different wine grapes, like other fruits, offer a range of flavors. I tell my waiters and customers to think of the fruit flavors as a spectrum, ranging from lean to luscious. Once you think about the actual flavors of different fruits, it is easy to arrange them across this spectrum. For now, let's look at familiar fruits:

LEAN	>	>	>	>	>	>	LUSCIOUS
Lemon	Grapefruit	Apple	Pear	Orange	Peach	Pineapple	Mango
Cranberry	Cherry	Raspberry	Plum	Blueberry		Blackberry	Fig

The flavors of different wine grapes and styles can also be arranged across this lean-to-luscious fruit spectrum. I will show you how to do this in Chapter 4, and also how to predict the fruit character of a wine from its label, even when you do not know which grape was used to make it. For now, just keep in mind that you cannot predict exactly what you will get when requesting a "fruity" wine, because the definition varies from person to person. That is why "fruity" is not a part of the Wine Buyer's Toolbox.

and sometimes by leaving them on the vine and letting nature take its course. In some parts of Germany, Hungary, Austria, and in France's Sauternes region a mold called botrytis (bo-TRY-tiss) attacks the grapes and shrivels them rapidly into raisins (it happens in other regions, too, but these are the most famous). The grapes don't look pretty, but the resulting wine is as decadent as nectar.

The French name for botrytis is *pourriture noble*, which means "noble rot." Anyone who has tasted a great Sauternes, or one of the great mold-flecked cheeses like Roquefort, would have to agree with the name. As the famous wine expert Hugh Johnson has said, leave it to the French to find nobility in mold! (They got it right.)

2. What the winemaker does during fermentation. The winemaker can control the amount of sugar and sweetness in a wine by stopping fermentation, either by lowering the temperature or adding alcohol. In the first case, the wine yeasts can't ferment at very low temperatures, so some sugar remains. This method is often used in making wines with light to medium sweetness, like white Zinfandel or Asti Spumante from Italy. Adding alcohol (usually to above 15 percent by volume) kills the yeast, thus stopping the fermentation. In wines made with very ripe grapes, the high alcohol is natural, and occurs without additions. In the case of fortified wines, a famous category including Port and Madeira, the winemaker adds alcohol to stop the fermentation. ("Fortify" means to make stronger—you've seen "fortified with eight essential vitamins and minerals," for example.) The additional alcohol stops the fermentation, leaving residual sugar, and sweetness, in the wine.

In my experience with waiters and consumers, even among the very wine-savvy, the idea that most quality wines are dry is a radical one. This is understandable, considering that chances are your first taste of wine was sweet, at least a little. For Baby Boomers, who currently comprise the biggest wine-buying segment of the population, their "starter" wines were the popular branded wines of the 1960s and 1970s—Blue Nun, Mateus, Riunite, and so on, which were all slightly sweet. Nowadays, white Zinfandel, with its slightly sweet style (although it is currently more fashionable to say "off-dry"), is very popular and one of the first wines many people sample. With these wines as your frame of reference, Is it dry? is a natural question when you are about to taste something new.

Another culprit in the confusion with "dry" is wine snobbery. Many so-called wine experts look on the popular categories of wine, such as white Zinfandel, with disdain, in part *because* of their sweetness. As if wine buyers weren't already self-conscious enough! Now we have the wine world equivalent of "real men don't eat quiche": Real wine drinkers don't drink sweet wines. That means for many buyers, "dry" says "I'm sophisticated about wine" whether they like the style or not. I hear it all the time from restaurant guests: "We only like dry wines. Can we have a bottle of the white Zinfandel, please?" That is serious wine schizophrenia, and the snobs are to blame.

Still, "dry" is a necessary descriptor for nonsweet wines. As your tasting experience builds, you will expand your vocabulary and your comfort zone using this and other wine words will broaden.

Crisp

The French often translate this wine adjective as "crispy." To Americans, it suggests "crunchy," which sounds like something that doesn't belong in a

THE PALATE

In wine terms, this is just a fancy word for "sense of taste," but with the emphasis on sense, not taste. Remember what you discovered in Chapter 1 about tasting—the tongue and its tastes (sweet, salt, sour, bitter) are team players in a bigger sensory effort. As you now know, "tasting" a mouthful of wine is really sensing it through smell and taste, plus sight and touch.

wineglass. But crisp is the most popular English word to describe the tingle, tang, tartness, zing, and liveliness of acidity in wine. And it is a very good thing when it is in balance with the wine's other components. This tasting will teach your palate what that means. You will find "crisp" to be quite useful, because many back-label descriptions on wine bottles use this word. And in Chapter 4, I will show you how to tell which wines will have especially crisp, vibrant acidity even when the back label doesn't specifically mention it.

Like any other fruit, wine grapes, and the wines made from them, count acidity as one of their natural components. The degree to which the acidity can be tasted in the wine depends mainly on two things:

1. The grape. Different grape types have different levels of acidity, just as other fruits do (a lemon versus a peach, for example). The general rule of thumb is that white grapes and white wines tend to have higher acidity than red grapes and red wines. And usually, the Riesling and Sauvignon Blanc grapes have higher acidity than the Chardonnay grape.

2. The wine's region of origin (where the grapes are grown). If the wine's region of origin is cool (farther from the equator), then the wine is likely to have more prominent acidity. This is because as grapes ripen in the sunshine and heat, their sugar level rises and their acidity level goes down. Think of a not-yet-ripe green tomato (sour) versus a vine-ripe, red tomato (juicy and sweet). In cooler growing areas, the acidity in the grapes remains higher. Whatever the acidity level of the grapes, low or high, it will be reflected in the wine (more on this in Chapter 4).

And what is the taste difference between low and high acidity in wines? The simple, intuitive answer is that more acidity tastes tangier or, in

I AM AN ACID FREAK

I love the crisp, tangy, vibrant, mouthwatering quality of acidity in wines. Wine is beautiful. It smells great, tastes great, feels great. But if I have to choose the best of its virtues, for me it would be the acidity, hands down. That's because in addition to loving wine, I love to eat, and the acidity in wine is what makes it taste so great with food.

wine lingo, crisper. Even though acidity is a taste perceived by the tongue, in many wines you will also notice a texture difference, and a different feeling in your mouth, between low-acid wines and high-acid, "crisp" wines (the wine word we are talking about, crisp, actually implies texture). Here is my description of the difference, which you'll want to refer to as you do the tasting below. You'll see that the contrast between high and low acidity is very distinct.

Low acidity: soft, plump, and smooth-feeling in the mouth

High acidity or "crisp": like an electrical charge going through your mouth—tangy, tingly, mouthwatering.

High acidity is similar to the pucker you get from a squeeze of lemon, but less tart than citrus fruit because the wine's other components add balance to this taste.

Oaky

Up until a few years ago, I did not teach about the term *oaky*, because I thought students would find it too obscure and confusing. But now I make sure to, for two reasons. First, oakiness is everywhere, and it is a prominent taste feature of many of the most popular wines on the market. Second, many oak-aged wines are labeled as such, making the term *oaky* a very useful addition to the Wine Buyer's Toolbox (more on this in Chapter 3).

Why would we want a drink based on grapes to taste like a wood? The answer to this question totally depends on your taste. I tell the waiters I teach to think of an oak barrel as a marinade for wine, and wine pros often refer to oak as "the winemaker's spice rack." Simply put, it adds aroma, flavor, body, and sometimes color, as our tasting will reveal. A lot of people like wines with this "oaky" style.

The tasting we're going to do will compare an obviously oaky wine with one that is made from the same grape but is not oaky, so you can see for yourself. And believe me, you will know right away, because "oaky" is a very distinctive, love-it-or-hate-it characteristic in a wine. The good news is that there are some very common label terms that tip you off to an oaky wine and I will show you how to spot them.

In contrast to the tastes of sweetness and acidity we previously explored, both of which come from the grape, oakiness in wine is put there by the winemaker. In fact, oak is one of the major methods a winemaker can use to affect the style of a wine. Wineries use oak barrels for winemaking in two ways:

- Oak Barrel–Fermentation The grape juice has to be put into some type of leak-proof container for fermentation. In ancient times it might have been a clay amphora. Nowadays, it is usually steel tanks or barrels. If the container used is an oak barrel, this can give an oaky character to the wine.

- Oak Barrel–Aging Many wines are aged for some length of time at the winery before bottling, anywhere from a few months to several years. Using an oak barrel as the aging vessel is another winemaking option that can give an oaky style to the wine.

Historically, using barrels for wine was a matter of practicality. Before the invention of stainless steel tanks, which are widely used for fermentation and aging nowadays, oak barrels were the best technology available. Barrels predated the invention of glass, and were much more durable. Above all, they were convenient for shipping on ocean voyages. In fact, the taste-enhancing effect of barrels on wine was discovered as a lucky by-product of ocean trade. All types of manufactured goods, from tools to foodstuffs, could be shipped in barrels. At the destination point, the barrels needed to be refilled with something—wine, for example—to provide ballast for the ships on their return trip. It wasn't long before people noticed that the wine actually tasted *better* after its time in the barrel.

HOW OAKY IS IT? Fermenting or aging a wine in oak barrels affects several aspects of its style. They are:

Color: makes white wines look darker

Aroma: makes red and white wines smell stronger

Flavor: makes red and white wines taste richer

Body/Texture: makes red and white wines feel fuller

As I tell the waiters I teach, using oak barrels is like turning up the volume on all of these components in the wine. When fermenting or aging with oak, winemakers have choices. They can just bump up the volume a notch, turn it up full blast, or go somewhere in between.

Here are the different ways wineries control the amount of oakiness in a wine:

- **Barrel Fermentation vs. Barrel Aging** The winemaker can choose just one or the other for a subtler oak effect, or do both to give a stronger oak character to the wine.

- **Time in a Barrel** The amount of time a wine spends in the barrel matters: The longer it spends in barrels, the oakier it will taste.

BARRELS AT THE SOURCE

In addition to the size, newness, and toasting of the barrels, wine professionals also talk about the source of the barrels, meaning where the oak trees themselves were grown (usually America or France). And you may see reference to *American* oak or *French* oak barrels on wine labels. Some pros say American oak barrels give a stronger or sweeter character to wine than French oak barrels, but I think the distinctions are usually too subtle for most people to notice.

Whether French or American, oakiness in wine is so distinctive that oaky wines tend to get a lot of attention from wine critics. When rating wines, critics' scores can be influenced by an oak character because it can make a wine stand out among those being tasted. The result is that sometimes a wine whose quality isn't necessarily better may get a higher score simply because the taster noticed it more due to the oak.

Obviously, if a wine is both fermented and aged in barrels it will naturally lengthen the total time the wine spends in oak.

- Age of the Barrels Before they're cut in half to become charming garden planters, wine barrels are reused by wineries from one harvest to the next. New barrels, when used to ferment or age wine for the first time, give the wine a stronger oak character than barrels that have previously held wine. It is similar to the idea of trying to reuse a teabag—a lot of the color, aroma, and flavor get steeped out the first time around.

- Size of the Barrels In this case, size matters—smaller barrels give the wine more oak character than large barrels. The reason is that in a smaller barrel, the wood surface area proportional to the volume of wine is higher, so you get more oak taste and scent. Some wineries use oak vats as large as Winnebagos. They don't give any oak character to the wine. Commonly used barrels include the *barrique* (*buh-REEK*), traditional to French red Bordeaux, which holds 225 liters (about 20 cases), and the Burgundy barrel (in

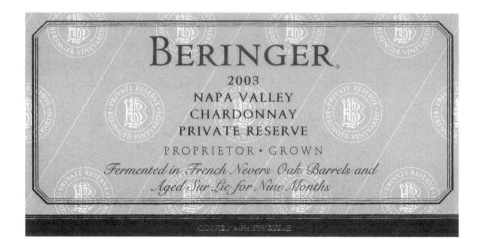

French, *pièce*, pronounced *pee-YESS*), which holds 228 liters and is traditional to French red and white Burgundy. In North America and the Southern Hemisphere, the first is used often for full-bodied red varietals; the latter for Pinot Noirs and Chardonnays.

- "Toast" of the Barrels At first, this always sounds strange to people, but it actually makes perfect sense. To curve and shape each barrel, the barrel maker, called a cooper, heats the wood by placing it over a fire. In the process, the interior gets toasted, or charred. This toasting affects the amount and style of oak flavor given to the wine. A *light toast* makes the wine lightly oaky; *medium toast* makes it more oaky; and *heavy toast* makes it very oaky. The reason is that toasting oak, like toasting bread, coffee beans, or marshmallows, caramelizes the starches, giving a stronger, richer flavor and a scent that tasters usually describe as toasty, smoky, sweet, or some combination of the three.

WHEN THE OAK CHIPS ARE DOWN

The bottle's label says "barrel select," yet the wine costs less than ten dollars. Knowing that oak barrels are one of the most luxurious ingredients in winemaking, you may well ask, How do they do it? It might be called a form of recycling. In making and repairing oak barrels, wineries and barrel manufacturers build up a supply of leftover pieces of wood. Resourceful companies put these chips and fragments of wood to good use as "seasoning" for their bargain-priced bottles, whose market price would never pay back the cost of actually aging in oak barrels. Some wine experts are snobby about this, calling it an imitation technique. I think that when skillfully employed, oak chips are a very good thing indeed—they make the oaky flavor so many people like affordable.

Sweet oak? Yes, sweet, but not sugary. I am often asked about this description, which you sometimes see in the winemaker notes on the back labels of bottles. Think how sweet-tasting an onion becomes if you cook it slowly, letting it brown and caramelize. And nature is full of aromas that smell sweet without the presence of a lot of sugar. Spices, such as cloves and cinnamon, are a great example of sweet scents that are not sugary, and some tasters note these spicy scents when drinking wines that are oaky. Vanilla is another one—everyone is taken by the sweet scent of a vanilla bean or vanilla flavoring, but on its own vanilla isn't sugary. Vanilla is a term very often used by professional tasters in describing the scent of an oaky wine. There is a reason for this: Traces of vanillin are present in the oak used to make barrels. (See the Beringer label opposite.)

There is one other very important trait that oak adds to wine—cost. Barrels are expensive to buy, clean, and maintain. They also wear out, and must be replaced far more often than stainless steel tanks, which are virtually indestructible. All of this adds up to higher production costs, which invariably get passed along in the bottle price. That makes our oak tasting very important. Let your taste decide about oakiness. Those who like that style will be willing to pay extra for it. And those who don't can save their money.

Tannic

The word may sound obscure, but this is one you will definitely want to get to know. In the last tasting in this chapter, we will learn the meaning of tannic, the word used to describe red wines with a lot of the substance known as tannin. You may recognize the word from the process of tanning leather, and yes, tannin is the substance used. In a wine context, tannin is a natural component of the skins, stems, and seeds of wine grapes. That is why it is notable in red wines, not white—the juice, while soaking with the grape skins to get the red color, also soaks up the tannin.

To the taster, tannin in wine is sensed not as a flavor but as a *texture* that you feel on the tongue and, when there is a lot of it, all over the insides of your mouth. It is probably a texture with which you are already familiar. Red table grapes often have noticeable tannin, as do other fruits—persimmons and plums immediately come to mind.

Wine tasters describe the feeling of tannin in many ways—drying, puckery, velvety. I have used them all, depending on the wine. I tell the waiters I teach that the feeling on the tongue is like accidentally biting the stringy part of the banana peel rather than the banana, or drinking hot tea that has steeped for too long (tea has tannin, too).

The amount of tannin in red wine can cover a broad spectrum, from low to high. Here is how I describe the range:

Low tannin: Hardly noticeable; the wine feels silky.

Medium tannin: Noticeable dry, tacky feeling, but smooth rather than harsh. (A waiter I once worked with told me, upon tasting this style, that it felt as though the inside of her mouth had been wallpapered in velvet and suede—the entire room agreed.)

High tannin: Ouch! Your tongue feels very puckered, dried out, and leathery.

The varied tannin levels in different wines are due to three main factors:

The grape: The amount of tannin in red grapes varies from one type to the next, according to the thickness of the grape skins—thicker-skinned grapes like Cabernet Sauvignon have more tannin than thinner-skinned varieties such as Pinot Noir. We talked about this in the last chapter in connection with color in red wines—the thicker-skinned Cabernet Sauvignon had a darker color than the thin-skinned Pinot Noir. Now you can see the obvious connection between tannin and color—as a rule of thumb, the darker the color of a red wine, the more tannin.

Amount of skin contact: You will remember this winemaking term also from our color discussion. It is the amount of time the grape skins soak with the juice: The longer the soak, the more tannin in the wine. The Zinfandel grape is a good example. When it is made as a blush wine, white Zinfandel, there is no tannin, and the wine feels completely smooth and crisp like a white wine (hence the name). But when it is made with long skin contact, as in a red Zinfandel, there is a lot of color and tannin.

Age of the wine: In everyday buying and drinking situations, this is not a factor, because most wines are rightly bought and consumed young. But some classic wine types, known for their very high tannin, can be allowed to age to reduce the harshness of the tannins. What happens during the aging process is that the tannins soften and integrate with the rest of the wine's components, making for a smoother, more balanced, and enjoyable drinking experience than when the tannins were so prominent in the wine's youth. Sediment is a common result of this aging process. During aging, the tannins bond with the color pigment in the wine and settle as a deposit in the bottom of the bottle. (See Chapter 10 for how to pour and serve a wine that has sediment.) With this background, now you're ready to take a taste tour of the Wine Buyer's Toolbox.

Drink Your Words—Tasting Dry, Crisp, Oaky, and Tannic

My wine students love this tasting because it is such an eye-opener. This is how it works. We taste a total of eight wines, grouped in pairs, with one pair to illustrate each of the major style terms in the Wine Buyer's Toolbox:

TASTING ORDER	STYLE WORD	WINES TASTED
First pair	Dry	Dry Riesling vs. Sweet Riesling
Second pair	Crisp	Crisp, high-acid Sauvignon Blanc vs. Low-acid Sauvignon Blanc
Third pair	Oaky	Chardonnay with no oak flavor vs. Oaky Chardonnay
Fourth pair	Tannic	Low-tannin Pinot Noir vs. High-tannin Cabernet Sauvignon

As with our tasting in Chapter 1, you have a few options. Choose whatever seems most convenient.

Option 1 Taste all four wine pairs in one sitting. This is what I do with my wine students. It takes less than an hour, and really helps to cement the meanings of each style term, because you can compare them to one another. If you don't have enough glasses to pour all eight wines at once, taste one pair at a time, empty your glasses, and pour the next pair. No need to rinse or wash the glasses between pairs.

If you do plan to taste all the wines in one sitting, taste the pairs in the order shown in the table, from dry to tannic. In Chapter 1, we tasted the wines from lightest to fullest in body. Look at this list; we are following the same pattern (remember, Riesling, Sauvignon Blanc, Chardonnay—light-, medium-, full-bodied). It is always best to taste wines from lightest to fullest, just as you traditionally serve the lightest food courses (salad or fish) in a meal first, ending with the heaviest (meat or cheese or dessert). This progression allows your mouth to gradually warm up to stronger tastes. Doing the tasting in reverse, tasting full-bodied wines first, can leave lingering flavors in your mouth that overpower the lighter wines to follow.

Option 2 Taste each wine pair on its own, whenever it is convenient. A good way to do this is to plan a dinner around one of the wine pairs. Do your tasting, then sit down to dinner and enjoy the wines with your meal. It is an easy thing to do at home, whether you are cooking or ordering take-out.

CHOICES, CHOICES

Choice is what going to restaurants is all about. You get to taste lots of different things, and you don't have to shop, cook, or do the dishes. And the trend just keeps growing. Restaurants across the country are offering more wines by the glass than ever, adding tasting menus, half-glasses, shared plates, and so on, all of which increases your tasting options for wines, and for different wine and food combinations.

This is also one of my favorite tastings to do with restaurant guests, especially if they can't decide which wine to choose. "You don't have to choose," I tell them. As with most good eateries these days, we offer a range of wines by the glass in the restaurants I work with. I simply offer my guests one of these pairs, by the glass or half-glass, so they have the chance to compare them, side by side. It is fascinating to taste the style differences, and to learn how trying the wines with food changes your perception of the taste. Sometimes your second-favorite of the wines will move into the top spot when tasted with food.

Tasting Setup: The Steps

Step 1. Buy the wines, choosing from the following list:

For each style term, choose one wine from List A, and one from List B.

Dry

1. DRY RIESLING

CALIFORNIA
Kendall-Jackson
Wente
Bonny Doon
Jekel
Trefethen

NEW ZEALAND
Brancott
Villa Maria

AUSTRALIA
Grosset
Pike's
Jacob's Creek
Penfolds Eden Valley

ALSACE, FRANCE
Trimbach
Hugel
Schlumberger
Albrecht
Josmeyer
Leon Beyer

2. SWEET RIESLING

CALIFORNIA & WASHINGTON
Columbia Crest Late Harvest
Chateau Ste. Michelle Late Harvest
Hogue Late Harvest

GERMANY
Riesling Spätlese or Auslese from the following wineries* (or your store's recommendation):
Selbach-Oster
Lingenfelder
Gunderloch
JJ Prüm
Burklin-Wolf
Dr. Fischer
Dr. Loosen
Strub
Kurt Darting

———————————

*Note: If you choose a German wine, ensure that the label doesn't say *trocken*, which means dry.

Crisp

3. HIGH-ACID SAUVIGNON BLANC

LOIRE VALLEY, FRANCE
Sancerre from the following wineries:
Jolivet
Michel Redde
Domaine Thomas
Château de Sancerre
Crochet

NEW ZEALAND
Brancott
Allan Scott
Cloudy Bay
Villa Maria
Nobilo
Stoneleigh
Seresin

4. LOW-ACID SAUVIGNON BLANC

CALIFORNIA
Simi
Benziger Fumé Blanc
Murphy-Goode Fumé Blanc
Kunde Estate
Kenwood
Matanzas Creek
Robert Mondavi Fumé Blanc
Merryvale
Meridian
Chateau Souverain
Iron Horse
Chalk Hill

Oaky

5. CHARDONNAY WITH NO OAK FLAVOR

BURGUNDY, FRANCE
Mâcon-Villages from the following wineries:
    Louis Latour
    Bouchard
    Jadot
    Verget
    Drouhin
Pouilly-Fuissé from the following wineries:
    Bouchard
    Jadot
    Château Fuissé
    Verget
    Drouhin

6. OAKY CHARDONNAY

AUSTRALIA
    Lindemans Bin 65
    Rosemount Show Reserve

CALIFORNIA
    Stonestreet
    Gallo of Sonoma
    Beringer Napa Valley
    Cambria
    Franciscan
    Matanzas Creek
    Chateau Souverain
    St. Francis

Tannic

7. LOW-TANNIN PINOT NOIR

CALIFORNIA & OREGON
    Calera Central Coast
    Estancia Pinnacles
    Buena Vista Carneros
    Byron
    Kendall-Jackson
    Clos du Bois
    Robert Mondavi
    Pepperwood Grove
    Parducci
    Meridian
    Sebastiani Sonoma County
    Firesteed
    Sokol Blosser

8. HIGH-TANNIN CABERNET SAUVIGNON

CALIFORNIA
    Franciscan
    St. Supéry Dollarhide Ranch
    Stonestreet
    Beringer Knights Valley
    J. Lohr Paso Robles
    Mt. Veeder
    Chimney Rock
    Frog's Leap
    Simi
    Merryvale
    Joseph Phelps

Step 2. Chill the white wines.

By the way, do not worry if they warm up a little as you're tasting. The exact serving temperature doesn't matter very much; in fact, overchilling wines mutes their flavor.

Step 3. Set up your glasses.

You will want to number the glasses as we did in the first tasting, with pieces of paper or a numbered placemat, especially if you are pouring all eight wines at once. And you may very well be doing this. I have a wine-loving friend who doesn't have a wine cellar because she doesn't have the storage space, and she doesn't like to wait years to drink a bottle, anyway. But she does have seven dozen wineglasses in her New York City apartment. Her favorite way to entertain is to invite friends over to taste and compare different wines. When people ask, What can I bring? she always has an answer: a new wine to try.

Step 4. Open the wines and pour them in number order, or one pair at a time, depending on which tasting option you have chosen.

If you are tasting just one pair of wines at a time, keep track of the order by pouring the wines left to right, with the List A selection on the left, and the List B wine on the right.

Again, one to one and a half ounces is good for a tasting portion. Afterward, you can pour more of your favorite, ideally with dinner.

Step 5. Taste the wines in order.

The First Wine Pair—Dry

This tasting will give you a clear understanding of dry and its opposite, sweet. Your first two wines are both Rieslings (a light-bodied white grape, as you learned in Chapter 1). The first Riesling has virtually no residual sugar, and is dry. The second Riesling contains a lot of residual sugar, and is sweet. Before you drink, follow the steps in this chart. Here is what you will find as you compare them:

WINE 1, DRY RIESLING	WINE 2, SWEET RIESLING
THE LOOK: Compare them against a white background.	
Pale yellow-green	Same grape, but this wine is darker. That's very common. The high concentration of sugar in the sweet wine often gives it more color.
THE SMELL: Swirl and smell Wine 1, then Wine 2.	
You remember this scent from Chapter 1—crisp and refreshing.	You'll find you can actually smell the sweetness. Here is how I describe the difference: The first wine smells like fresh fruit; the second wine smells like pie or jam made from that fruit—sweet and sugary.
THE TASTE: Now sample the wines, first Wine 1, then Wine 2.	
After Chapter 1, this is a familiar taste. Plenty of refreshing, lip-smacking Riesling flavor here, but no sweetness.	Compared to the other Riesling, this is like a dessert. You can taste the sugar here, and you can also feel it—that syrupy texture in your mouth. The sweetness really lingers in the aftertaste, too.

Give yourself time and go back and retaste these wines. After Wine 2, drink some water or take a bite of plain bread to clear your mouth of sugar before you go back to the dry wine. Otherwise, it will be like drinking orange juice after eating a brownie—kind of sour. I always find that people are enchanted by the sweet wine in this tasting. This type of wine is irresistible with, or as, a dessert.

The Second Wine Pair—Crisp

In this tasting, we explore wine's acidity, one of its most distinctive ingredients. As I pointed out, crisp is the word most often used by wine pros to describe wines with vivid acidity. Tangy, tingly, bright, mouthwatering, and lively are also ways to describe the acidity in wine. I don't usually refer to wine as tart or sour because these words sound slightly negative, and acidity in wine is anything but.

The two wines for this tasting are both made from the white Sauvignon Blanc grape (which is medium-bodied, as you learned in Chapter 1). The first Sauvignon Blanc has very prominent acidity and tastes very crisp. The second tastes a lot less acidic or crisp. Here is what you will find as you compare them:

WINE 3, NEW ZEALAND SAUVIGNON BLANC OR SANCERRE FROM FRANCE	WINE 4, SAUVIGNON BLANC FROM CALIFORNIA
(white Sancerre [*Sahn-SAIR*] wines, which are named for the region, are always made from Sauvignon Blanc)	(some American wineries use the name fumé blanc [*foo-may BLAHNC*] instead of Sauvignon Blanc)
THE LOOK: Compare the colors of the wines against a white background.	
Straw yellow	This looks very similar to Wine 2, but perhaps a touch darker (my experience is that not everyone agrees on this; in any case the colors are very similar).
THE SMELL: Swirl and smell Wine 3 first, then Wine 4.	
Remember the very distinctive scent of Sauvignon Blanc from Chapter 1? Here it is again in all its pungent glory—tangy and vibrant.	This one probably smells a little less pungent. It is still distinctively Sauvignon Blanc, but a little riper and richer in the aroma.
THE TASTE: Now sample the wines, first Wine 3, then Wine 4.	
This is one of my favorite wine tastes, making me feel as though someone grabbed me by the collar and gave me a shake. It reminds me of a squeeze of lime but better, because it is balanced with more fruit taste.	This has a softer, plumper feeling in the mouth, and a juicier taste. To give you a more concrete reference point, comparing the two wines is similar to comparing the taste of a green tomato versus a ripe, red tomato.

I have found that this comparison surprises many tasters. People often start out expecting not to like the crisper, tangier Sauvignon Blanc style. But by the end of the tasting they are usually asking for the name of the wine and where they can buy it.

The Third Wine Pair—Oaky

In this tasting, we explore wines with an oaky style. The two wines for this tasting are both made from the white Chardonnay grape (which is full-bodied, as we discussed in Chapter 1). The first Chardonnay has no oak flavor, just the pure character of Chardonnay. The second tastes notably oaky. Here is what to look for as you compare them:

WINE 5, MÂCON-VILLAGES OR POUILLY-FUISSÉ FROM THE BURGUNDY REGION OF FRANCE (white Burgundy wines, which are named for the region, are virtually always made from Chardonnay)	WINE 6, CHARDONNAY FROM CALIFORNIA OR AUSTRALIA
THE LOOK: Compare the colors of the wines against a white background.	
Straw yellow	Straw yellow to yellow-gold, and noticeably darker than Wine 5.
THE SMELL: Swirl and smell Wine 5 first, then Wine 6.	
Pure, inviting Chardonnay character.	Someone turned up the volume. You can't miss the oakiness—the scent is much richer and more intense.
THE TASTE: Now sample the wines, first Wine 5, then Wine 6.	
Tastes great. You get the Chardonnay character in a refreshing, pleasant style.	This is a full wine. Concentrate on how your mouth feels, and you will really notice the richer texture. And the taste difference? That is the character of "oaky" Chardonnay.

Your taste told you that the differences were dramatic. The oaky character in wine, when present, is so distinctive, it is no wonder that oaky wines get a lot of attention from wine critics. My students often tell me they come away from this comparison with no clear preference. If you liked both wines, then this gives you a taste of why Chardonnay is so popular these days. It can be made in a variety of styles and still puts its best foot forward.

If you had a very strong preference for one wine or the other, you have learned some valuable buyer's info: If you strongly preferred Wine 5, you probably are not a fan of oaky wines. You can spend your time and money exploring the fabulous world of nonoaky wines. I have two things to say about that. First, when it comes to the big-name winery brands that you see in every store, proceed with caution. They usually cater to the oak-lover. Second, there is a world of exciting unoaked wine in store for you. Look at the list of wine suggestions above for a starting point. Then look in Chapters 5 and 6 for more suggestions.

If you strongly preferred Wine 6, oak is for you. It will be pretty easy to find what you are looking for, because most of the popular big-selling winery brands emphasize wines with an oaky character. My list of wine suggestions above also shows lots of choices. And in Chapter 3 we will learn all the label clues that tip you off to an oaky wine so you can choose your own.

The Fourth Wine Pair—Tannic

This tasting will teach your tongue what tannin is—a texture, not a taste. Some people like wines with a lot of tannin, and some prefer wines where the tannin isn't as prominent. Here we feature a Pinot Noir (low tannin) versus a Cabernet Sauvignon (high tannin) so you can see the difference. In later chapters we will explore the clues on the label (grapes, regions, etc.) that tip you off to wines that are especially tannic. Here is how the two wines compare:

WINE 7, PINOT NOIR FROM CALIFORNIA	WINE 8, CABERNET SAUVIGNON FROM CALIFORNIA
THE LOOK: Compare the colors of the wines against a white background.	
Translucent ruby-pink—you can see through it.	Inky reddish-purple—this wine is obviously darker (nearly opaque), letting you know right away that it will probably be fuller-bodied and more tannic than Wine 7.
THE SMELL: Swirl and smell Wine 7 first, then Wine 8.	
This is the Pinot Noir scent you became familiar with in Chapter 1.	And this is the now-familiar Cabernet Sauvignon. You cannot smell tannin per se, but you can certainly note the character of the Cabernet grape, which we know to be a tannic one.
THE TASTE: Now sample the wines, first Wine 7, then Wine 8.	
You know the taste of Pinot Noir. Now concentrate on the texture. It is silky, satiny-smooth. If you notice any of the drying sensation on your tongue, it will be very subtle.	You will feel the tannin all over your mouth—cheeks, gums—not just your tongue.

Do you like the tannic wine? Many red wine fans like that style very much because it's bold and intense. Although I love Pinot Noir, I enjoy the tannic Cabernet Sauvignon, too. It immediately makes me think of food—specifically, a great steak or a good piece of cheese. That is because tannin is very easily tamed by protein and fat, both of which coat your tongue, letting the tannin slide right past without drying it out. Now you see why these are two of the classic wine and food matches: red wine with steak, and red wine with cheese. Next time you head out to a steakhouse for red meat, you'll know exactly what wine to order.

Speaking of knowing what to order, let's do a progress report. You have learned the taste and style of the Big Six wine grapes, and equipped yourself with the Wine Buyer's Toolbox of major wine style words—body (light, medium, full), dry, crisp, oaky, and tannic. In fact, just these two easy tasting lessons put you in about the ninety-fifth percentile for wine knowledge, which is way ahead of most restaurant waiters and wine shop clerks. But this isn't about competition. It is about feeling comfortable choosing a wine that fits your taste. You are now equipped to do that.

But we're only just beginning. You don't need to learn everything there is to know about wine. But there is a lot more that I want to share with you that will make your wine-buying life easier and more economical, and your wining and dining life (whether at home or in a restaurant) immeasurably more exciting. It's time to apply your wine knowledge to unlocking the simple secrets of the wine label.

CHAPTER THREE

News You Can Use on the Wine Label

Congratulations are in order. By now, you know how to ask for a wine that is light-, medium-, or full-bodied and (more important) what it will be like when you do. You know the taste and body style of the white grapes Riesling, Sauvignon Blanc, and Chardonnay; and the reds Pinot Noir, Merlot, Cabernet Sauvignon, and Syrah—the Blue Chips of the wine grape world. And finally, you are equipped with the power tools in the Wine Buyer's Toolbox—dry, crisp, oaky, and tannic. In short, when it comes to wine, *you rule*.

You could stop here, if you weren't having so much fun cruising the wine shops, head high, exploring your new mastery of at least two-thirds of what's there. You could hang up your tasting glass if you weren't basking in the glow of your new status with restaurant waiters as you deftly handle most any wine list. But if you think *that's* fun, let me tell you this: We've barely scratched the surface. No doubt about it, you have hit your stride, but this is also where the wine buyer's equivalent of endorphins kicks in. It seems effortless to go on to new heights—and it is. I'll show you how.

In this chapter we will do two things. First, we will look a bit more closely at three of the major elements in the Wine Buyer's Toolbox—body style, oakiness, and tannin—because there are quite a few easy label cues that will help you pinpoint these styles. Second, we will go beyond the major grape varieties and toolbox terms to some other helpful label words, and our tasting lessons will explore the different styles and flavors that they reveal. What we'll learn here is mainly designed for supermarket and wine shop situations, when you have a chance to scope out everything the front and back labels have to say. When you can put your hands on the bottle and read the label yourself, you have a much better opportunity to learn about the wine. But there is also a new trend in wine lists that will allow you to make better decisions just from reading the listing.

WHO'S PUTTING WHOM ON THE SPOT?

The next time you are feeling intimidated buying wine in a restaurant, remember who is paying the check. If anyone should feel performance anxiety, it is the server or wine waiter, whose job it is to make you feel comfortable and, ideally, to impress you with a wine recommendation in whatever price range you specify, not the other way around.

The Progressive Wine List

In the past decade or so, there has been a growing movement in many restaurants across the country to revamp the way their wine lists are structured. I think most diners would applaud this, because the traditional way of setting up a wine list, by country and region, leaves a lot of people squirming. What is a thirsty person supposed to do with wine list sections like France, Italy, and the United States? Unless you are very familiar with the wines from these countries, there is no way to figure out the wine styles so you can order something. It's crazy.

Enter the Progressive Wine List. This is a wine list in which the choices are arranged according to their style. For years, the Napa Valley's Beringer Winery has been a major proponent of this concept, using their staff of wine experts to help restaurateurs around the country reformat their lists to make it easier for guests and staff to understand them. When I first joined Windows on the World in 1990, the cellarmaster gave me a tip about the wine list on my first day. "The wines in each category are arranged by style, from light- to full-bodied." We didn't call it a Progressive

Wine List then, nor did we tell customers about it. But it was a powerful tool for all of us on the service staff.

A customer might say, "I'm considering these two Chardonnays. How do they differ?" And I could answer, "Well, ma'am, the Beringer (farther down on the Chardonnay list) is slightly fuller in body." Whether I had actually tasted that wine or not, I had something genuinely helpful to tell the customer.

Typically, the Progressive Wine List goes further with its categories than just body style, using groupings such as "Mild, Fruity, Sweet" or "Stronger-Tasting Dry White." The same idea is also happening in wine retail stores, championed by the wine-store chain called Best Cellars, which offers every-day-priced wines arranged according to style categories they devised—fizzy, fresh, soft, luscious, juicy, smooth, big, and sweet. I think this is a good thing, both in retail and in restaurants, but it still requires a well-educated service staff to understand and be comfortable with words like fruity and dry.

Of course, now when *you* see a Progressive Wine List, as you will more and more, you will be completely comfortable. When I write wine lists, I also arrange my wines from light- to full-bodied, but by grape variety rather than taste characteristics, because I think customers are more comfortable with grape names than with wine descriptions. Either way, it's more power to you, the customer, and that is what matters.

WINE LIST HELL

What do people do when confronted with an impossible wine list? They don't even bother asking their waiter. Bad lists are just as confusing to the waiters as to the guests. Instead, people ask for iced tea. So much for the idea of a beverage that will actually enhance the meal. A tiny minority of guests will go ahead and bravely search until they find something that sounds familiar—a big winery name or a comfortable style like Pinot Grigio. But that isn't very satisfying. You could have had the same wine experience at home for a lot less money. I believe that if restaurants are going to charge more than retail, as they must to cover the extra overhead costs of running a restaurant, they've got to try harder. To me, that means wine lists with a user-friendly format and a reasonable selection and pricing. They make an effort with food. Why not the wine, too?

Body Style: What the Label Tells You

Outside of a restaurant, however, you'll nearly always be making your decision based on reading wine labels. Let's explore what the label has to offer (in addition to the usual suspects like grape variety) to help you predict the style of the wine inside.

As always, we start with body. It is really helpful to know the body style of a wine, because so often that influences your choice. In summer, with lighter fare and hot weather, you probably look for lighter-bodied wines. And how about with that big-ticket sirloin in a steakhouse? You probably won't get the most enjoyment out of your meal drinking a delicate, light-bodied wine. By the same token, it's obvious that you don't want a monster red with your aunt Peggy's salmon croquettes. And then there is also your personal preference to consider. I have one friend who only ever drinks big, bold Cabernet Sauvignons, regardless of the circumstances. It's what he likes.

You know how to identify the body styles of the major grape varieties (the Big Six). But there is another very powerful tool on wine labels to help you predict the wine's body style. It's the Percent Alcohol by Volume. For this information, you can thank the U.S. government, which requires wineries to put the wine's alcohol percentage on every bottle label.

Alcohol content is one of the more helpful tools to the buyer. Simply put, to the taster, *alcohol is perceived as body in a wine*. So when you taste two wines side by side, one with lower alcohol and one with higher, you will generally perceive the wine with the higher alcohol percentage as fuller-bodied. Judging a wine by alcohol content is especially useful when:

- you're considering wines with regional names, rather than a grape name whose body style you know;

- you're looking at wines made from grapes other than the Big Six (and you undoubtedly will, either on your own or after reading about them in later chapters of this book);

- you're trying to decide between two similar wines, such as two different Chardonnays, and need to determine how their styles compare.

The government gives wineries some leeway in labeling the alcohol percentage on their wines—they need only be accurate within 1.5 percent of the actual wine. For the consumer, this is mostly an issue on the high end of the Table Wine percentage range, where a wine's actual alcohol content may be above that shown on the label. That is because a winery pushing the upper 14 percent limit would have the incentive to understate the alcohol in their wine, to avoid a higher tax. But even if the alcohol percentage of a wine *labeled* 14 percent is slightly underreported, you already know what to expect—full body.

To sum up, you can learn about a wine's body style just by looking at the percent alcohol by volume listed on the label. Here is a summary of the range of alcohol percentages for table wines, and the body style to which they generally correspond:

Light body: 7–10.5 percent

Medium body: 10.5–12.5 percent

Full body: Above 12.5 percent

Tasting for Body, Part II

Let's try it. I will give you two percentage alcohol/body comparisons—one with white wine and one with red. You can try the reds and whites separately, but I recommend that you eventually do both tastings. With either tasting, you can make an evening of it. Try the wines, then follow with dinner so you can see how each of them tastes with food.

White Wine

Our white wine tasting compares two Rieslings, one from Germany that is light in alcohol, and one from Alsace in France, where the Rieslings generally have higher alcohol. This is because the growing region is warmer and sunnier, and as we have learned, grapes get riper in sunnier regions, and riper grapes give more alcohol and thus fuller-bodied wines.

This is the third Riesling tasting we have done in this book and, if you are like most people, probably your third Riesling tasting ever. That's because I love Riesling, and I am hoping that by now you also see its virtues. It's great stuff.

LOWER ALCOHOL WHITE, GERMAN RIESLING	HIGHER ALCOHOL WHITE, FRENCH ALSACE RIESLING
Choose among these styles of German Riesling, which range from 7 to 10 percent alcohol—Riesling Kabinett from the following wineries: Selbach-Oster, Strub, Burklin-Wolf, Christoffel-Berres, JJ Prüm, Dr. Fischer, Robert Weil (or your store's recommendation; check especially the alcohol percentage on the label).	These usually range from 12 to 13.5 percent. Here are some wineries from which to choose: Trimbach, Hugel, Weinbach, Leon Beyer, Schlumberger, Deiss, Sparr, Schoffit, Dirler, Blanck, Zind-Humbrecht, Kreydenweiss.
THE LOOK: Compare them against a white background.	
Pale yellow-green	Also yellow-green, but often a touch darker
THE SMELL: Swirl and smell the German Riesling first, then the French Alsace Riesling.	
You'll smell the delicate and beautifully fragrant scent of Riesling.	You'll smell the Riesling character, but pay close attention here. You might perceive the higher alcohol from the smell, because your nasal passages can actually *feel* the alcohol vapors.

Concentrate on the feeling of the wine—its weight, body, and intensity. It will seem delicate, almost ethereal in the mouth. There is no shortage of flavor, but the weight of the wine is cloudlike—light-bodied.

This is completely different. You will feel the richness and full-bodied, mouth-filling, almost oily texture. That is due to the wine's higher alcohol content.

Red Wine

Now on to the red wine. This will compare two Merlots, one from Bordeaux in France, and one from California. Again, the difference in alcohol in the wines is due to different amounts of sunshine in the growing season. Bordeaux's Merlots are lighter in alcohol because the vines generally get less sunshine than those in California. This is a subtler comparison than the white wine tasting, because the alcohol percentage difference between these two is not as dramatic as it was in the whites. Still, you will be able to perceive the body difference.

LOWER ALCOHOL RED, MERLOT FROM BORDEAUX, FRANCE

HIGHER ALCOHOL RED, CALIFORNIA MERLOT

Choose among these Bordeaux Merlots: Christian Moueix, Michel Lynch, B&G, Mouton-Cadet, Baron Philippe de Rothschild St. Émilion

Here are some good examples from which to choose: Kunde, Wente, St. Francis, Gallo of Sonoma, Benziger, Markham, Robert Mondavi Napa Valley.

THE LOOK: Compare them against a white background.

Ruby red

Dark purplish-red. The darker color comes as no surprise. You have already learned that deeper color usually implies fuller body.

THE SMELL: Swirl and smell the Merlot from Bordeaux first, then the California Merlot.

Here is the familiar smell of Merlot, very juicy and inviting.

You might notice the feel of the alcohol in your nasal passages with this scent. You will also notice the smell of the extra ripeness these grapes achieve in their warmer growing region.

THE TASTE: Now sample the wines, first the Merlot from Bordeaux, then the California Merlot.

This is textbook Merlot—medium-bodied, good red wine flavor, soft, not heavy.

Concentrate on the body. You will notice the richer, thicker mouth feel, almost a plumpness to the wine—in other words, fuller body.

The Truth About Table Wine

The term *Table Wine* is a source of some confusion in this country. Specifically, many people think that it refers to the category of mediocre-quality, jug-style wines. But actually, Table Wine is a U.S. government term, referring simply to wine ranging from 7 to 14 percent alcohol by volume, which dictates the level at which it is taxed (lower alcohol products like beer are taxed less; higher alcohol beverages like spirits are taxed more).

The confusion is understandable because in European wine-growing countries, "table wine" does refer to basic-quality, everyday jug wines. Look on the labels even of great wines in any wine store in this country, and you will see the (tax) term Table Wine. You can avoid headaches (literally) when you are in Europe by remembering that their definition of table wine *does* refer to the lowest quality category.

Oaky, Revisited

You can often judge a wine's body from the label according to the grape variety, or the alcohol content. But there is yet another major body indicator with which you are also familiar—oakiness. That information is often right on the label, too.

By now you know "oaky" very well. In Chapter 2, you learned that oaky wines have more intense color (for whites), aroma, flavor, and texture. Tasters perceive that greater intensity, especially of the flavor and texture, as fuller body. As you tasted for yourself, that oaky character is very distinctive, and usually comes with a higher price tag.

So how can you know which wines will be oaky before you buy them? Luckily, you can do so with ease, especially with the varietal wines that are so popular these days. Look for these "oaky" indicators right on the label:

Barrel Fermented

Barrel Aged or Oak Aged

Barrel Select or Barrel Selection

Barrel Cuvée (*cuvée* is French, and in this sense just means selection)

Oak Barrel or Oak Cask (nothing unclear about that)

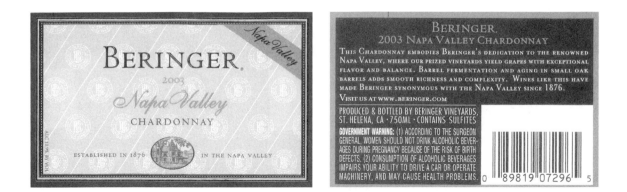

These label terms are most often seen on white wines. But many red wines are also barrel fermented or barrel aged. In fact, because red wines generally are fuller-bodied than whites, their flavor can support a lot of oakiness without it seeming overpowering.

OVER-THE-TOP OAK

Professional tasters use the term *overoaked* to describe a wine whose flavor is so dominated by oak that the rest of its attributes are masked—in other words, too much of a good thing. Cooks and chefs often try to steer clear of very oaky wines, because they can clobber the taste of good cooking. But like other flavors, the right amount of oak is a matter of personal taste.

When it comes to red wines, I recommend that you look at the back label (this is obviously easier at the store, but your tasting exercises will familiarize you with reds you can knowingly order in a restaurant). Quite often, the back label tells you what oak treatment the winemaker used to make the wine, or gives the winemaker's description of what the wine's oaky style tastes like. Here are some examples from real reds in my wine rack right now:

- "spicy vanillin oak" On a Lindemans Cabernet Sauvignon from Australia. Recall that in Chapter 2 we learned of the presence of vanillin in the wood used to make oak barrels.

- "aged for one year in oak barrels" On a DeMartino "Prima" Cabernet Sauvignon from Chile. As we learned previously, the length of time a wine spends in oak barrels affects the degree of oakiness in the taste.

- "Aged in small oak barrels, this highly acclaimed wine has an elegant, smooth finish . . ." On a BV Private Reserve Cabernet Sauvignon from California. Remember the effect of barrel size on a wine's level of oakiness, with smaller barrels giving a stronger oak character than large ones.

Tannic, Take Two

Tannin, to remind you, is a texture, giving a distinctive mouth feel as well as body to red wines. Wine pros refer to this combination of the body and tannin in a red wine as its "structure," a term sometimes found in the descriptive notes on a back label. There are some other common label terms that refer to the tannin level in wines. Think back to your tasting of a lower-tannin Pinot Noir versus a higher-tannin Cabernet Sauvignon. Or better yet, repeat the tasting with the same or different wine selections for the fun and additional practice, and consider these descriptions as you compare the two wines.

Lower tannin: smooth, supple, soft, silky

Higher tannin: firm, structured, velvety, chewy

Expanding Your Vocabulary

It is now time for us to think outside the box—the Wine Buyer's Toolbox, that is. We are going to explore some more exotic wine descriptions. As you will soon taste for yourself, these are the nuances that make wine *wine*, the synapse-revving subtleties and funky quirks that can make this glorious beverage seductive, sometimes breathtaking, occasionally even weird, and a lot more interesting than grapes could ever be. And what you will discover about wine as you explore is absolutely fascinating. In one little taste of wine, there is so much more to seduce your senses than you could ever hope to find in anything else you drink. And it's all because of fermentation.

There's no need to get deeply into the chemistry of it all. Learning fermentation science is the winemaker's job. For the buyer, it's *sensory* chemistry that matters. What is exciting to learn about fermentation is its powerful impact on pleasure. It is the reason wine is so much more exciting than grapes, and Scotch whisky is more fascinating than barley.

If you are skeptical, consider more familiar territory—cheese. "Milk is milk is milk," a Napa Valley winemaker once said to me. "But think of the hundreds of great and very different cheeses that start out as the same bland beverage!" In both cheese and wine, we owe all those great scents and flavors to the fermentation process. In addition to converting the grapes' sugar into alcohol, fermentation also produces traces of chemical compounds that mimic aromas and flavors in nature—from apples and cinnamon to rotten eggs and green pepper (most of the time the flavor compounds present in wine are good aromas and flavors, but not always).

I think this is one of the reasons wine-tasting descriptions, which can get downright funky, sometimes make people nervous—particularly the ones that make no reference at all to grapes. I always tell my students, "Grape juice tastes like grapes, but wine tastes like . . ." There are literally thousands of possibilities. And I have found that once wine drinkers learn that there is a bona fide reason for all the complexity in wine aromas and tastes, they suddenly become open to them, and to enjoying a new, higher pleasure quotient from each and every glass. That is exactly what we are looking for.

I have been "collecting" the different words on wine labels for a long time, so that each time I teach a wine class, I am (I hope) ready with answers to all the questions I'm asked. I could write a whole book on wine descriptors alone, but for now, I'll cover the major ones as well as, for the trivia buffs among you, some of the more obscure ones. (I don't advise flaunting the more exotic wine vocabulary at your next cocktail party. You'll come off like a wine snob—and no one likes those.) Among all these, the terms that are used most often warrant a tasting lesson, so that you can experience firsthand what they mean. That's where we'll start.

Tasting for Butter

As this tasting will reveal, you don't have to be an expert taster to note a pleasing buttery aroma in some wines, especially Chardonnays (maybe *that's* why Chardonnay is America's number one selling white varietal wine). For many people, this is one of the strangest wine-tasting descriptions—after all, we're talking about a nondairy product. There's fermentation at work again. The process creates, in some wines, a trace component called diacetyl (*die-ASS-uh-teal*)—the same flavoring used in the "butter"-flavored oil you get on your popcorn at movie theaters.

If you are curious about diacetyl, pick up a bottle of butter flavoring in the spice-and-baking section of your supermarket. It is made of diacetyl, and smelling the flavoring will give you a great frame of reference for the "buttery" scent in wines. Then you can bake a cake, because this is the flavoring to use in your frosting.

Although you could taste just one wine with buttery character, I think it is helpful to have, for this tasting, a contrasting wine with which to compare it. So the first wine tasted will be a Chardonnay without buttery character, compared to a buttery Chardonnay.

Turn to page 21 if you need a review of the steps to set up a tasting.

NONBUTTERY CHARDONNAY: MÂCON-VILLAGES OR POUILLY-FUISSÉ FROM BURGUNDY, FRANCE.

Choose from among these French white Burgundies without buttery character:
Mâcon-Villages: Bouchard, Jadot, Drouhin, Duboeuf, Verget; Mâcon-Lugny Les Charmes; Pouilly-Fuissé: Château Fuissé, Bouchard, Jadot (or your store's suggestion).

BUTTERY CHARDONNAY: FROM AUSTRALIA, CALIFORNIA, OR WASHINGTON

I am giving you choices from all three places:

Australia: Lindemans Bin 65, Rosemount Diamond Label, Château Tahbilk, Chateau Reynella, Devil's Lair

California: Beringer Napa Valley, Sebastiani Sonoma County, St. Francis, Iron Horse, Buena Vista, Kunde Estate, Bonterra, Cambria, Gallo Laguna Ranch

Washington: Columbia Crest Grand Estates, Chateau Ste. Michelle

THE LOOK: Compare them against a white background.	
Straw yellow—The color is as you expected, because you have already tasted wines from this region.	Straw yellow to yellow-gold—The color is somewhat deeper.

THE SMELL: Swirl and smell the French Chardonnay, then the California, Washington, or Aussie Chardonnay.	
This scent has the clean, pure, and inviting Chardonnay character.	Butteriness in wine is usually most marked in the aroma. You can't miss it. Still, the scent of Chardonnay comes through as well, making for a very pleasing aroma overall.

THE TASTE: Sample the wines, first the French Chardonnay, then the California, Washington, or Aussie Chardonnay.	
By now, this flavor is your old friend—crisp, delicious Chardonnay.	In the taste, the buttery character comes on more subtly than in the aroma, but you will still notice it. Some other points: The acidity is softer and less crisp compared to the first wine, and the body is a little fuller.

Tasting for Grassiness

The descriptions *grassy* and *herbaceous* throw people off at first. "Why on earth would I want to drink a wine that tastes grassy?" But for fans of the Sauvignon Blanc grape especially, this can be a very exciting and delicious attribute—a distinctive signature in the same way that single-malt Scotch lovers adore the "peaty" style of their favorite whisky. I have found that with most wine drinkers, it is a matter of getting familiar with the grassy character, just as you have come to understand an oaky taste, which on paper doesn't sound particularly appetizing, either.

In any case, grassy and herbaceous (or herbal) are terms used to describe wines, especially Sauvignon Blancs, that are marked with scents similar to that of fresh-cut grass, fresh herbs, or raw or cooked vegetables. Take a moment at the wine shop to scan the back labels of a few Sauvignon Blancs, and I bet you will spot this description. You can try one of your finds, or taste any of the following wines to get a sense for what grassy/herbaceous means. As you are tasting, pay particular attention to the scent, which is where the grassy/herbaceous character makes its strongest statement.

CALIFORNIA SAUVIGNON BLANC	FRENCH SAUVIGNON BLANC	SOUTHERN HEMISPHERE SAUVIGNON BLANC
Silverado	**LOIRE VALLEY SANCERRE**	**NEW ZEALAND**
Duckhorn	Lucien Crochet	Cloudy Bay
Honig	Domaine Thomas	Stoneleigh
Hanna	Pascal Jolivet	Villa Maria
Voss	Michel Redde	Babich
Robert Mondavi Fumé Blanc	Château de Sancerre	Nobilo
Frog's Leap		Brancott
Geyser Peak	**BORDEAUX**	
	Michel Lynch Sauvignon Blanc	**SOUTH AFRICA**
	Château Carbonnieux	Mulderbosch
	Château La Louvière	Thelema
		Brampton

THE LOOK: Look at the wine against a white background.

The color range is pale yellow-green to straw yellow.

THE SMELL: Swirl the glass, then smell.

You'll get the grassy/herbaceous aroma immediately—you probably won't forget this style any-time soon. Specifically, tasters may notice similarities to these scents: grass, hay, tarragon, green bean, green tomato, asparagus

THE TASTE: Now sample the wines.

One taste will erase your skepticism about this style, because although they are quite racy and lively, these wines do not actually *taste* of grass and hay. You may note some delicate herbal ac-cents along with the Sauvignon Blanc fruit flavor (which we will explore further in Chapter 4). The herbal nuances make this wine style especially suited to foods that are considered hard to match—such as salads, sushi, and chile-laced ethnic foods (Mexican, Thai, and Indian).

SAILING ALONG ON CLOUDY BAY

I consider New Zealand's Cloudy Bay Sauvignon Blanc to be not only a benchmark example of a grassy wine, but also a benchmark wine, period. It is so individual that it's worth the search to find it. Your best bet may be to look for it in better restaurants. Although its price has crept up, it is not unreasonable. Since it's in high demand, the importer reserves much of the stock for restaurant wine lists.

CLOUDY BAY

SAUVIGNON BLANC 2004
MARLBOROUGH

ALCOHOL 13.5% BY VOLUME
PRODUCT OF NEW ZEALAND

Tasting for Spice

Pop music aside, *I* was the original Spice Girl. I am crazy for spicy wines, both white and red, because I find their exoticism, complexity, and unpredictability to be incredibly exciting. If your palate is easily bored, these wines are guaranteed to keep your interest. "Spicy" on a wine label can refer to scents of both sweet spices and savory ones. Some of the common ones that professional tasters refer to in wine include:

Savory: Black pepper, white pepper, cumin, coriander, mustard powder

Sweet: Cinnamon, ginger, cloves, anise, licorice, nutmeg, allspice

The wines with the most obvious spicy style are usually made from Syrah grapes, or the Big Six, although you may have looked at the back labels of some oak-aged Cabernets or Merlots and seen them described as spicy, too. Without a doubt, the oak aging that is so common with Pinot Noir, Merlot, Cabernet Sauvignon, and Syrah lends a spiciness that tasters often pick up on. But usually the result is a subtler stamp of spice than you will find in the inherently spicy grapes and wine styles we are discussing here. I want you to taste wines that are especially known for their spicy character. I think you will love them, and you'll definitely notice their distinctive taste and compatibility with food.

Spicing Up Your Cellar

In terms of sales, the Big Six grapes are so dominant in this country that you'd assume the rest of the wine grape landscape is practically off-limits to most buyers. On the contrary, it's a buyer's paradise. As soon as you branch out of the Big Six mainstays of Chardonnay, Cabernet, and Merlot, you have a huge price advantage. The staple grapes in the Big Six are bastions of comfort for most wine drinkers, which means wineries can comfortably charge a premium for them. But a wine made from a no-name grape, or a blend of grapes, has to go to extra lengths to convince the wary buyer. I think that's one of the main reasons Syrah/Shiraz has come on so strong: the Aussie Shirazes in particular offered incredible prices for the quality in the 1980s and 1990s to get buyers' attention; it worked! Some of the other value-for-money options in this wine category are similarly rewarding.

But that is just one of the virtues of the spicy family of wines. Another is that they are some of the best wines in the world with food. It all makes sense, really. Aside from *amour* and *amore*, food is what the French and Italians do better than anyone else. If you have traveled there or have European friends, you know that these cultures treat even the simplest of repasts as an art form. And while it is true that some of the world's greatest and most expensive wines come from Europe, what most people in France and Italy drink daily is wines from spicy, no-name grapes. Considering how well they eat and drink, I think this strategy deserves some attention.

The fact is that many of the so-called no-name grapes are some of the world's greatest in terms of the wine quality they produce. But they are not necessarily on the tip of every buyer's tongue. First, often they are not as widely grown throughout the world as the Big Six. Second, they are often blended with other grapes and listed not under varietal names, but under regional names (which may themselves be famous). Some examples include:

Sangiovese: You might not know this red grape name, but you have probably heard of Italian Chianti, for which it is the main ingredient.

Tempranillo: As a varietal wine, this red grape is an up-and-comer, but in the Spanish regional wines Rioja and Ribera del Duero, it is world famous.

In this tasting, I will show you two of my favorite spicy wine styles, one white and one red, so you can experience the excitement first hand.

White

The Gewürztraminer (guh-VURTS-truh-mee-nuhr) Grape

For German-language speakers, this grape sends its message loud and clear. *Gewürz* translates to spicy, *traminer* means grape. And it is aptly named, as you will taste for yourself. Choose either an American or French one from the list below.

AMERICAN GEWÜRZTRAMINER	FRENCH GEWÜRZTRAMINER FROM THE ALSACE REGION
Hogue Cellars	Hugel
Navarro Vineyards	Trimbach
Beringer	Lucien Albrecht
Fetzer	Pierre Sparr
Chateau Ste. Michelle	Leon Beyer
Meridian	Schlumberger
(or your store's recommendation)	(or your store's suggestion)

THE LOOK: Look at the wine against a white background.

The color is straw yellow to yellow-gold.

THE SMELL: Swirl the glass, then smell.

Give yourself a moment to really take it in. You may sense ginger, clove, nutmeg, and allspice. Many people also detect aromas of some spicier fruits, such as lychee nuts and apricots.

This wine is medium- to full-bodied, and the flavor definitely echoes the scent. It is easy to see why many people like Gewürztraminer with exotically spiced foods such as Chinese and Thai.

Given the grape name, you may be asking, Why no German Gewürztraminer? The surprising fact is that very little Gewürztraminer is grown in Germany. Alsace in France is the most famous region for this grape, and the United States, though a small player, makes some high-quality versions.

Red

Syrah, aka Shiraz (Suh-RAH *and* Shuh-RAHZ, *respectively*)

For me, this grape was love-at-first-taste. It has everything—luscious texture, rich flavor, full body, and of course that irresistible spice. Syrah's traditional home is France's Rhône Valley, between Lyon and the Mediterranean, where the vines alternately bask in the sunshine and struggle against the brutal wind called the Mistral.

Beyond France, a lot of winemakers tell me Syrah will be "the next big thing" from Washington, and it's a definitely grown in importance in California over the last decade. Finally, under the Aussie moniker Shiraz, it is without a doubt the biggest thing Down Under, and has been for a very long time. In fact, some of the most famous Australian Shiraz wines are made from vineyards that are older than the folks who drink them—in some cases a lot older (read on for more about "old vines"). For this tasting, I will suggest selections from all three areas. It would be fun and delicious to try one wine from each place.

FRENCH SYRAH	AMERICAN SYRAH/AUSTRALIAN SHIRAZ
These versions are all from the Rhône Valley, and named for their growing region (in bold). The names following each region are alternate wineries from which to choose.	**CALIFORNIA** The best Syrah areas are Mendocino and the Central Coast AVAs.
CROZES-HERMITAGE Jaboulet Alain Graillot Colombo Chapoutier Chave	McDowell Joseph Phelps Vin du Mistral Cline Cellars RH Phillips Qupé Andrew Murray Edmunds St. John Echelon Jade Mountain
CÔTES DU RHÔNE Perrin Reserve	**AUSTRALIAN SHIRAZ** Penfolds Kalimna Bin 28 Wynn's Michael
ST. JOSEPH Jaboulet Chapoutier	d'Arenberg "The Footbolt" Leasingham Bin 61 Hardy's Nottage Hill Château Tahbilk
CORNAS Clape Colombo (or your store's suggestion)	Wolf Blass Peter Lehmann "Clancy's" (or your store's suggestion)

THE LOOK: Look at the wine against a white background.

Syrah/Shiraz is deeply colored, from ruby red to inky purple.

THE SMELL: Swirl the glass, then smell.

It's an intense wine. The great thing about Syrah/Shiraz is that very often, both savory *and* sweet spices come through. Its signature scent is freshly ground black pepper, so start by looking for that—take in the scent of a few cranks on your pepper mill for a reference point, if you like. You may notice cumin or a dried chili pepper aroma, too. Give your sniffer a few seconds' rest, and then go back—chances are you will find something new: anise, licorice, clove, nutmeg, allspice, eucalyptus, mint. Syrah is capable of all that, and more.

THE TASTE: Now sample the wines.

You will notice the full body, and also tannin—ample but balanced and not overpowering. In the taste, the spicy character overlays lots of ripe, rich Syrah flavor.

WATCH WASHINGTON

Syrah is hot stuff on the Washington wine scene, and it's exciting. The acreage planted in Syrah is growing rapidly, and the soils and climate conditions certainly seem right to ripen this big, brawny grape. In my tasting, I've found the wines to have rich fruit and great structure. However, most are short on the spice factor that I consider to be a signature for this grape. So for now, there are no Washington Syrahs in my spicy wines tasting. Stay tuned!

Tasting for Floral

Let's first clear up a misconception: Floral does not mean a wine that tastes like perfume (although it's easy to understand how a label-reader could jump to that conclusion). But some wines have an intoxicating perfumelike *aroma*. Floral is yet another style description that applies chiefly to the wine's scent, although the flavors are still of fruit.

The Nose Knows

The last chapter dealt with "Putting Flavors into Words," yet as we continue exploring wine descriptions, we keep coming back to where we began: the nose—yours and, now, the wine's. Wine professionals and bottle labels often refer to a wine's scent as its "nose," as in "a wine with a spicy nose." Even when we looked at basics like the Big Six wine grapes, we found the scent most revealing of each grape's character. As we look at the rest of the label, you'll see that many of the major wine words and descriptions focus on scent. As we already learned, it all comes down to the amazing capabilities of the nose (yours) to discern the finest of distinctions and variations in all the scents nature has to offer. Smelling a floral wine is like smelling perfume. Your nose cannot necessarily isolate individual blossoms, but you get an overall impression of flowers.

Shalimar, Ornellaia, Chanel No. 5, Le Bouge, Obsession, Opus One—these are famous fragrances, and famous wines. Can you pick which is which? The similarities between fine fragrances and fine wines don't stop with the luxurious names (and prices). Like wines, the scents of fragrances rely on a "layering" of often very exotic combinations of different aromas, which change and gain complexity when combined in an alcoholic base, which is also common to both.

FRAGRANCE	WINE
Scent evolves with exposure to air	Scent evolves with exposure to air
Heat of your skin releases and changes scent	Heat in your mouth releases and changes flavor (scent)
Everyone's chemistry and preferences are different	Everyone's chemistry and tastes are different
You can smell the complexity	You can taste *and* smell the complexity

There is, however, a very big difference. For perfumers, fragrant essences, either captured from nature or chemically derived, are the raw materials from which to craft alluring scents. Winemakers must coax their flavors and scents from the vineyard, and then the fermentation process. Mother Nature throws so many variables into the mix that most winemakers say they look at their life's work as one big experiment, for which they get only one harvest per year to check their progress. Many tell me they owe their best results to a little bit of gut feel, a lot of luck, and, mostly, a great vineyard. It is no wonder the world's most famous vineyards are considered hallowed ground. And in the case of fermentation, despite extensive ongoing research, relatively little is known about how its chemical reactions result in complex scents in wine, and thus very little is in the winemaker's control. Bible readers might say it was meant to be that way: "[The Lord] brings forth food out of the earth; and wine that maketh glad the heart of man" (Psalms 104: 14–15).

If you are not a gardener of exotic flowers, a great way to familiarize yourself with these different scents is to head to the mall. Candle shops and stores specializing in fragrant cosmetics, such as The Body Shop or Caswell-Massey, often display extensive lines of products (candles, aromatherapy oils, etc.) that let you take in the individual scents of these flowers. I once worked with a perfumer to develop a tasting of wines whose scents mimicked the essences in a range of very famous perfumes.

Some of the most common floral scents associated with wine are orange blossom, honeysuckle, lilac, lavender, lily, hyacinth, jasmine, and hibiscus. In my experience, floral is one of the harder wine terms for tasters to relate to, probably because most of us come in contact with these exotic scents only rarely. Just keep an open mind as you continue experimenting, and you may find that you develop an appreciation for floral characteristics in wine. On the other hand, if this style doesn't really click for you, don't worry about it. Remember that the purpose of this vocabulary is to open your eyes to all the sensory possibilities in wine, and thus add to your enjoyment. You need not waste time with words that don't further the cause.

Although there are some red wines with floral characteristics, it is mostly a signature of certain white wine styles. Here is a tasting of a wine often celebrated for its signature floral character. The grape is the Muscat, a variety with ancient origins and widely grown throughout the world for both eating and winemaking. The Italian name is Moscato, and the wine we are going to taste is Moscato d'Asti (*Moh-SCAH-toe DAH-stee*), a lightly sparkling wine that is the sister wine to the popular Asti Spumante, both from the Piedmont region of Italy.

I have found that people love this wine style once they try it. It has a lovely light spritz, a touch of sweetness, light body, and, of course, that signature floral scent. It is also low in alcohol, making it a great brunch wine—it beats a mimosa any day. The name Moscato d'Asti follows a naming pattern common in many Italian wines: the grape, Moscato, attached to the town or region, Asti (more on this in Chapter 7).

MOSCATO D'ASTI

These are all wineries that make delicious Moscato d'Asti:

Rivetti "La Spinetta"
Michele Chiarlo* "Nivole"
Paolo Saracco
Bruno Giacosa
Vietti
Mionetto
Marco Negri

If your local shop suggests a brand not listed here, I'd go with their recommendation. Moscato d'Asti wines are remarkably reliable.

THE LOOK: Look at the wine against a white background.

The wine is straw yellow, with delicate bubbles. Sometimes there is a faint pinkish tinge to the color.

THE SMELL: Swirl and smell.

This is floral. I would not be surprised if you are tempted to dab this behind your earlobes and wear it as a fragrance. (But remember there is some sugar here, so it could get sticky.) I usually detect mostly orange blossom and honeysuckle, but also lily and hyacinth—scents of spring. The main fruit scents of Muscat are grape (one of the few wines that smell like grapes), tangerine, mandarin orange, apricot. There is sometimes ginger as well in this highly fragranced wine.

THE TASTE: Now sample the wine.

The fruit flavors are simply beautiful—orangey and grapey, like the scent. The delicate bubbles and light body make this a truly pleasant, quaffable wine. Note the slightly sweet taste, as well. Aside from brunch, this is lovely as an aperitif and with spicy oriental and Indian foods.

---

*A "ch" in Italian is pronounced as a "k" sound, as in "zucchini." Thus *Mee-KEH-leh Kee-AHR-low.*

Label Lingo: Style Words

As we have discovered, knowing the major wine words on a bottle label can help you know what you are buying. For the curious among you, here are the meanings of some other terms often found on wine labels—some of them informative, others just plain outlandish. Why do wineries put some of these more wine-geeky statements on their bottles? I think they're just going a little overboard in their zeal, like passionate devotees of anything. Still, when they resort to wild lingo, they usually lose the rest of us along the way. In the wine world, I have spotted some over-the-top technical wine terms, such as "canopy management," on the back labels of even bargain bottles. I call them Stupid Label Tricks because they tell the average buyer very little, if anything, about the style of the wine inside.

Words Related to Style

Bright This word usually comes with an attachment—bright fruit, or bright acidity. It means the fruit flavor or acidity grab your attention right at first sip, as one of the wine's most prominent characteristics. Wines with this description can be especially refreshing.

Exotic Just as it applies to other things, this description suggests unusual and alluring characteristics in wine. It often refers to wines with a floral or spicy style, or with flavors beyond your typical fruit bowl, such as tropical fruits or rare berries. But with wine, the sky is really the limit.

Food friendly Food-friendly wines are especially good tablemates, with taste characteristics like spiciness and vibrant acidity that match well to a wide variety of foods, without overpowering or clashing.

Malo-lactic fermentation Yikes! Sounds scary. This is a second fermentation that winemakers use to soften the edgy taste of acidity in wine. It converts sharp-tasting malic acid into softer-tasting lactic acid, a contrast similar to the difference between a Granny Smith apple (tart) and a Golden Delicious apple (milder). It is routine in red winemaking—without it, many red wines would taste harsh. When white winemakers use malolactic fermentation, it gives the wine a softer style that is sometimes buttery.

Notes, hints, and tones These words are used when a wine displays "just a touch" of a particular scent or flavor, as in the "grassy notes" of some Sauvignon Blancs, "hints of buttery character" in certain Chardonnays, "vanilla tones" from oak aging, and so on.

Varietal character A wine with varietal character displays the typical scents, flavors, body, and style of the grape (varietal) used to make it.

Quality: Where It Comes From

Some of the most advanced label lingo is a group of words connected to quality, but before we can understand or use them, we need to examine what quality means in some detail.

When it comes to wine, the usual tendency is to link quality to price. But there is a trap here into which many buyers fall: The belief that price and quality are neatly proportional, as in the twenty-dollar bottle is twice as good as the ten-dollar one. You certainly have a right to expect better quality for a higher price, but supply and demand, marketing hype, and brand recognition also figure into pricing. It is frequently true that you can pay more and get better wine, but it is not the case that you *must* pay a lot for good wine. Let's look at quality in wine, both how it is achieved and how it tastes.

What makes quality wine? Insert "food," "shoes," or any other product in place of "wine," and the answer to this question is basically the same. Quality comes from two things: excellent raw materials (the "garbage in, garbage out" principle), and skilled handling of those raw materials to maximize their potential.

Great Wine Is Made in the Vineyard

In the case of wine grapes as the raw material, a lot of factors influence the quality level. Vineyard location, soil, and topography make a quality difference since grapes are like any plant. Consider your garden tomatoes. Some locations work better than others, depending on the type of soil, the drainage, sun and shade patterns, and the amount and timing of watering. The same factors affect the quality of grapevines' output.

Here are some interesting points to note about wine growing:

Bad soils make good wines. What is unusual about vines in this context is the type of soil needed for best results. While most farmers look for fertile ground, wine grape growers know that poor soils low in organic content make the best wines. The reason is that fertile soils promote vigorous growth, causing the vine to feed its energy to the green parts of the plant—the leaves and shoots—rather than to ripening the fruit.

Example: In France's famous Burgundy region, the hillsides, where soils are rocky and poor due to erosion, are home to the best-quality vineyards. Vine plots on the flat land, where the soil is richer, produce more ordinary wines that typically sell at a fraction of the price of the hillside-grown wines.

Vines should work for their water. For most vegetables and fruits, an ample water supply is crucial to how the garden grows. Grape vines need plenty of water, too, but how and when they get it has a major impact on wine quality. As grape growers say, vines should struggle for their water, and they don't like "wet feet." The struggle results in a healthier plant, and more flavorful grapes, by encouraging the vine to devote its energy to root and grape growth, the good stuff, rather than excess leaves. "Wet feet" refers to roots planted in soils that hold moisture. Since vines are prone to rot in damp conditions, well-drained soils suit them better. That is why great vineyards are often those engineered for good drainage—sloped, or rocky, or both. Nature can do the engineering, or technology. In preparing a new vineyard wineries may use earth movers to engineer vineyard slopes and drainage where they didn't previously exist.

Example: Chile's vineyards are known for their access to virtually unlimited irrigation water—the melting snow runoff from the nearby Andes Mountains. Historically, this allowed high production quantities but limited Chile's quality potential. A new wave of Chilean wineries is improving quality by avoiding overirrigation. The top-quality Casa Lapostolle winery uses "dry farming"—no irrigation at all.

Growing season weather is critical to quality. This answers the question, What makes a "good year" or a "good vintage"? The amount and timing of sun, rain, wind, and so on directly affects the flavor quality of the grapes, and thus the wine. Some years are better than others—just as with your tomatoes.

Viticultural methods make a major quality difference. Many winemakers say "Great wine is made in the vineyard." They focus on the term I used above, "wine growing," rather than "winemaking." This philosophy emphasizes tasks done in the vineyard to promote the health of the vines and the resulting quality of the grapes and wine. Some of the big things are pest and weed management, managing the soil's nutrition, and pruning. The successful tomato gardener hoes, controls bugs, adds nutrients to the soil, and desuckers the plants (removing the spindly green growth so the plant's energy concentrates on ripening its produce). The quality-grape grower's tasks are similar. Tasks for cutting off the vine's excess growth include pruning (removing excess buds) and shoot-thinning (removing the excess green parts).

Lower yield is associated with higher quality. The yield is just the output of grapes or juice per vine plant. It is one of the foremost quality factors. Even the healthiest vine's capacity to ripen fruit is finite, in the same way that the productive capacity of a machine or a person has limits. Wine growers actively control each plant's yield and shape by pruning, as you would with trees or rosebushes. But what is interesting is that all of the quality factors mentioned above directly affect yield as well. Here's how:

- Poor soils give lower vine yields than fertile soils. The rich soils of California's Great Central Valley, source of most of California's "jug wines," easily yield thirteen tons per acre of grapes and up. The less fertile soil for a top Napa or Sonoma vineyard might yield two or three tons per acre.

- Less water gives lower yields. In France's famous Bordeaux region, 1961 was a drought year with one of the smallest, and finest-quality, grape crops ever. A lot of irrigation, or rain near harvest time, can swell the grapes, raising the yield but also diluting the flavor. Just imagine pouring a glass of wine, then adding water. Wouldn't taste as good.

- Bad weather can lower yields. In spring, a storm can knock off the vine's flowers, which are its future grape clusters. This happened in parts of California in 1998, and the crop was very small.

- Certain viticultural practices can lower yields. Pruning is the grape grower's main method for yield control. Quality-minded grape growers prune aggressively, cutting off excess buds (from which grape clusters would form), to reduce each vine's yield. And many of the top vineyards even "green prune," cutting off some grape clusters before harvest so that the remaining ones will have the best flavor possible. The clusters drop to the ground, making for very expensive fertilizer.

Skilled Handling

We know what goes into good grapes. Now let's look at the human factor in the quality equation. It is logical enough to assume that a skilled and experienced winemaker can make the most of the grapes, whatever their quality level. Certain wineries in every region are known for making consistently good wines, year in and year out (more on this in Chapter 8). Mother Nature is in control of so many of the factors affecting grape quality, but an experienced vintner can improvise and adjust in the face of whatever surprises she may spring and still make good wine. And in a great year with great grapes, they are capable of true artistry.

What does quality wine taste like? Really great? Not necessarily. I have seen it all too often when, with much eager anticipation, a customer splurges on a famous bottle. Mentally, he prepares for an out-of-body wine-drinking experience. He drinks. His reaction ranges from underwhelmed to "Yuck!" He concludes: "Something's wrong with me. I guess I just don't get this wine thing." If that sounds familiar, here is what I would like you to understand about tasting and drinking quality wine:

Quality is in the eye of the beholder, or at least the sensory aspect of it. You may recognize and respect the quality components and workmanship in a car or a home or a pair of shoes, but they may not be to your taste. Similarly, it isn't worth paying extra for a quality wine if it is not your style.

Quality wine can taste weird, or even yucky. Most people have been stung by an experience like the one above. I always tell waiters to avoid steering customers toward the most exclusive, and expensive, bottles on the wine lists I create, despite their quality reputation. That is because a wine's fame may be based on its *potential* to taste great after years of age. Such wines, when opened and served before that potential is reached, can really disappoint. And some quality wine styles are an acquired taste. Their fame may be owed to a very distinctive style that is not instantly attractive to all comers. Think of the first taste of a stinky gourmet cheese for the person weaned on supermarket American singles, or the first sip of Guinness stout for the Budweiser drinker. It is sensory shock-therapy, and not necessarily pleasant.

Quality is sometimes inversely proportional to quantity. That is because it is easier for wine growers to focus on, and make the most of, smaller vineyard plots and/or smaller lots of wine—say, a few carefully tended barrels rather than a whole fleet of super-sized vats. A good analogy is this: Think of a hand-tossed pie from your local pizzeria that is made to order versus pies found in the frozen-food section of your supermarket. The quality will be different, but so will your expectations, and the price.

Quality spans the price spectrum, from bargain to mega-bucks bottlings. For everyday-priced wines, say in the ten-dollar neighborhood, quality means a notably tasty wine that consistently stands out against similar-priced wines.

For mid-priced wines, my quality standards are especially strict. That is because these wines represent a "trade up" for most wine drinkers ready to try something new, and I say the bet should pay off handsomely. Mid-priced means different things, but for our purposes, assume from fifteen to thirty dollars in a retail store. I think most people, even with money to burn, consider higher prices a serious splurge.

For the increased price I expect complexity and balance. First, *complexity*. At first sip, the wine should command all your sensory attention, putting every synapse through its paces with scents, tastes, and textures. By the way, if you are not *giving* the wine all your sensory attention, at least at first, by tasting the way I have taught you, then the wine doesn't stand a chance, no matter the price. Then should come balance, a pleasure plateau, much like a runner's endorphin rush, when all your senses have risen to the occasion and you can just relax and enjoy a complete, sustained deliciousness that kicks in after the first few tastes.

For splurge wines, can you expect an out-of-body drinking experience? Sometimes, yes, these wines can be breathtaking, bewitching, unspeakably seductive (frankly, so can some of the mid-priced wines—*those* are the real treasures). As mentioned above, sometimes such wines may have a very unique style to which your tastes may not be accustomed, or they may need bottle age to reach their ultimate potential. As prices escalate, eventually a point of diminishing returns is reached, at least in terms of taste. This is because more than quality is factored into price: rarity (supply and demand), a high critic's score, or a famous reputation (the vineyard or the winemaker) are some of the major features that some buyers are willing to pay more for—sometimes a lot more. That is a personal decision, for which this book and lots of tasting experience will prepare you.

The bottom line is that learning what you like will help you develop your own definition of quality. As you sample and learn more, you can expect that definition to evolve as your tastes evolve. For me, that is what makes wine so exciting.

Back to Label Terms: Words Related to Quality

Canopy management I have seen this term on the back label of a *seven-dollar wine*. Canopy management refers to the way grape growers trellis the vines on wires or stakes to enhance the ripening process. A good thing, yes, but on a seven-dollar-wine label? Please.

Clonal selection Another head-scratcher, even for sophisticated buyers. Grape vines, like other living things, can mutate, so the same grape variety can have multiple versions, each with distinctive characteristics of size, flavor, aroma, and so on. The different versions are called clones. Winemakers may select a clone, or several of them, for the special character it will give to the wine or for its suitability to their particular vineyard conditions.

Complex Ordinary wines can seem just wet and ho-hum. A complex wine commands your attention, revving up your senses with its scents, flavors, and textures, and luring you back to the glass for more.

Dry-farmed This term has zero meaning to the average label reader. Now you know that excess water or easy access to water causes the vine to waste its energy on leaf growth rather than on producing ripe and flavorful grape clusters. Growers who dry farm often do so to coax the maximum flavor from the grapes. They may put this term on the back label because they want you to be aware of the extra efforts they make to increase quality.

Old vines Keep your eyes peeled for this term. It often means wine with extra complexity. As vines mature, they are capable of producing grape clusters with greater complexity and flavor, which can translate right to the wine. Not all wines from old vine sources mention that on the label, but here are some styles to look for: red Shiraz wines from Australia, red Zinfandels from California, and many French wines, where the label term is *vieilles vignes* (*vee-ay* VEEN-*yuh*).

Poor soil For an already dubious wine buyer, "poor soil" on a back label could seem like a warning sign. But as we have learned, poor soil encourages the vine to concentrate on fruit ripening rather than leaf growth, leading to better quality. Similarly, "well-drained soil" is good because wet vineyard soils can lead to rot and other vine ailments, while soils with good drainage promote healthier vines.

Terroir (*tear-WAHR*) This is a French term referring to the distinctive growing conditions of each vine plot (vineyard location and slope, weather and soil). Many, including me, believe terroir is displayed in the wine as a unique and special taste character. Other specialty products capture a similar idea of distinctive growing areas—Vidalia onions from Georgia; prosciutto di Parma from Parma, Italy; Kona coffee from Hawaii; and so on.

Unfiltered This term is both trendy and controversial. That is because the influential wine reviewer Robert M. Parker, Jr., has criticized the use of filtration, common in winemaking, because he believes it strips the wine of flavor and character. Some wineries agree with him, others do not. I don't think you need to worry whether this term is on your wine label. It is not a guarantee you will love the wine.

Yield, low yield Lower vine yields mean fewer clusters and less juice produced per plant. This usually gives more flavorful, complex-tasting grapes and wines.

Should you memorize these words? If you want to, but it is certainly not necessary. The memorable attributes of wines that you enjoy will make a big impression on their own without you working hard to memorize a vocabulary list. When you *do* find styles that you especially like (or dislike), refer to this chapter and put words to it—a smooth Pinot Noir, a buttery Chardonnay, a spicy Shiraz, a grassy Sauvignon Blanc. This will enable you to read labels and find similarly styled wines on future shopping trips, or to comfortably describe your style preferences to a wine merchant or waiter. Still more power to you, and we haven't even addressed all the fruit descriptions on the label.

Read on, precocious taster. In Chapter 4 we will mine the wine label and raid the produce section so that you can understand all those fruit-style descriptions. I will also give you a road map to help predict which fruit styles you are likely to find in a wine just by looking at its label or wine list entry.

CHAPTER FOUR

A Flavor Map
of the Wine World

". . . flavors of dark cherries and raspberries . . ."

". . . apples and pears with a hint of citrus . . ."

". . . rich, tropical fruit flavors . . ."

This is a major turning point on our wine route. We are leaving the test track of wine tasting, where we defined our fruit flavor descriptions in terms of the Big Six wine grapes so that you could learn the distinctive styles of each. Now we are ready to hit the open road and explore the entire spectrum of fruit flavors in wine.

Putting Fruit Flavor on the Map

Let me introduce you to what I call the Flavor Map, a guide to understanding the full range of fruit flavors found in all the quality wines produced in the world. About fifteen years ago I left a budding career in investment banking to pursue my passion—wine. In the field of wines, keeping abreast of the market means you taste hundreds of wines every week. I found that the best way to learn was to taste with people who were more experienced than I, and to listen to their descriptions. One day I listened to judges in a wine competition toss around dozens of different fruit and style descriptions—yet every wine they were tasting was made from the

Chardonnay grape. I asked one of them, "Why so many different styles?" "Because the grapes are grown in drastically different climates," she told me. "The taste in the bottle is a reflection of the amount of heat and sun in the growing region."

That made a huge impression on me. And cleared up a lot of confusion. I had experienced the broad range of flavor possibilities in grapes like Chardonnay, Pinot Noir, Merlot, and so on. But short of tasting and trying to memorize the style of every wine on the market (which I'll tell you right now is impossible), I could think of no way to predict the style of any particular bottle. Now I had a starting point that made a lot of sense—climate warmth and sunshine. Pineapples require lots of sun to grow and, as you will discover with our tastings, so do exotic, tropical fruit-flavored wines. That is how the Flavor Map was born.

Apples, mangos, cherries, figs, raisins ... wines are capable of just about every fruit flavor at the farmer's market, and you know it's not just because of climate. As we have already discussed, part of the answer is fermentation, which is what makes wine taste like wine. Once the yeasts get hold of grape juice, what started out as a pleasantly sweet liquid can be transformed into a drink of incredible complexity, with tastes and aromas not just of grapes but of other fruits as well. And alcohol, the other major by-product of fermentation, amplifies those flavors and scents, just as it intensifies the scents in perfumes and the flavored extracts used in baking.

You also know for the most part which wines will have which specific flavors. From our tasting comparisons, you are quite familiar with one of the factors that influences a wine's fruit style, namely, the grapes used. Certain grapes are associated with a unique style "signature," such as grassy and herbaceous notes in Sauvignon Blanc, floral flavors in Muscat, and the spice of Gewürztraminer. And as we discovered in Chapter 1, all of the major wine grapes have distinct fruit-flavor profiles. For example, the aroma and taste of the Riesling grape are different from that of Chardonnay. Our tastings in this chapter will let us explore and define more precisely the fruit character of each of those grapes, and our use of the Flavor Map is going to make sure you remember them without having to do any memorization.

Why Do You Need a Flavor Map?

The fact that all the major wine grapes have distinctive flavor styles does not mean that all wines made from them are the same. The excitement of wine is that each bottle of a type still has its own unique attributes, just as one thousand sunsets or a thousand beautiful brunettes can be spectacular, each in a different way. Many people find this diversity (you might call it unpredictability) to be one of the most intimidating aspects of wine.

But rise above the confusion and you will see that these variations really mean *possibilities*. Obviously, to comfortably explore and enjoy all of these possibilities, you need a simple and precise way to predict how the fruit flavors will differ between, say, two Chardonnays or between an Oregon Pinot Noir and a California bottling—before you buy them. New taste sensations are one thing; a "flavor shock" is something else, especially if you are hoping to impress a date, the boss, or the in-laws.

This is why I developed the Flavor Map. It shows you how to predict which fruit flavors to expect from various wines, even bottles that are completely unfamiliar to you. We'll do this by examining the growing region on the label or the wine list entry, and answering one question about that region: Is it a cool place or a warm place?

Getting into the Climate Zone of Wine

The Flavor Map is based on climate, another major factor that shapes wine style. It's specifically concerned with the amount of warmth and sunshine where the grapes are grown. The principle behind the Flavor Map, which the tastings in this chapter will illustrate, is this: *Very diverse wines, when grown in the same climate zone, share a striking family resemblance in terms of their fruit-flavor profile.*

The Flavor Map charts this by dividing the wine world into climate-style zones:

Cool climate zone: cool/less sunny

Moderate climate zone: temperate/moderately sunny

Warm climate zone: warm/very sunny

And it shows which specific fruit flavors characterize each zone. This means that, from Australia to Zeltingen in Germany, and from Airen (the world's most widely planted wine grape) to Zinfandel, you can predict the fruit style of any wine if you know the climate zone in the region where it was grown.

"Cool Style" versus "Warm Style"

Before we focus on specific fruit tastes, it is helpful to first understand broadly how wine styles compare across the cool-to-warm climate zone spectrum. Classifying wines as "cool climate" or "warm climate" gives the taster very powerful clues to body and acidity, too. For virtually all wine types, here is how the taste components differ from a cool climate to a warm climate:

	Cool Climate Zone	Warm Climate Zone
SUN	Less sunny	Very sunny
ACIDITY	Crisp and tangy	Soft and smooth
BODY	Light	Full
FRUIT STYLE	"Green," lean and tart	Ripe and luscious

The Flavor Map plots these characteristics, adding all the different fruit flavors. On the left side, you see the climate zones. Following what you learned in elementary school geography, areas that are farthest from the equator are cool and less sunny; climates become warmer and sunnier as you get closer to the equator. On the right side, you see the fruit-flavor styles typically associated with each climate zone, for both white and red wines, ranging from tart and crisp fruits to ripe and luscious flavors. First, look at the legend opposite, so you can see what fruit flavors are associated with each climate zone.

Explore your taste memory and imagine this flavor range—for example, from tart green apple to plump peach to luscious mango for whites, and from sour cranberry to juicy plum to rich concentrated raisin for reds. Remember the lean-to-luscious fruit spectrum we saw in Chapter 2's discussion of the word *fruity*? You can see that the climate in the growing region is a logical basis for that flavor range.

It's that simple. Better still, you don't have to memorize the Flavor Map, or carry it with you wherever you go, because it is based on common sense. If you live in the Northern Hemisphere, it is easy to remember which fruit flavors typify each climate zone from cool to warm if you think about the fruits that typically grow in each. For example, let's begin with the major white wine fruit flavors. Crisper (tart, tangy) tree fruits like apples and pears grow in cooler, less sunny areas (generally at higher latitudes, in the north). For the Northern Hemisphere, think Maine and Washington.

By contrast, luscious, exotic fruits like pineapples and mangos grow in warm, sunny, and tropical areas closer to the equator (Hawaii, the Caribbean, Mexico). In the moderate zone you find citrus fruits (orange, lemon, lime, tangerine), stone fruits (peaches, apricots, nectarines), and melons. As you can see, unless you have led a strictly meat-and-potatoes life, you are well equipped to put your knowledge of these fruits and where they grow to work for you in a wine context, without a lot of tedious memorization. Our tasting lessons using the Flavor Map will simply reinforce what you already know.

At first glance, it might seem simplistic to reduce the wine world to just three style zones (cool, moderate, warm). But looking at the delicious range of flavors shown in the Flavor Map, you can see that it in no way diminishes the range of Pinot Noir's pleasures, for example, or the many faces of Chardonnay. In fact, the Flavor Map showcases all that diversity and character, and gives you access to it whatever your budget.

FLAVOR MAP OF THE WINE WORLD

		White Wine Fruit Flavors	Red Wine Fruit Flavors
	Cool Zone	apples, pears, quinces	cranberries, red currants, red cherries, pomegranates
	Moderate Zone	citrus (oranges, lemons, limes, tangerines, grapefruits), peaches, apricots, nectarines, melons, kiwifruits	black cherries, blackcurrants, blueberries, blackberries, plums, raspberries, strawberries
	Warm Zone	mangos, pineapples, papayas, guavas, bananas	figs, raisins, prunes
	Main Wine Regions	Warm Spots	Cool Spots

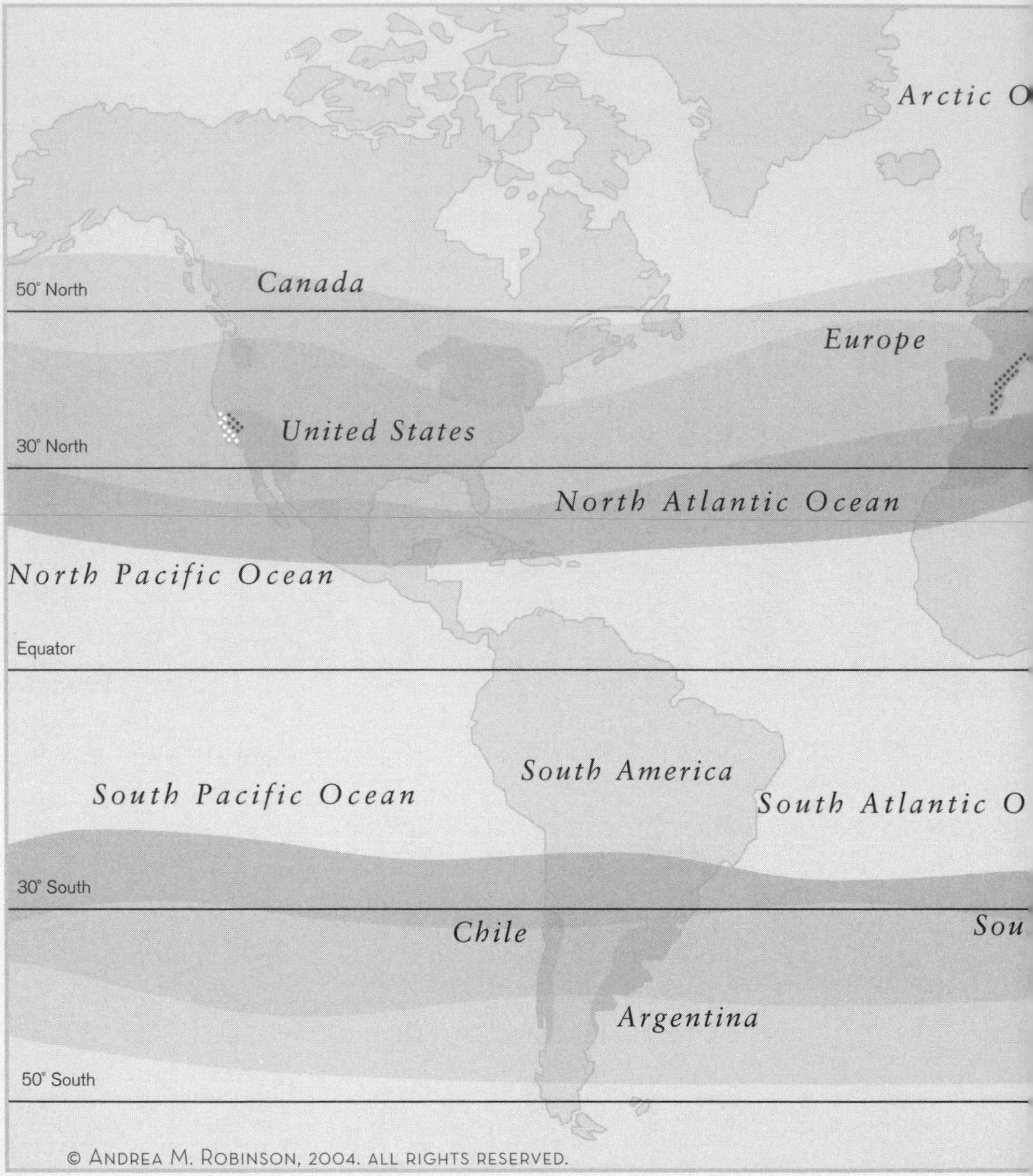

Arctic O

50° North

Canada

Europe

30° North

United States

North Atlantic Ocean

North Pacific Ocean

Equator

South America

South Pacific Ocean

South Atlantic O

30° South

Chile

Sou

Argentina

50° South

MAJOR WINE REGIONS OF THE WORLD
MAPPING THE CLIMATE ZONES AND FRUIT FLAVORS OF WINE

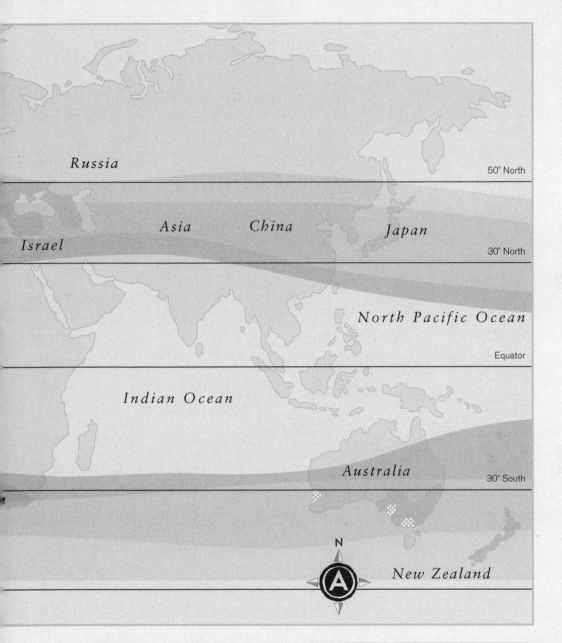

Russia

Asia   China   Japan

Israel   30° North

North Pacific Ocean

Equator

Indian Ocean

Australia   30° South

N

A   New Zealand

50° North

FLAVOR MAP OF THE WINE WORLD

		White Wine Fruit Flavors	Red Wine Fruit Flavors
	Cool Zone	apples, pears, quinces	cranberries, red currants, red cherries, pomegranates
	Moderate Zone	citrus (oranges, lemons, limes, tangerines, grapefruits), peaches, apricots, nectarines, melons, kiwifruits	black cherries, blackcurrants, blueberries, blackberries, plums, raspberries, strawberries
	Warm Zone	mangos, pineapples, papayas, guavas, bananas	figs, raisins, prunes

Main Wine Regions	Warm Spots	Cool Spots

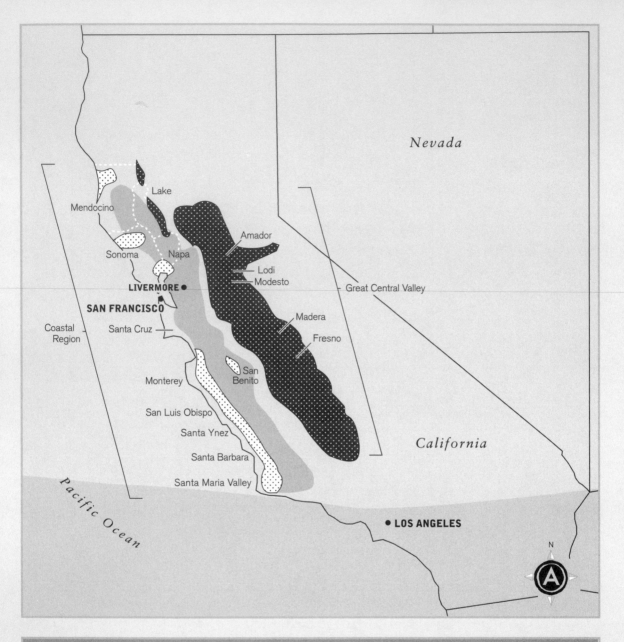

Nevada

Lake

Mendocino

Amador

Sonoma   Napa

Lodi
Modesto

LIVERMORE •

SAN FRANCISCO   Great Central Valley

Coastal   Santa Cruz
Region   Madera

Fresno

Monterey   San
                      Benito

San Luis Obispo   California

Santa Ynez

Santa Barbara

Santa Maria Valley

Pacific Ocean

• LOS ANGELES

N

CALIFORNIA FLAVOR MAP

		WHITE WINE FLAVORS	RED WINE FLAVORS
☐	Cool Zone	apples, pears, quinces	cranberries, redcurrants, red cherries, pomegranates
☐	Moderate Zone	citrus (oranges, lemons, limes, tangerines, grapefruits), peaches, apricots, nectarines, melons, kiwifruits	black cherries, blackcurrants, strawberries, blueberries, blackberries, plums, raspberries
☐	Warm Zone	mangoes, pineapples, papayas, guavas, bananas	figs, raisins, prunes
☐	Main Wine Regions	● Warm Spots	◌ Cool Spots

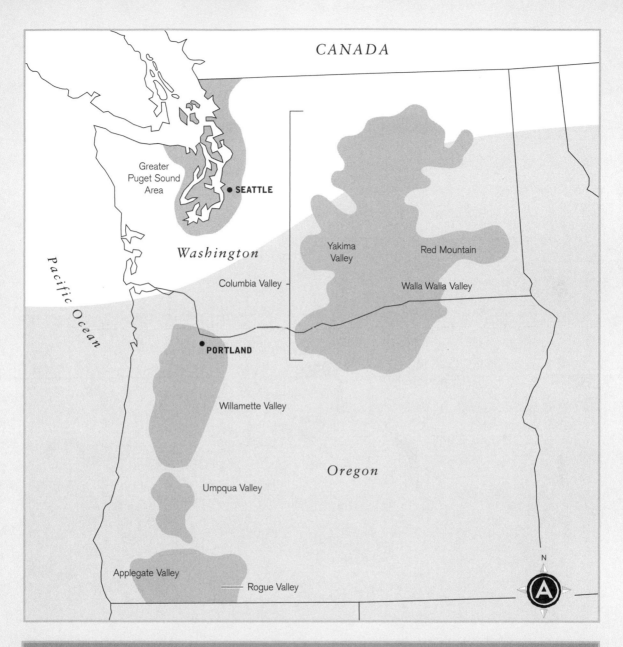

CANADA

Greater
Puget Sound
Area

● SEATTLE

Washington

Yakima
Valley

Red Mountain

Columbia Valley

Walla Walla Valley

Pacific Ocean

● PORTLAND

Willamette Valley

Oregon

Umpqua Valley

Applegate Valley

Rogue Valley

N

WASHINGTON AND OREGON FLAVOR MAP

		WHITE WINE FLAVORS	RED WINE FLAVORS
	Cool Zone	apples, pears, quinces	cranberries, redcurrants, red cherries, pomegranates
	Moderate Zone	citrus (oranges, lemons, limes, tangerines, grapefruits), peaches, apricots, nectarines, melons, kiwifruits	black cherries, blackcurrants, strawberries, blueberries, blackberries, plums, raspberries
	Warm Zone	mangoes, pineapples, papayas, guavas, bananas	figs, raisins, prunes
	Main Wine Regions		

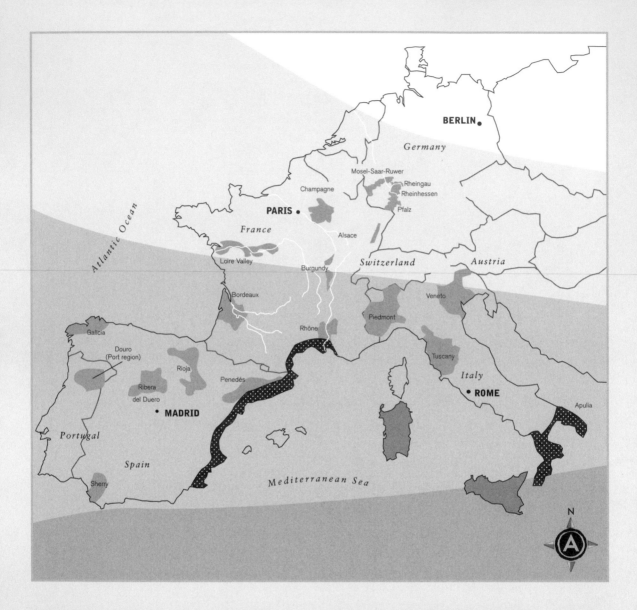

EUROPE FLAVOR MAP

		WHITE WINE FLAVORS	RED WINE FLAVORS
	Cool Zone	apples, pears, quinces	cranberries, red currants, red cherries, pomegranates
	Moderate Zone	citrus (oranges, lemons, limes, tangerines, grapefruits), peaches, apricots, nectarines, melons, kiwifruits	strawberries, black cherries, blackcurrants, blueberries, blackberries, plums, raspberries
	Warm Zone	mangos, pineapples, papayas, guavas, bananas	figs, raisins, prunes
	Main Wine Regions	Warm Spots	Cool Spots

There are three steps to using the flavor map:

1. Look at your wine label.
2. Find the wine's region of origin (the place where the grapes were grown)—Australia? Pouilly-Fuissé in Burgundy, France? Napa Valley, California?
3. If, in your mind's eye, you can place the wine's growing region into either the cool-style zone, the moderate zone or the warm-style zone of the Flavor Map, you can get a very good idea of the wine's fruit style.

Tasting Techniques of the Pros

When professionals do wine tasting, classifying wines as "cool climate" or "warm climate" is one of the first steps, especially when they are doing what is called "blind tasting." A blind tasting does not mean the participants are blindfolded. It means that the taster is given a glass (or several) of wine to identify based solely on its look, smell, and taste—a feat that can seem amazing to the average person. I was thirty years old when I passed the blind tasting in my Master Sommelier exam and won the title Best Sommelier in America. I did not grow up in a wine business family. (Although my dad and I once made a stoneware crockfull of Concord grape wine when I was seven. To my mom's chagrin, during fermentation it bubbled out all over the laundry room floor. It was very sweet, very sticky, very purple—and the taste was really vile.) But where I lacked encyclopedic tasting experience, I compensated with technique, including the cool climate/warm climate trick. Obviously, it is a very powerful tool for the blind taster. In our tasting comparisons, you will see how easy it is to use the same technique to help you as a buyer.

The Flavor Map and the Bottom Line

I am referring to *your* bottom line, of course. Even if you are not hankering for broader taste and style options than you get with the big brand-name varietal wines, money is a practical reason for broadening your wine horizons. You buy these big-name wines because they are recognizable and fairly consistent. But as with other products, you often pay extra for the "insurance" of a heavily advertised brand versus a lesser-known winery of comparable quality. It is what I call the "comfort premium," and it is especially prevalent in wine, a decidedly *un*comfortable subject for many buyers. Without a doubt, the branded varietal wines are a great jumping-off point for getting started in wine. But if you use tools like the Flavor Map to branch out into new choices that offer truly great value for the money, both your pleasure and your pocketbook stand to gain.

The Rising Cost of Comfort

For years, I used the Flavor Map premise to teach waiters, but never thought of it as something particularly useful for consumers. What I have seen in the wine industry has changed my mind. I call it "price creep." In the last ten years, the price of nearly every well-known, nationally available wine has seen a steep increase—from 15 percent to 25 percent or more. I am sure you have felt the sting. The bargain bottle that used to be $7.99 is now $9.99, your $10 bottles are now pushing $12 to $15 or more, and so on across the price spectrum. I taste these wines every day, and I can tell you that with very few exceptions, the quality of what is in the bottle is the same, and sometimes poorer. You're paying more, but you don't get more in terms of flavor. These days, anyone looking to maximize their flavor-per-dollar has no choice but to explore the alternatives.

Wine professionals like me who choose wines for stores or restaurants take great joy in uncovering the wine world's unsung heroes. We're always looking for wine selections that are long on quality and flavor but short on name recognition and thus priced lower to get your attention.

But you don't have to be a professional to find these deals. You can inquire about these wines when shopping or dining out, especially at smaller stores and restaurants where the buyer is often on the premises. All you need to do is ask. Try something like "What are the best values you've uncovered lately?" or "Have you discovered any sleepers recently in the ten-dollar-a-bottle range?" A lot of people are afraid to do this for fear of looking cheap, but trust me, you will have one excited merchant or wine waiter on your hands if you give them a chance to show you something new. One of my favorite wines to sell when I was Cellarmaster at Windows on the World was an obscure twenty-dollar bottle of red Côtes du Rhône (*Coat dew ROAN*) from France. That wine *rocked*. It thrilled my guests every time, and I loved that.

The Flavor Map in Action

Now that you understand the basic model, let's look at how you can put the Flavor Map to work for you in stores and restaurants.

Predicting the fruit flavors of Big Six varietal wines from unfamiliar wineries.

We might as well start with Chardonnay, because in the world of varietal wines, it rules. For wineries everywhere, it is truly the grape of choice, and with good reason. Its adaptability to a wide variety of growing conditions is virtually unequaled in the grape world. From the cool, frost-prone hills of the Chablis region in France to sun-baked South Australia, and practically everywhere in between, Chardonnay grows well and makes good (and sometimes great) wine.

On the buying side, Chardonnay is the wine market's equivalent of a Blue Chip stock. It virtually sells itself, and buyers confidently ask for it by name, whereas in the 1970s and 1980s, people used to order "chablis" (the generic stuff) or "a glass of dry white wine." In fact, some wineries joke that Chardonnay is really the accountants' favorite grape, because, for cash flow, it is practically a sure bet. Without exaggerating, I can say that for the average restaurant diner free-falling in a black hole of self-doubt (translation: looking at the wine list), Chardonnay is manna from heaven. In short, Chardonnay is to wine what steak and vanilla ice cream are to food—a safe haven.

But there is a catch. The truth is, you can only really count on getting the comfort of this quirk-free, plain-vanilla Chardonnay style from big, well-known winery brands, which are deliberately crafted in a crowd-pleasing, middle-of-the-road style to maximize market share. That is helpful information to be sure, but then there are hundreds of other Chardonnays in the shop and on the restaurant wine list. How on earth can you get some idea of what *those* wines will be like?

I first put the Flavor Map to work to solve exactly this problem. When I started as a sommelier-in-training at New York's Windows on the World restaurant, our thousand-selection wine list included Chardonnays from regions that spanned the globe. California bottlings and French white Burgundies (all made from Chardonnay) figured prominently, but also represented, in an amazing array of styles, were Argentina, Australia, Italy, New York, New Zealand, Oregon, Spain, South Africa, Texas, Virginia, and Washington State. With Chardonnay accounting for about 60 percent of our sales in the early 1990s, it became clear to me that my waiters and I needed to know how to quickly guide our guests toward a choice that would suit their style preferences and their menu selections. Otherwise, we'd never sell anything but the top ten or so brands, which is boring, both for the sommelier and the guests.

For waiters and guests, and for every Chardonnay lover, the Flavor Map is the perfect tool. Knowing what style to expect from a particular bottle is as simple as looking at the label and knowing a little geography. For example, take two Chardonnays, one from the Burgundy region of France, which is a cool place, and another from sunny Australia. Now think of the white wine flavors of the Flavor Map, from the cool zone to the warm zone. If you want the crisp, refreshing, applelike style of Chardonnay that comes from a cool climate, buy the French; if you prefer the ripe, luscious, tropical-fruit style of a warmer climate, the Australian bottling is the way to go.

It's instantly empowering. Whether you are faced with a wall of Chardonnays (or Cabernets, or any other grape) at the wine shop, or a wine list that doesn't offer any familiar names at a price you are prepared to pay, you can use the Flavor Map. It will help you confidently select a bottle based on your style preferences, your budget, your menu, or all three.

Perhaps even more important, you can also branch out without taking a big risk. In other words, regardless of which grape or style you are looking for, you no longer have to limit your choices to wines you already know.

Predicting the fruit flavors of regional and brand-name wines you haven't tried before.

I introduced the Flavor Map in the context of varietal wines, such as Chardonnay, which list the grape on the label. But the Flavor Map works just as well for regionally named wines and brand-name wines (wines with a trademark or fantasy name rather than a grape or region). Take, for example a Mâcon-Viré (which is named for its growing region in Burgundy, France) and the brand-named wine Quintessa, from Napa Valley, California. Burgundy is a cool region, so you can look at the Flavor Map and predict that the Mâcon-Viré (made from the Chardonnay grape) will have an apple and pear style, and you will be correct. Napa Valley is a moderate-to-warm climate, which clues you in to the berries-and-plums style of Quintessa.

What if you are not familiar with the climate zone of a particular growing region? For most well-known wine regions, you can certainly follow your knowledge of geography and your intuition. For the others, refer to the Flavor Map, which shows all the major growing regions in each climate zone.

The Flavor Map and Climate

Before we get to tasting, I want to emphasize an important point about the Flavor Map. Once again, it takes you back to the label and, like the other buying tools and techniques we've explored, converts what's there into style information that is easy to understand without a lot of memorization or technical knowledge. This is why the Flavor Map highlights what is obvious about growing regions: the climate zone of each, based mostly on latitude. As a rule, fine wine grapes grow successfully between the 30th and 50th parallels of latitude, north and south of the equator. Farther from the equator the weather is too cold, the grapes won't fully ripen, and chances are the vines will freeze and die in winter. Too close to the equator and you've got tropical heat that keeps the vines from going dormant (perfect for your winter vacation getaway but not for grape vines). Vines need the winter rest period to build energy to grow the next year's crop.

The aspect of climate that affects flavor most of all is the amount of warmth and sunshine during the growing season. And when it comes to these, there is more than latitude at work. One of the other major factors is weather, which is ever-changing.

A Change in the Weather

Some wines print a growing season weather report on the back label, but I think it usually means little to the buyer. The Flavor Map, however, works well year in and year out, because it reflects the *average* weather in each region. Vexing though they may be, the vagaries of weather are what make each vintage unique. In years of unusual growing season weather, here is what happens:

In a cool year, less warmth and fewer hours of sunshine mean the grapes do not ripen as thoroughly. In slightly cool years, the wines' fruit style edges toward those flavors of the cooler climate zones. So, for example, the fruit flavor of Australian Chardonnay in a cool year might taste less tropical and more applelike. In extremely cool years, the grapes in some regions may not ever reach sufficient ripeness to make quality wine—in plain English, "a bad vintage."

In a warm year, the corollary is obvious. Warm-weather years will yield fruit flavors that edge toward the exotic flavors of the warmer climate zones. French red Burgundy is a great example of this. In the warmest years, the wines taste of ripe raspberries and black cherries instead of the leaner, tart, cool red berry flavors (cranberry, redcurrant, and sour cherry) of average years. In general, wine drinkers tend to love exotic fruit flavors. This means that quite often, a warm year and "a good year" (or a great one) are considered synonymous.

Microclimate

Besides latitude and weather, there's also "microclimate," which the Flavor Map accounts for in simple terms. Microclimate simply refers to the growing conditions in a particular spot. Interestingly, the conditions even in vineyards that are quite close to one another can vary a lot. Have you ever visited a seaside town and found yourself cool or comfortable near the shoreline, but sweltering on the town square just a short distance inland?

Similarly, many wine regions have pockets or subsections where the microclimate differs quite a bit from the overall climate in the region. On the detailed Flavor Maps I have shown you the major ones. They are noted as Warm Spots and Cool Spots, which signals that they are warmer or cooler than average for their climate zone, and thus clues you in to how their fruit-flavor styles differ from the norm. There are quite a few causes for microclimate variations, but the two major ones—bodies of water and altitude differences—are very easy to understand.

BODIES OF WATER If you think of my seaside town example, then the significance of a nearby body of water is logical. Specifically, bodies of water temper climate extremes—cooling down hot spots and warming up cool spots, as in the famous wine regions, Germany and California.

Germany's great wine regions (Rhine, Mosel, Nahe, etc.) are all named for the rivers flowing through them. The rivers reflect the sun's light and heat onto the vines clustered on their banks, and they also maintain airflow, which helps reduce the risk of frost late in the growing season. In fact, without her rivers, most of Germany would just be too cold to grow wine grapes at all. This explains why most people rightly think of Germany as a beer country—where it is too cold for grapes, they grow and brew grain.

Many people think of California as a warm place—understandably. But its top wine regions all share one thing in common: They hug the coastline, where cool ocean breezes temper the heat. This is why all the famous regions—from Napa and Sonoma in the north to Santa Barbara in the south—share a moderate climate zone, sprinkled here and there with a few hot spots that are blocked from the ocean's influence, usually by mountains. Farther inland is the Central Valley, the source of jug wines and basic "California" bottlings, and one big warm spot. On the label, it is increasingly common for California wineries to make reference to cooler-climate vineyards, to emphasize their use of grape sources that are considered to be of higher quality than those in the hot Central Valley.

THE COASTAL DIFFERENCE You see the word *coastal* prominently displayed on a broad array of California wines. Some famous wineries like BV (Beaulieu Vineyard) have developed entire "Coastal" product lines. The reasons are both viticultural and traditional. In terms of wine production, California's moderate and cooler coastal zones are considered to produce better-quality grapes than the warm Central Valley. This is because regardless of where you are in the wine world, temperate growing conditions are acknowledged to result in grapes with more refined flavor and better balance than hot conditions, where the grapes ripen fast and their acid is lower. As we noted previously, acidity is an important preservative of a wine's flavor, balance, and complexity.

On the viticulture side, there's a marketing reason for this interest in the coast. You might have noticed that, on moderately priced wines these days, "Coastal" shows up on labels a lot more than, say, "Napa Valley." A few years ago, a vine ailment called phylloxera (*fuh*-LOCK-*sir*-*uh*) struck California, hitting famous coastal zones like the Napa Valley especially hard. To maintain production levels, wineries had to source fruit from other coastal growing zones, and also develop new ones. The term *Coastal* is typically used for wines that are blended from a lot of different coastal regions, or from coastal regions that lack consumer name recognition.

In terms of tradition, delineating a wine as Coastal distances it from the products of the Central Valley, whose quality reputation suffers from the fact that its warm growing conditions have long been exploited for generic and jug wine production—the lowest common denominator in terms of quality. The fact is that, as varietal wines have gained favor over generics in the past few years, the trend in this region has turned toward wines with improving balance and notably higher quality, with the jug stigma on the wane. Stay tuned.

Although you need not memorize the details of each region, you should keep in mind the significant quality impact of bodies of water (oceans, rivers, lakes) on the world of wine.

The list of famous wine regions below underscores this point:

Region	Water Body
Coastal California (Napa, Sonoma, etc.)	Pacific Ocean
Bordeaux, France	Gironde River and tributaries
Rhône Valley, France	Rhône River
Loire Valley, France	Loire River
Germany's top vineyards	Mosel, Rhine, and Nahe Rivers

ALTITUDE   Altitude is rarely cited on wine labels, but I mention it here because it, too, helps explain some of the cool spots on the Flavor Map. If you think of snow-capped mountains in summer, this one is obvious. Very simply, a higher altitude makes for a cooler microclimate. Australia is a warm place, but you would hardly recognize the usual Aussie characteristics in the Rieslings and Chardonnays grown in the Adelaide Hills and Eden Valley districts, which are at higher altitudes and thus show up as cool spots on the Flavor Map.

A Taste Tour of the Flavor Map

Aside from a corkscrew, your best tool to navigate the Flavor Map is an open mind, and maybe a bit of poetic license. This is important to remember as you do the tastings in this chapter. By now, your senses of smell and taste are well-honed, so you are going to notice the fruit-flavor differences in the wines as you compare them. But you may not yet have the words for the flavors; that comes with experience, which is, of course, what the tastings are for. As we taste, I will help you with the vocabulary. If you don't agree with one of my descriptions, insert your own. The fruit styles on the Flavor Map are reference points for the taster, not hard-and-fast rules set by the Wine Police.

Sampling the Local Flavor

Some fruit descriptions for wine, like apples, have universal acceptance because most everyone is familiar with them. But there are many fruits that are local to a particular area. As such, it can get a little confusing when they are used to describe a wine. Here are the ones commonly used by wineries and on bottle labels, with their source and a short description of the style.

Blackcurrant British and French tasters use this moderate-zone fruit flavor to describe the classic taste of Cabernet Sauvignon, yet it leaves many Americans in the dark because blackcurrants are not widely grown here. (I finally found a farm growing them in upstate New York, and went there just to taste them.) A related word is cassis, which is the liqueur made from blackcurrants that you can find in liquor stores if you want to learn this flavor and scent. Another thing to try is blackcurrant jam or preserves, sold in supermarkets and specialty food stores.

Redcurrant This is a flavor sometimes attributed to Pinot Noir.

These, too, are rare in the United States, although I have occasionally seen them fresh at farmer's markets and upscale groceries. They are tart and tangy. You can sample redcurrant jelly to get an idea.

Gooseberries Another British term that is classically used to describe Sauvignon Blanc from cool zones. It is an extremely tangy flavor. I have seen gooseberry preserves sold in gourmet stores, but they are very sweet, so you don't quite get the pungently tart effect.

Quince Europeans use this term, although quinces are increasingly available in this country. When raw, they have a mouth-puckering feel that is almost tannic, so the description usually refers to quince when sweetened and cooked, as preserves or a candylike paste. It has a slightly spicy, rich apple-pear taste.

Lychee Rather than being local to a specific area, the lychee fruit description is quite widely used for one very distinctive grape—the Gewürztraminer. But since lychees, a native of southeast Asia, are so exotic, many who read the word *lychee* on a back label might not be familiar with it. Remember our taste of "spicy" Gewürztraminer in Chapter 3? Try canned lychees, which are available in Asian groceries and supermarkets (next to the Chinese food ingredients), and you will see that it's the perfect fruit descriptor for this spicy grape.

Flavor Mapping the Big Six Varietal Wines

These tastings will put the Flavor Map into sensory terms, showing you the cool-to-warm climate range of fruit styles in our Big Six grape varieties. Although we're tasting Big Six wines, my wine suggestions will not be limited to bottles with the grape on the label. That way we may include, as we have in past chapters, famous regional wines that are based on the Big Six grapes.

These tastings will also illustrate another enlightening fact about wine grapes—namely, that each has its own climate affinity. For example, Pinot Noir gives its best results in cooler climates, while Cabernet Sauvignon flourishes in a moderate to warm climate. As you will see, these affinities for climate zone are a great clue to the basic fruit style of each grape—in other words, those flavors that make a Pinot a Pinot, and so on.

Riesling

Riesling is a grape that grows best in climates that are cool, edging into moderate—Germany and Alsace, France, are its strongholds. Austria, Canada, New York's Finger Lakes district, and the coolest parts of Australia and New Zealand also achieve greatness with Riesling. California and Washington State make small amounts of good Riesling, too, including dessert wine styles.

Consequently, our tasting will feature just cool-zone and moderate-zone Rieslings. With the Flavor Map, you could predict what tastes to expect—apple and pear flavors from the cool zone, stone fruits such as peaches from the moderate zone. As any experienced taster would tell you, that is a perfect summary of the Riesling grape's fruit style. Many pros find Riesling to have a floral style, especially in wines coming from the cool zone. (Wineries do not produce "oaky" Rieslings, because oak overpowers the delicacy of the Riesling style.)

COOL-ZONE RIESLING, GERMANY & ALSACE, FRANCE

Choose a German Riesling Kabinett or Spätlese from any of these wineries (or your store's recommendation):

JJ Prüm, Gunderloch, Lingenfelder, Dr. Fischer, Fritz Haag, Dr. Loosen, Strub, Darting, Schloss Johannisberg, Robert Weil

Alsace, France: the classic wineries mentioned before: Trimbach, Hugel, Deiss, Sparr, Albrecht, Weinbach, Dirler, Leon Beyer, Schlumberger, etc.

MODERATE-ZONE RIESLING, AUSTRALIA, CALIFORNIA, AND WASHINGTON

Australia: Grosset, Pike's, Mt. Horrocks, Penfolds, Jacob's Creek

California: J. Lohr, Bonny Doon, Kendall-Jackson, Jekel, Beringer, Trefethen, Smith-Madrone

Washington: Eroica, Hogue, Columbia Winery, Chateau Ste. Michelle

THE LOOK: Compare them against a white background.	
Pale yellow-green	Also yellow-green, but perhaps a touch yellower

THE SMELL: Swirl and smell the cool-zone Riesling first, then the moderate-zone Riesling.	
With cool-zone Riesling, green apples ranging from Granny Smith (tart) to Golden Delicious are the common fruit styles. For floral scents, you might notice honeysuckle, or just "flowers" with no particular one standing out.	There may be some cool-zone scents here, too (it is Riesling, after all), but look also for peach, apricot, and all manner of citrus—orange, lemon, tangerine, etc. Quite lovely and a bit more exotic.

THE TASTE: Now sample the wines, first the cool-zone Riesling, then the moderate-zone Riesling.	
Notice its delicate, light body and fruit flavors that echo those you smelled—green apples. The acidity (due to the cool zone) may also come through as slightly lemony.	The flavors mirror the orchard-in-a-glass scents: peaches, apricots, citrus, and so on. The slightly fuller body from the moderate climate is also apparent.

Riesling Scorecard

Professional Riesling's flavor and scent are very expressive. In fact, it could be said that Riesling presents virtually an archival rendering of its growing conditions—the vintage (weather), the soil, the region, even the person who made it. Nonetheless, its signature style always comes through—orchard fruits, from apple and pear to citrus to stone fruits, and sometimes floral character, thanks to its home base in cool-to-moderate climate zones. Also thanks to the cool climate, its style is marked by vibrant acidity.

Personal I adore Riesling. Hopefully, this tasting has highlighted some of its virtues for you, too. You already know how I feel about acidity, but I also love the depth of fruit flavor you get on such a sleek, ultralight frame. The late harvest versions are some of the best dessert wines in the world. Try them, too.

Sauvignon Blanc

Like Riesling, this is another grape with cool-to-moderate climate affinity, but there are some major differences. First, Sauvignon Blanc's best regions, while cool to moderate, are closer to the equator, and thus warmer, than Riesling's. As such, its flavors are different and can be noticeably riper. Second, I am sure you remember from Chapter 3 the very distinctive grassy/herbaceous character of Sauvignon Blanc. This is especially evident in the cool-climate versions. The cool-zone strongholds for Sauvignon Blanc are the Loire Valley's Sancerre and Pouilly-Fumé regions, and New Zealand's Marlborough district. These versions rarely use oak. By contrast, the main moderate-zone regions for Sauvignon Blancs—Bordeaux, France, and coastal California—often use oak as a complement to their fuller fruit style. It is also common practice in these two regions to blend in Sémillon (*Sem-ee-YOHN*), another white grape that further enriches the fruit style.

Fumé blanc is what a lot of American wineries label their Sauvignon Blanc wines. The name, originally coined by the famous Robert Mondavi winery, was inspired by the classic French Loire Valley Sauvignon Blanc region, Pouilly-Fumé and the wines from there, which used to be called "blanc fumé" due to the morning mists that looked like smoke (fumé) rising off the vineyards. Generally, American Fumé blancs are among the fullest-bodied styles of Sauvignon Blanc, due to the warmer grape source (usually California versus the Loire Valley and New Zealand), and the common practice of aging this style in oak barrels.

Choose among these styles of Sauvignon Blanc:

COOL-ZONE SAUVIGNON BLANC

LOIRE VALLEY SANCERRE
Lucien Crochet, Domaine Thomas, Pascal Jolivet, Michel Redde, Château de Sancerre, Cotat

LOIRE VALLEY POUILLY-FUMÉ
Alphonse Mellot, Didier Dagueneau, Ladoucette, Henri Bourgeois

NEW ZEALAND SAUVIGNON BLANC
Cloudy Bay, Brancott, Stoneleigh, Villa Maria, Nobilo, Babich, Goldwater

MODERATE-ZONE SAUVIGNON BLANC

CALIFORNIA
Simi, Murphy-Goode, Dry Creek Vineyards, Rochioli, Chalk Hill, Matanzas Creek, Meridian, Cakebread Cellars, Kenwood, Robert Mondavi, Benziger, Ferrari-Carano

BORDEAUX, FRANCE
Château Rahoul, Blanc de Château Lynch-Bages, Château La Louvière, Château Carbonnieux

Pale yellow-green to straw yellow	Similar to the cool-zone wine, but often a bit darker.

The scent of cool-zone Sauvignon Blanc is notably tart—sour apple comes to mind. And the grassy/herbaceous style usually comes through, sometimes quite pungently. That herbaceous character reminds some people of vegetables—asparagus and canned green beans are commonly cited.	Moderate-climate Sauvignon Blanc is often marked by citrus—particularly more pungent citrus fruits such as grapefruit and lime. But in wines from the warmest fringe of the moderate zone, richer, riper fruits come through, such as honeydews and cantaloupes, along with peach and nectarine.

Granny Smith apple, tart and tangy are the flavors here. This also makes me think of a green apple Jolly Rancher candy.	The moderate-zone fruit flavors are like the scent—much richer and riper, sometimes ranging to downright exotic in some of the California bottlings. They also mirror the fruits in the scent—citrus and melon.

Sauvignon Blanc Scorecard

Professional Like Riesling, Sauvignon Blanc usually has vibrant acidity. It is medium-bodied, and the classic flavor descriptions range from tart apple to citrus (especially lime and grapefruit) to honeydew melon and peach. Overlaying the fruit is that signature grassy, herbaceous style.

Personal I constantly recommend Sauvignon Blanc because it offers great stylistic range, excellent availability and value for the money, and it's delicious. Even the lowest-priced examples have character and retain the grape's signature style, while the top-end examples, which are world class, almost never reach the stratospheric pricing of top Chardonnays. And, of course, we already noted how Sauvignon Blanc's herbaceous character gives it great food affinity.

Chardonnay

Chardonnay is truly the chameleon grape. As already pointed out, its success throughout the wine world, from cool to moderate to warm zones, is legendary. In this tasting, we will emphasize the most famous versions from each zone, for two reasons. First, they will be easy to find when you're shopping. Second, these standard-bearers are the styles with which you should be familiar, because they are the paradigms, literally, to which the rest of the Chardonnay world aspires. They are also the styles that anchor the Chardonnay offerings on most restaurant wine lists.

Cool Zone Burgundy, France, is our reference point for cool-style Chardonnay. Almost all French white Burgundy is made from Chardonnay. The wine suggestions here come from Burgundy regions whose wines best represent the cool style: Mâcon, Pouilly-Fuissé, and Chablis. These regional wines traditionally are not oak aged, thus allowing the pure fruit style to come through.

Moderate Zone Coastal California is the paradigm here. The wine selections will emphasize the coastal zones that are best known for high-quality Chardonnay. Most of these wines have some oak-barrel contact during fermentation, or aging, or both. However, I have chosen balanced versions in which the fruit flavor is not overpowered by the oak.

Warm Zone Australia will show us the Chardonnay style in its most exotic, tropical version. (I have also included a few choices from California's warm spots.) Oak is certainly a factor in this wine style, but again, I have chosen balanced wines that let the fruit shine through.

The wine choices here are divided into two price categories: $15 and under, and then $16 to $35. Whatever you choose to taste, make all three of your selections from the same price bracket, so that you are comparing wines of roughly equivalent quality. This lets you really focus on and distinguish the varied fruit flavors of each style zone; in this way you can experience the amazing range of this grape.

PRICE BRACKET*	COOL STYLE	MODERATE STYLE	WARM STYLE

$15 and under	Burgundy regional wines:
	  Mâcon (usually has a suffix such as -Villages or -Lugny): Jadot, Bouchard, Verget, Les Charmes, Duboeuf, Bonhomme, Manciat-Poncet, Drouhin
		California Varietals:
		  Echelon, Estancia Pinnacles, Gallo of Sonoma, Chateau St. Jean, Kendall-Jackson, Mirassou, Wente
			Australian Varietals:
			  Lindemans Bin 65, Chateau Reynella, Château Tahbilk, Wolf Blass, Jacob's Creek Reserve
			California: RH Phillips Barrel Cuvée, Kunde, St. Francis, Beringer, Kenwood

$16–35	Pouilly-Fuissé:
	  Bouchard, Château Fuissé, Jadot, Michel Picard
	Chablis:
	  Grossot, Laroche, Moreau, Long-Depaquit, William Fèvre (or your store's suggestion)
		Calera Central Coast, Robert Mondavi Carneros, Morgan, Byron, Sonoma-Cutrer, Acacia, Cambria, Buena Vista, Iron Horse, Trefethen	Australia:
			  Devil's Lair, Rosemount Show Reserve, Knappstein-Lenswood, Cape Mentelle, Scotchman's Hill, Bannockburn
			California:
			  Chalk Hill, Stonestreet, Simi Reserve, Matanzas Creek, Merryvale

*Approximate, prices vary by market

COOL-ZONE CHARDONNAY	MODERATE-ZONE CHARDONNAY	WARM-ZONE CHARDONNAY

THE LOOK: Compare them against a white background.

Pale yellow-green	Pale yellow-green to straw yellow	Yellow-gold. The wines are often darker in the warm climate zones, as though the grapes get a "tan" from the extra sunshine.

THE SMELL: Swirl and smell each of the Chardonnays in climate-zone order: cool, moderate, warm.

Take your time and concentrate on each of the scents and how they compare to one another.

Even in the scent, you may notice that Chardonnay's cool style seems less tart compared to Riesling or Sauvignon Blanc —ripe pear and soft apple (think Golden Delicious) rather than super-tart Granny Smith. Quince, if you are familiar with it, may also come through.	Fruit-salad-in-a-glass—lemon, orange, tangerine, peach, and melon. Each wine differs slightly in the dominant fruit scents. Many California bottlings put their winemaker's fruit descriptions on the back. Check the label and see if you agree.	Exotic. The scent is redolent of ripe pineapples and mangos (and I'm often reminded of banana splits from my childhood). There are also traces of some of the more exotic moderate-style scents, often mandarin orange, apricot, and peach.

THE TASTE: Now sample the Chardonnays in style order: cool, moderate, warm.

Like the scent, the flavors are delicate and soft, with a bit of refreshing tartness from the acidity—kind of like biting into a fresh apple.	Lots of fruit flavor here, just as in the aroma—lemon, orange, peach, and so on. This is the juicy, fruity, lip-smacking style for which California Chardonnay is famous. Do not be surprised if you taste apple, too. It often crosses over into this style.	Luscious. The exotic warm-zone fruit flavors echo the scents and are much richer and riper than the moderate and cool versions. Some wine critics refer to this as a "blockbuster" Chardonnay style due to its richness and succulence.

Chardonnay Scorecard

Professional No wonder Chardonnay is celebrated throughout the wine world for its stylistic range and quality. You have just sampled three very different styles, all of them worthy. Given that range, can anyone characterize this chameleon grape? Despite its diversity, I think you *can* articulate Chardonnay's signature—it is fruit. Compared to the rest of the Big Six whites—the delicate and floral Riesling, the tangy and herbaceous Sauvignon Blanc—Chardonnay's style is fruit-driven, which surely explains its unparalleled popularity. Who doesn't love fruit? Even the pickiest children will drink apple juice or eat a banana. Fruit gives us decadent flavor without excess. That is Chardonnay at its best.

Personal Mine is a love-hate relationship with the Chardonnay grape. Here's why: As I have already pointed out, much of what is sold in this country is solidly middle of the road in terms of style. The big wineries achieve this by blending grapes from many regions, cool to warm, with the result that no particular style stands out in the final wine. Look at the labels of the big-selling, branded Chardonnays and you are likely to see "California" listed as the region, indicating a broad range of grape sources (usually including the hot Central Valley), versus a more specific, high-quality area such as Central Coast, Sonoma, or Santa Barbara. As I explained already, these wines are crafted for broad appeal and consistency. They are easy to buy *because* their style is standardized.

But there is a trade-off. Quite often, flavor and character get lost in the pursuit of quantity and homogeneity in winemaking. This is frequently the case when you are comparing mass-market versus handcrafted products. For example, a fast-food meal provides sustenance. But a gourmet repast, or a home-cooked meal lovingly prepared, can become a dining experience that stirs your senses and makes memories.

Similarly, the best wines can capture your sensory imagination, too. Unfortunately, in today's market, I find that the Chardonnays that fill this bill are few and far between. And believe me, I taste dozens of them every week in search of good ones to offer my guests. Truthfully, 90 percent of them taste pretty dull and generic—alcohol without flavor.

Let me be clear. I do not expect everyday-priced wines to deliver a mind-blowing experience—that is unrealistic. And you are not always seeking a cerebral drinking experience, anyway. A casual cocktail, picnics, leftovers, and numerous other everyday situations just call for something tasty to drink, not a masterpiece. At every price point, the best wines are the ones that make your palate sit up and take notice, at least briefly (and sometimes even knock your socks off). Those are the wines I have recommended here.

Pinot Noir

Pinot Noir, like Riesling for the whites, grows best in climates that are cool, edging into moderate. Its historic home is the Burgundy region of France, whose wines have been famous for centuries. Oregon's Willamette Valley (*Will-AM-ett*, not *Will-uh-METT*) also specializes in Pinot Noir, as do the coolest parts of coastal California (especially the Russian River Valley, Carneros, Monterey, and Santa Barbara) and Australia (notably the Adelaide Hills and Yarra Valley districts). Finally, New Zealand, which has quite a cool climate, is starting to emerge as a big source for quality Pinot Noir, often at good prices for the quality.

Pinot Noir from all the major regions is typically oak aged, but the amount of oakiness is matched to the intensity of the fruit. Thus, the cool-zone wines whose fruit is more delicate see less oak (either shorter time in oak, fewer new barrels, or both), while the more intense fruit in the moderate-zone wines can support more oak. Even within a region, winemakers adjust their oak formula to the fruit quality, which can vary a lot from one year to the next. In the right dose, oak enhances the wine's scents and flavors without overpowering the Pinot Noir fruit character.

In keeping with its climate affinities, our tasting will compare cool-zone and moderate-zone Pinot Noirs. The Flavor Map indicates the range of fruit styles that will characterize these wines—cranberries and red cherries in the cool zone, raspberries and black cherries in the moderate zone. And these are indeed the classic Pinot Noir descriptors. My tasting list is broken into price brackets, and as with the Chardonnays, you should choose wines from the same bracket for your comparison.

PRICE BRACKET	COOL-ZONE PINOT NOIR: BURGUNDY, OREGON, NEW ZEALAND	MODERATE-ZONE PINOT NOIR: CALIFORNIA

$25 and under	**BURGUNDY**
	Mercurey: Perdrix
	Santenay: Lequin, Olivier Leflaive
	Chorey Côte de Beaune:
	    Tollot-Beaut
	Bourgogne: Bouchard, Groffier,
	    Jadot, Girardin (or your store's
	    recommendation)
	
	OREGON
	Willamette Valley Vineyards, Rex Hill,
	    Sokol Blosser, King Estate,
	    WillaKenzie, Benton Lane
	
	NEW ZEALAND
	Vavasour, Brancott, Spy Valley
		CALIFORNIA
		Calera Central Coast, Meridian,
		    Estancia Pinnacles, Gallo of
		    Sonoma, Robert Mondavi Napa,
		    Byron, Saintsbury Garnet,
		    Ramsay, Clos du Bois, Buena
		    Vista, MacMurray Ranch,
		    Cambria, Sebastiani, Echelon,
		    Au Bon Climat, Acacia (or your
		    store's recommendation)

$26 and over	**BURGUNDY**
	Mercurey: Faiveley, Juillot, Louis
	    Latour
	Santenay: Jadot, Belland, Potel
	Savigny les Beaune: Bouchard, Leroy
	Nuits St. Georges: Gouges, Engel,
	    Perrot-Minot, Rion
	
	OREGON
	Domaine Drouhin, Adelsheim,
	    Chehalem, Ponzi, Bethel Heights,
	    Panther Creek, Domaine Serene
	
	NEW ZEALAND
	Martinborough
		CALIFORNIA
		Domaine Carneros, Marimar
		    Torres, Chalone, Iron Horse,
		    Dehlinger, Robert Mondavi
		    Carneros, Sanford, Saintsbury,
		    Kent Rasmussen, Etude, Merry
		    Edwards, Chateau St. Jean, Belle
		    Glos Clark & Telephone

COOL-ZONE PINOT NOIR	MODERATE-ZONE PINOT NOIR
THE LOOK: Compare them against a white background.	
Dark pink to translucent ruby red	Ruby red to violet. The color is denser in the moderate-climate styles, though still limpid (not opaque).
THE SMELL: Swirl and smell the cool-zone Pinot Noir first, then the moderate-zone Pinot.	
The predominant scents are of tangy red berries—cranberry, cherry. If you are familiar with redcurrants, you might smell them, too.	Here the scents are riper, black cherries and raspberries, but still with a tang that makes your mouth water. You might also note a whiff of sweetness from the oak.
THE TASTE: Now sample the wines, first the cool-zone Pinot Noir, then the moderate-zone Pinot.	
We return to that delicate, silky Pinot Noir texture. Like the scent, the taste is tangy and mouthwatering, all red berries with a little bit of spice.	Compared to the cool-zone wine, the acidity in this one is less prominent, making the style taste less tart and more juicy, with flavors of dark, ripe summer berries.

Pinot Noir Scorecard

Professional Ah, Pinot! Many wine pros share the view that, at its best, the grandeur of Pinot Noir is unsurpassed by any other wine. They also share the view that Pinot Noir is one unreliable grape. Consistent success with it is maddeningly elusive, particularly in its famous home base of Burgundy. Still, vintners there and the world over continue to tussle with this picky, difficult-to-grow vine, seduced by the possibility of that grandeur. This is why, in wine circles, Pinot Noir is often referred to as The Grail of winemaking—or, by some, the Heartbreak Grape.

Of all the major growing regions, California is the most consistent, followed by Oregon and then Burgundy. (As a relative newcomer, New Zealand Pinot Noir's record there is still too young to call, but most pros are excited about the potential.) Supply (not much) and demand (it *is* The Grail) conspire to make even the most basic Pinot Noirs pricey compared to the other grapes in the Big Six. But devotees of the gorgeous flavor and silken texture of great Pinot are willing to pay—and to ride the style roller coaster from one vintage to the next.

Personal As I have already confessed, Pinot Noir is my favorite grape in the world (I give it extra points for being a major component in my all-time favorite wine—Champagne, of which more in Chapter 6). It is the wine of my dreams—the limpid violet shimmer, the perfumed berry scent, but most of all the silken texture, which leaves me speechless. Needless to say, I taste a lot of Pinot Noir, and the recommendations here are my favorites for flavor and consistency. I have even included my special discoveries—exceptions to the pricey rule that you could afford to drink every day. Let's keep them between us, shall we?

Merlot and Cabernet Sauvignon

Merlot and Cabernet Sauvignon, both of which flourish in moderate climates, leave us little to explore in terms of varied fruit styles. The moderate climate zone of the Flavor Map paints a very accurate picture of these grapes' fruit character, ranging from dark berries (blackberry, blueberry, blackcurrant) to plums. In fact, they are so consistent and similar in terms of flavor style that the most famous examples, the great chateau wines of Bordeaux, are usually blends of this dynamic duo. Elsewhere in the wine world, varietal Merlots and Cabernets often contain in their blend a dollop of their counterpart grape for balance. California even created a wine category, called Meritage (rhymes with heritage), for such blends made in the Bordeaux tradition.

Of course, there is still significant style diversity among Merlots and Cabernets from different regions and wineries, but the distinctions are not so much about fruit style. Rather, the notable style differences come in the areas of body, from medium to full, and flavor intensity, from subtle to strong.

We explored the first of these, body, in Chapter 3, when we compared a Merlot with a lower alcohol percentage to one whose percentage of alcohol by volume was slightly higher, illustrating the fact that, to the taster, alcohol is perceived as body. In that tasting, I pointed to the percentage of alcohol on the label as an obvious indicator of the wine's body, but now you have another label clue—the region. Although we broadly classified them as moderate, the Cabernet and Merlot growing zones do vary somewhat, with Napa Valley generally warmer than Bordeaux, for instance. So you could predict that for wines of comparable quality, the Napa versions would be slightly fuller than their Bordeaux cousins.

Flavor intensity can vary based on a wine's quality level, although not always in exact proportion. For both Merlot and Cabernet Sauvignon, the range goes from uncomplicated everyday styles to the super-intense boutique and collectible Merlot- and Cabernet-based wines from places like Bordeaux in France, California, and Washington State. In Chapters 6 and 7, our tastings of French and Italian wines will illustrate how flavor intensity varies according to a wine's quality level.

As for subtle versus strong flavor intensity, I will defer this tasting comparison to Chapter 5, which highlights the subtler flavor intensity of classic European regional wines, compared to the new wave varietals and blends that emulate them. In that chapter, we will also explore the body differences, and the reasons for them, in more detail. For purposes of exploring the Flavor Map, we'll compare Merlot with Cabernet Sauvignon to see their subtle similarities and distinctions.

Aside from their basic fruit flavors, Merlots tend to be medium-bodied with medium tannins (more than Pinot Noir, equal to or less than Cabernet Sauvignon) and some oak aging (from just a little for everyday Merlots, to very long aging in new barrels for very upscale wines, whose fruit is powerful enough to support lots of oak). To the taster, oak is perceived in the everyday wines as a subtle grace note, while in the upscale versions, it is usually a prominent feature in the wine's overall style.

Cabernet Sauvignon is generally full-bodied, with ample tannins that should be matched by the fruit intensity. Its fruit tastes are classically described as blackcurrant and cassis, along with the rest of the moderate-zone fruit family (dark berries and plums). Oak aging plays the same role here as with Merlot, a subtle note in the style of everyday Cabernets, and a more prominent oaky character in the upscale versions.

I have noticed, while tasting so many Merlots and Cabernet Sauvignons in search of wines for the wine lists I write, that there are more similarities than differences in their fruit flavors, just as the Flavor Map would suggest. As such, the tasting I present here is a comparison of these two grapes, so that you can explore the subtle differences, but also see the family resemblance. The tasting list is again broken into price tiers, so that you can compare a Merlot and a Cabernet from the same price tier. If your store has them, a Merlot and a Cabernet from the same winery make an especially interesting comparison; you can really focus on the character of each grape, because the winemaker and winemaking style are the same.

PRICE BRACKET	MERLOT	CABERNET SAUVIGNON
$20 and under	(You may also refer to Merlots in our previous tasting lists.)	(You may also refer to Cabernets in our previous tasting lists.)
	Washington State: Columbia Crest, Columbia Winery, Hogue Cellars, Covey Run, Hedges, Chateau Ste. Michelle	California: Clos du Bois, Wente, Canyon Road, Geyser Peak, Estancia, J. Lohr, Blackstone, Sterling Vintners Collection, BV Napa, Simi
	California: Gallo of Sonoma, Wente, Blackstone, Meridian, Bogle	Chile: Casa Lapostolle, Los Vascos, Veramonte, Concha y Toro Casillero del Diablo
	Chile: Veramonte, Montes, Casa Lapostolle, Dallas Conte	
$21–$35	Washington State: Canoe Ridge, L'Ecole No. 41, Columbia Red Willow, Powers, Andrew Will	California: Mt. Veeder, Frog's Leap, Beringer Knights Valley, St. Supéry Dollarhide Ranch, Stonestreet, Clos du Val, Robert Mondavi Napa
	California: Franciscan, Benziger, Markham, Pine Ridge, Rutherford Hill, Robert Mondavi, Stonestreet, St. Francis	

THE LOOK: Compare them against a white background.

Dark ruby red. Merlots are typically lighter in color than Cabernets of comparable quality, but there are plenty of expectations, so yours may in fact be darker than the Cabernet you are tasting.

Ruby red to dark purple. The color is sometimes denser in Cabernet, but do not be surprised if the colors are the same, or if your Merlot is darker.

THE SMELL: Swirl and smell the Merlot first, then the Cabernet Sauvignon.

The predominant scents are of plums and dark berries. You may also note scents that we have come to associate with oakiness, such as a sweet character, vanilla, or spice.

The scents are quite similar, but if you have had the chance to smell blackcurrant preserves or cassis syrup, as I suggested above, see if you detect those scents here.

THE TASTE: Now sample the wines, first the Merlot, then the Cabernet.

The flavors are really quite similar. Even very experienced tasters would be hard-pressed to guess which was which from the flavors. But as you compare them, concentrate on the body and tannin, both of which you should feel rather than taste. Does the Cabernet Sauvignon have more tannin? Does the Merlot feel softer and smoother? You may find, as I often have, that the two are more similar than different.

Merlot Scorecard

Professional A late-nineties explosion in popularity and worldwide plantings put Merlot neck-and-neck with Cabernet as the top-selling red grape in the U.S. But as production mushroomed, quality slid toward mediocrity, forcing buyers to get more choosy and prompting many to reach out for Shiraz and other alternatives. Still, there are many worthy Merlots. For everyday-priced wines, California and Washington are the most successful regions, although Bordeaux, France, also offers some good proprietary, varietal Merlots. Chile makes dozens of everyday-priced Merlots, but in my opinion these as a group have not lived up to their potential, at least so far. In upscale Merlots, I think red French Bordeaux is the quality leader; however, you will not find the varietal listed on the labels of its best Merlots, which are regionally named wines. (I will show you how to identify them in Chapter 6.) Washington and especially California are also very big in the upscale Merlot business, and although the quality of the wines is sometimes quite high, the prices always are. I have shown here some of the wines that I think consistently deliver the goods.

Personal The bottom line to me is this: Merlot makes perfectly good—but rarely great —red wines. I sometimes think the real reason it got so hot in the nineties was the name

—just two syllables. It is my theory that a less frightening pronunciation makes for an easier sell, which gives Merlot a distinct advantage over *Cab-uhr-NAY Sow-veen-YONE*. I also find that Merlot's reputation for soft (low) tannin is more theoretical than real. Wineries have started to veer away from the smooth-style Merlot people fell in love with. Now, many of the boutique bottlings are made in the style of topflight Bordeaux, which are built for aging in the cellar rather than current drinking, and thus have a lot of tannin. Finally, Merlot came to the fore in tandem with the widely publicized health benefits of moderate red wine consumption, which probably helped boost its popularity. I advise caution when buying Merlot at the everyday price points; many of the offerings are pretty industrial and plain. Although the top-end wines do not always deliver on the soft tannin promise, they can be excellent. Unfortunately, there aren't many available in the middle price range, although many of the high-priced bottlings are starting to come down to prices commensurate with their middle-of-the road quality.

Cabernet Sauvignon Scorecard

Professional Cabernet Sauvignon has long been famous as the main ingredient in most of the top red French Bordeaux, and it's certainly the calling card of California's two best-known wine regions, Napa and Sonoma. Several other regions have just scratched the surface of their potential for making good-to-great Cabernet Sauvignon. Among them are Argentina, Australia, parts of Italy, and South Africa, with Washington State and Chile in particular worth watching.

Personal For my money, Cabernet Sauvignon trumps Merlot nine times out of ten. It usually offers better value for the money, and I am always amazed at how well the distinctive style of the grape comes through even in the everyday bottlings. I also think its reputation for higher tannin than Merlot is a bit miscast. Even in its traditional home of Bordeaux, France, and throughout the rest of the Cabernet-growing world, the so-called modern style of winemaking is used to make Cabernets that have softer tannins. This change in winemaking and wine styles, which recognizes the fact that few wine drinkers have the space and patience to "cellar" wine before consuming it, took place long before the start of the Merlot craze.

Syrah/Shiraz

Syrah/Shiraz grows best in moderate to warm climates. Because Australia's market dominance with this grape puts so many warm-climate versions on store shelves and wine lists, I generally rank it as fuller-bodied than Merlot/Cabernet, although there are certainly exceptions. In terms of flavor, the moderate and warm climate zones' signature fruit flavors aptly characterize the Syrah/Shiraz style, ranging from plums and soft berries like raspberry to deeper fruits such as black-skinned berries and figs. I generally find that, depending on the sources, Syrah/Shiraz tends toward the wilder, more exotic dark fruits—boysenberry and blackberry, for example—as compared to the subtler plum and blackcurrant fruit of Merlot and Cabernet. In the warmest climates, the dark fruit flavors of Syrah/Shiraz often taken on a still richer stewed or dried character—imagine stewed prunes, dried figs, date, raisins, or even mincemeat and you get the idea.

For the tasting to explore these differences, we'll take a slight departure from the climate zone approach, for two reasons. First, the climate zone differences for Syrah/Shiraz are subtle and, I think, not particularly clear to the average label-reader. For example, Washington's Columbia Valley might be called a moderate climate for Syrah, as compared to Australia's warm-climate McLaren Vale for Shiraz—but only well-studied wine pros are likely to know this. Second, I've found that across climate zones, quality level seems to be the key factor in the fruit intensity of the wine—the higher the quality, the deeper and richer the fruit. Imagine the difference in apple flavor intensity of a fast food joint apple turnover versus a handmade apple pie or tart from an artisan bakery, and you get the idea.

So to sample these fruit style differences, we'll compare two wines—one with everyday quality, the other of ambitious quality, to show how the fruit intensity steps up from softly ripe to quite sumptuous as you ascend the quality ladder. You may wonder why this happens. My research hasn't yielded a definitive answer, but we can make some educated assumptions based on the factors we covered in the "Quality: Where It Comes From" section on page 72. Specifically, there's the vineyard source—as we've learned, grapes from a flat, fertile site that's easy to tractor-farm will be less intense than those grown in top hillside sites where the vines have to fight for their moisture and nutrients. Furthermore, grape growers usually farm each vineyard according to its potential. In the top vineyards, they're likely to restrict grape yields and to tend each vine individually to maximize its potential to make the ripest, most concentrated grapes possible. And as we've learned, the more intense the grapes, the more intense the wine. This tasting will illustrate that perfectly. To make the most of the comparison, try to use one of the same-source wine pairs listed here to compare an everyday- versus an ambitious-quality wine from the same winery. In this way, you'll see a common theme: the higher-quality bottlings across the climate zones yield the most intense fruit style.

	MODERATE CLIMATE SYRAH/SHIRAZ	WARM CLIMATE SYRAH/SHIRAZ
Everyday Quality	Washington State: Columbia Crest Two Vine Syrah, Columbia Winery Columbia Valley Syrah California: Geyser Peak Shiraz	Australia: Rosemount Diamond Label Shiraz, Penfolds Rawson's Retreat Shiraz, D'Arenberg "The Footbolt" Shiraz, Lindemans Bin 50 Shiraz
Ambitious Quality	Washington State: Columbia Crest Reserve Syrah, Columbia Winery Red Willow Vineyard Syrah California: Geyser Peak Reserve Shiraz	Australia: Rosemount Balmoral Syrah, Penfolds Kalimna Bin 28 Shiraz, D'Arenberg "The Dead Arm" Shiraz, Lindemans Reserve Shiraz

THE LOOK: Compare them against a white background.

Dark ruby-red, often with a fuchsia pink–tinged rim that's typical of young red wines.

Darker ruby-purple. The color is clearly denser, as you'd expect from more concentrated grape sources. Swirl the glass to see the tears, and you may notice they are more color-stained, too—a sign of the wine's greater concentration.

THE SMELL: Swirl and smell the everyday-quality wine first, then the ambitious-quality one.

Soft plum and berries, especially raspberries. At this quality level the grapes may not yield much of the spiciness we expect from varietal Syrah/Shiraz.

Berry ka-boom! Boysenberry and black raspberry jam, plus often fig compote and raisins or stewed prunes. There's also spice—sweet baking spices like cinnamon and clove, plus savory black pepper spice.

THE TASTE: Now sample the wines in order, focusing on the fruit flavor and the body.

The fruit flavors echo the scents—softly ripe plum and raspberry and a juicy texture. The tannins and body are medium-full.

This wine is a mouthful—the flavor of wild black fruits is laced with spices, chocolate, and even licorice. You can taste the greater concentration, like a fruit pie filling that's been simmered to evaporate the water and concentrate the flavor. You can also feel the greater richness as fuller body and thicker tannins.

Syrah Scorecard

Professional I have noticed some slippage as the Syrah/Shiraz grape's popularity has skyrocketed. Whereas you used to be able to count on getting this grape's signature spiciness in even the everyday versions, that's no longer consistently true. That said, I think the overall quality-for-the-money proposition is still a good one for buyers. The way to make sure you get the best deal is to go with producers I've mentioned here, or the personal recommendations of a good wine merchant. With so many new $12-and-under names coming on the market, good retailers are snapping them up and recommending them to their regular customers who are tired of the same-old, same-old. So ask!

Personal As the enormous growth of Syrah/Shiraz plantings continues worldwide, I'm optimistic that quality across all price points will continue to improve. It will have to, to keep consumers trying all the new labels. For all of us red-wine lovers, that'll keep it fun—yummy wines, affordable prices, and always something new!

Beyond the Big Six—Using the Flavor Map for Regional Wines and Other Grapes

Of course, there is wine life beyond the Big Six, and having discovered the delicious options of these grapes, you won't want to stop there and miss out on the rest of the wine world, including regional wines, proprietary wines, and other varietals beyond the Big Six. For these wines, which come up in so many everyday buying situations, the power of the Flavor Map is really compelling.

- For example, imagine you're in downtown St. Louis, where the French Brasserie menu has two reds available by the carafe—Beaujolais and Côtes du Rhône. You're having a heavy, rich braised veal shank, but you're not sure which to order. Geographically, you know that Beaujolais (a part of Burgundy) is cool zone, and Côtes du Rhône is warm zone. Using the Flavor Map, you theorize that the Beaujolais's flavor is probably light and cherry-like, and the Côtes du Rhône heavier—closer to prune and fig. Since your dish is heavy, too, you choose Côtes du Rhône—and the flavor is exactly as you predicted.

- You want a white wine, but you're ready to try something new. The shop clerk suggests Vouvray, a wine named for its region in the Loire Valley. You have never heard of that particular one, but since it's from the cool Loire you foresee a lighter body and apple/pear flavor profile, which is spot-on.

- You take a client to dinner in Little Italy, and she says she doesn't like heavy wines. You skip the big, raisiny red from sunny Sicily in favor of a delicate, cherry like Valpolicella from northern Italy. Good call.

- The new steakhouse down the street is featuring the famous Argentinian beef, and Malbec, a red grape you have never heard of. But since the growing zone is moderate to warm, you expect berry and plum flavors in this wine. You get what you bargained for.

- The name of the Australian wine on the in-store display, Bin 45A, means nothing to you. The back label lists the Grenache, Cinsault, and Mourvèdre grapes—strike two because you've never heard of them either. But the region, the Barossa Valley, is one of Australia's warm spots. You conclude that this juicy, raisiny red will be the perfect complement for your mom's steak au poivre. You're right, and so is the price.

No doubt about it: The Flavor Map makes broad generalizations about wine styles, and also lumps together very diverse wine types into the same fruit-flavor family. But that's okay, because, for one, it's generally accurate. Take the example of these cool-zone white wines—French Chablis, Loire Valley Vouvray, Italian Pinot Grigio, and Riesling from Alsace, France. Is apple and pear (the cool-zone fruit family) really an accurate description for all of them? Absolutely.

Second, generalizing about wine styles helps you to grasp them without in any way detracting from their individuality. Rabbit, duck, frog's legs, squab, alligator, and rattlesnake—over my illustrious eating career I have tried them all, and each was introduced to me in the same way: "Tastes like chicken." Of course, they're quite different, but it got me in the ballpark of knowing what to expect. As a wine drinker, isn't that all you want?

CHAPTER FIVE

Old World, New World

The Secret Weapon of Sommeliers

The hard part of this wine course is over. By design, the first four chapters of this book were the most rigorous. I didn't give you labeling laws and soil types to memorize, but that was because we're taking a different approach to wine. I *did* ask you to apply more of your senses, your imagination, and your spirit of adventure than you might ever have before. I also asked you to open and taste quite a few bottles, so that you might have experienced a little "sommelier's elbow" (long gone by now—if not, keep training). If at times it has seemed a little intense, that's good, because I know that at least some of that intensity comes from a new level of pleasure in your wine drinking. In the process, you have learned a lot about different wine styles, including which ones you like; and I have shown you how, by using a few easy tricks of the trade, you can find them by reading the label.

In the traditional wine world, my teaching approach is most unorthodox, especially the Flavor Map chapter. Now I'm going to give you another high-powered clue to the taste of every wine you see in the store or restaurant. Again, it is found right on the label and is, like the Flavor Map, intuitive. Best of all, it's even simpler.

Old World vs. New World

This technique, which I call Old World/New World, helps you predict the flavor style of a wine based on one of the most obvious things on the label:

the wine's country of origin. And it is trivially easy to use. **Step One** is this: In your mind, divide the wine world into two parts, the Old World, and the New World.

The *Old World* of wine is Europe and includes her classical wine-growing countries—France, Italy, Spain, and Germany—but also Greece, Hungary, Austria, and Switzerland. Probably you have seen few, if any, wines from this last group in your store. This doesn't mean the wines are not good. They're just not widely exported to this country, either because the quantities made are small or because the styles are not well known here.

The Czech Republic, Bulgaria, Romania, and Russia are also technically part of wine's Old World, but their political status precludes much market presence outside their borders. Bulgarian wine is one exception. It competes at a high enough quality level to have a substantial presence in United Kingdom wine shops and supermarkets. The American market could be next.

The *New World* includes the United States, whose wines you know so well and are our top sellers; Australia and Chile, whose wines began to take off here in the 1980s; and finally, three relatively new kids on the wine block—Argentina, New Zealand, and South Africa.

Step Two: Read the wine label, identify the wine's country of origin, and then, using the definition above, decide if it's an Old World wine or a New World wine. Here's what that tells you, in simple terms:

Old World: subtler-style wines

New World: bolder-style wines

I will explain these styles in detail, and our tasting lessons will showcase them. But first, here is a little background on the Old World/New World concept.

The Secret Weapon of Sommeliers

I did not invent this. The definition of Old World and New World countries and their respective wine styles is a long-standing convention in the wine trade. In fact, Old World/New World is a major tool in such constant use by sommeliers and wine professionals that it is practically part of the subconscious, in the same way that mouse maneuvers are second nature to a computer geek. Without really thinking about it, we use it to make wine recommendations, to match wines to food menus, and to decide if a wine belongs on our wine lists or store shelves.

You might wonder why such a great buying tool has remained pretty much under wraps outside the wine trade. I am not really sure of the reason. The cynic in me thinks that perhaps it is related to job security—we want you to need us pros to explain and reveal all of wine's subtleties to you. But in truth, the average time I got to spend on guest wine recommendations usually can be counted in seconds. For the typical sommelier, any given night is a juggling act of tables to be visited, bottles to be opened, and glasses to be topped up. And you, the guest, have better things to do, too—deals to close, lovers to seduce, future in-laws to impress, or whatever. Most of the time, you do not really want, or need, to "talk wine" with me. In my experience, something along the lines of "The Sancerre is really delicious, and you'll love it with your goat cheese salad" is usually enough wine talk for most customers.

A more likely explanation for the secrecy is that this tool takes the Old World and the New World and makes a big generalization about their wine styles—something wine professionals typically hate to do. This is because most wine lovers, both amateur and professional, just cannot bear to undersell the subtleties of wine, which are what seduced us in the first place. I think professionals reason that it's okay for us in the trade to use this quick trick, because we are already disciples of the grape, so we're in no danger of limiting ourselves to a vanilla and chocolate view of wine's (truly infinite) taste possibilities.

I know from experience, however, that if someone is completely in the dark about a wine style, they probably will never try it. This is true even with wine buyers for whom money is no object. When it comes to something they are about to eat or drink, the vast majority of the time, people want *some* idea of what to expect. So rather than making someone "peel the onion," so to speak, to get to all that wine has to offer, I would rather, when possible, show them how to cut to the chase, so they can confidently and efficiently experiment with everything that is out there. Otherwise, they probably *will* limit themselves to one or two basic, familiar styles (the vanilla and chocolate of wine) that barely scratch the surface of its pleasure and taste possibilities.

In fact, I think the peel-the-onion theory is what is behind wine's elitist reputation in this country—it seems like a rite of passage imposed by the wine trade. Most people can't be bothered with it, and the results are obvious: People are drinking mass-market wine (or beer or soda) and missing out. Wine is already complicated enough. A "trade secret" like Old World/New World can open doors for wine drinkers at any knowledge level, so I felt it should be shared.

Old World Subtlety versus New World Boldness— Why the Difference?

The style of Old World wines (mostly French, Italian, Spanish, and German selections in the average store) is generally subtler, more refined, and more understated. That does not necessarily mean light. Contrast that with the New World wine style, which can be described as bolder, more intense, more lush, or more opulent. The shorthand comparison we used above puts it most succinctly—subtle (Old World) versus bold (New World).

There are two root causes of the overall style difference between Old World and New World wines, both of them compelling. These are: the different growing conditions, and the differences in tradition and taste.

First, the differences in Old World versus New World growing conditions bring about the subtle versus bold contrast in their wine styles. Most of the classic, Old World wine-growing regions have temperate climates, generally ranging from cool to moderate. As you tasted in Chapters 3 and 4, a cool-to-moderate climate for growing the grapes generally yields lighter body and less intensity in the wine. Most of the New World countries, by contrast, have their wine regions concentrated in warmer, sunnier spots, which make for fuller-bodied, bolder-style wines. Let's recall the cool- to warm-climate fruit spectrum in the Flavor Map:

CLIMATE			
	COOL	MODERATE	WARM
Fruit style	Lean	Ripe/juicy	Overripe/lush
White wine fruit flavors	Apple/pear	Citrus/peach/melon	Mango/pineapple
Red wine fruit flavors	Cranberry/cherry	Berry/plum	Fig/prune
Overall style	Subtle/elegant	Medium intensity	Bold/intense

The last line of this chart simply layers the Old World/New World style comparison on top of the fruit flavor differences we have already explored through tasting the same grape grown in different climate zones. Remember to think of the cool to moderate to warm spectrum not as three discrete style categories, but rather as a style range with almost infinite possibilities at every point along the continuum—the very thing that makes wine so exciting and offers a lifetime of delicious exploring.

The Old World is also more likely to have poor, rocky soil. In the Old World, where wine history stretches back centuries, wine growing emerged almost by accident. Grape vines were planted in places where pretty much nothing else of value would grow. In an agricultural economy, as countries like France, Italy, Spain, and Germany once were, it made sense to use every inch of land for some crop. And as we pointed out in Chapter 3, vines love to tough it out in poor, low-fertility soil, often owing their higher quality, subtlety, and elegance to the struggle. Let's look at some examples:

One of the world's most famous wine regions is Bordeaux, France. Its highest quality, most collectible, most expensive wines come from vineyards whose soils are beds of almost pure gravel, often fist-size, with barely any dirt even visible. I know this firsthand, having picked grapes during the harvest of 1990. Unlike high arbor-type grape vines you might have seen, these clusters grow close to the ground, so you often have to kneel to get them—and it really hurts to kneel on a pile of fist-size rocks for three weeks straight. (At least 1990 was a good year.)

The great Port wines come from vineyards in the Douro (*DUHR-oh*) region of Portugal. The vineyards are planted on terraces cut into steep cliffs that rise up on either side of the Douro River. Here, there is really no soil at all, but rather pure rock, so dynamite is used to blast a hole for planting each vine.

The Mosel (*MOE-zuhl*) region of Germany is named for the Mosel River. Her best vineyards are planted on banks of almost pure slate that rise up from the water at nearly a 30-degree incline. They are so steep that during harvest, the pickers must secure themselves with ropes like rock climbers, to keep from slipping.

The second reason for the style differences between Old World and New World wines is differences in Old World and New World tastes and traditions. In most Old World wine countries, wine (and life) revolves around food. As such, wines are crafted as culinary tablemates, styled to share the stage as a supporting actor and complement to the food. Look at the food itself. From the classic sauces of French haute cuisine to the mellow suckling pig of Spain to the pastas and risottos of Italy, there is no shortage of deep, rich flavor, but it's generally not bold, intense flavor. At least, not when compared to American cooking, home of barbecue, Buffalo wings, and chili, and where the top-selling condiment is salsa; or to the Asian fusion of Australian cooking; or South America's blistering chimichurri.

This different aesthetic—Europe's subtle-and-understated to the New World's bold-and-splashy—emerges not just in wine and food but wherever taste is expressed. Europe gave us classical music; America rock 'n' roll and rhythm and blues. European fashion expresses subtlety and refinement; we broadcast our attitudes and feelings on T-shirts and caps. Europe's architecture is represented by stone castles and stately manor houses; the New World's by imposing skyscrapers in steel and glass. Sure, there's plenty of cross-pollination in this globally oriented world, but these iconic examples of Old World versus New World cultural styles come from tradition and taste.

And so it is with the wine styles. Europe's classic wines are literally bottled tradition, sometimes many centuries in the making. They respect the trial-and-error experience of countless generations to develop the combination of grapes, vineyard farming practices, and winemaking methods to yield a particular wine style that will make the most (in terms of wine quality) of each plot of land or vineyard region. This explains a lot about the European convention for using not grape varietal but rather regional wine names—a district (Champagne), a town (Margaux), a vineyard area (Sancerre), or even a single estate (Château Latour)—the plot of land where the grapes were grown rather than the grapes themselves. We are familiar with so many European regional names—Chianti, Chablis, Beaujolais—but it's hard to imagine a wine called just "Napa."

So linked are these regional names to the quality reputation of Old World wines that, beginning in the 1930s in France, the major Old World countries wrote into law minimum standards for each important growing area. The purpose was to stop the use of famous regional wine names by vintners who didn't uphold the style and quality tradition of the region in question. The laws are known as *appellation laws*, because "appellation" means a place-name that has a wine style associated with it. There are appellations for other things—Roquefort cheese from France, which is legally defined; Walla Walla onions from the eponymous town in Washington State; and prosciutto di Parma, the famous Italian ham from Parma, Italy, also legally defined, are examples. With wine, the idea is to ensure that what gets bottled under any particular wine appellation upholds the authentic style of that appellation. (Both the Italians, with Chianti, and the Portuguese, with Port, lay claim to being first with the idea of wine appellations. But the French model is the modern standard for appellation laws.)

Controlling Authenticity of Old World Wine Styles

Following are the names of the appellation laws for the top-quality regions in each major Old World wine country. The laws control the authenticity of the wine style associated with each appellation by specifying the following things:

- Permitted grapes—for example, you can't use Cabernet Sauvignon grapes to make Champagne

- Boundaries of the growing area; to be named to an appellation, the grapes must come from within its boundaries

- Maximum vineyard yield (which is a form of quality control, as we noted in Chapter 3)

- Minimum alcohol content—helps to ensure the grapes reach a minimum level of ripeness before they are picked

- Viticulture—controls some vineyard practices like irrigation

- Vinification—this usually controls minimum aging requirements, among other things

Depending on the country, the following words are what you will see on the label of any Old World wine made according to their appellation law's standards.

The **French law**, on which all the others were modeled, is called *Appellation d'Origine Controlée (AOC)*, which translates as "controlled appellation of origin." It is sometimes shortened to Appellation Controlée (AC).

On some labels, the appellation name is written in the middle, as in Appellation Pouilly-Fuissé Controlée.

Italy's law is called *Denominazione di Origine Controllata (DOC)*, which means "controlled denomination of origin," the same concept as France's AOC. There is also a higher level for a few of Italy's top regions, called *Denominazione di Origine Controllata e Garantita (DOCG)*. The *Garantita* adds a "guarantee" of more rigorous authenticity and quality controls.

Spain's law is called *Denominacion de Origen (DO)*, or "denomination of origin." Like Italy, they also added a higher rank to this law, *Denominacion de Origen Calificada (DOC)*. *Calificada* means "qualified," again implying stricter quality controls. At present, only Rioja has full DOC status. The Priorat region has been elevated to DOC, but as this book goes to print is still in the process of being added to the official Spanish DOC registry.

Germany's top-quality rank is identified as *Qualitatswein mit Pradikat (QmP)*, which translates as "quality wine with distinction." Typically, though, Germany's wines at this quality rank, which often are Rieslings, also list the grape name on the label.

It is standard practice in the wine trade to refer to these by their abbreviations, such as AOC for France and DOC for Italy, so don't get bogged down by the pronunciations.

An extreme example will illustrate the point of all of these rules and regulations. Suppose you paid thirty dollars for a bottle using the "champagne" name, only to find that the wine inside was not the elegant, bubbly, and complex treat you expected, but rather some cheap jug wine. Your trust in the "Champagne" name would be utterly compromised. You can understand why the Europeans object to some New World countries' use of names like chablis and burgundy on our jug and bag-in-box wines.

If all the rules and legalese strike you as tradition run amok, well, there are some in the wine trade who would agree, saying these strictures inhibit innovation and freedom of expression in the Old World. Others point to the quality and style diversity of the great wines—French Burgundy, Bordeaux, and Champagne; Italian Chianti and Barolo; Spanish Rioja; and so on—and conclude that these traditions are indeed worthy. You have to keep in mind the Old World point of view. It focuses on letting the vineyard, not the winemaker, express itself to the max. The freedom of expression is left up to Mother Nature.

Terroir

There is a word for the notion of the supremacy of the vineyard—or rather, the French have a word for it. It is called terroir (*tear-WAHR*), and it is the idea that the smell and taste of a wine can and should actually reflect the character of its particular vineyard. It is also the idea that gets wine lovers talking about the merits of Château X versus Château Y, or how the wine from this vineyard in the north of the Chablis region is more elegant than the one from the vineyard planted farther south.

But you don't have to probe that level of detail to appreciate the notion that different growing conditions give different characteristics to wine, in the same way that any living thing is a reflection of its environment. Artisanal cheesemakers will tell you that the taste of their cheese changes as the diet of their cows (or goats or sheep) changes from spring to summer grasses, then to winter feed. The flavor of Pacific northwest salmon and Alaskan salmon is different in part because of the different habitats and diets of the fish. When it comes to wine, the Old World view is that "wine is made in the vineyard," so the vintner's job is simply to shepherd into the bottle the character of the vineyard—nuances, subtleties, and all. *That* gets to the heart of the Old World subtlety of style that we've been talking about. You'll be able to explore some of these nuances with the tastings in Chapters 6 and 7.

It also makes for an obvious contrast with the New World riff, which is often about making a splashy statement. This grew out of the fact that there was little in the way of tradition to dictate styles or limit experimentation. What's more, there was a lot to prove in comparison to the venerable classic wines of the Old World, whose reputations precede them and often garner them top prices in the marketplace. In that context, put yourself in the shoes of a New World winemaker. How do you get the attention of the wine critics, the merchants, and the buying public? You can focus on quality, to be sure, but against the quality reputations of the Old Guard wines, that may not be enough. You may have to make a little noise. I believe that's why the New World wines often epitomize the lush and bold wine style, as a way to differentiate themselves, to create a signature.

What About "Earthy" Wines?

The waiters I train often express confusion about wines being described as "earthy." They think back to the time they made mud pies as children and actually took a taste; or to the gritty remnants of sliding into home plate during softball season. I find that when it comes to wine, the term *earthy* is harder for people to get used to than is the taste it describes. Generally, people love the taste of wines that are commonly described as earthy—Italian Chianti, French white and red Burgundy and Rhône wines, Spanish Rioja, among many others—but are not attuned to describing them as such. It certainly comes up as a positive attribute in other things—for example, potatoes are earthy; many great cheeses are known for a certain earthy funkiness; mushrooms are earthy. But if you do not relate to this term when you taste wines, it doesn't matter. Just don't let it put you off, because earthy is used a lot by the wine trade—often, and this is an interesting point, to identify the subtlety and terroir characteristics of Old World wines.

The New World counterpoint to the Old World's earthy style, used quite often on back labels and in critics' tasting notes, is "fruit-driven" or "fruit-forward." These terms mean that the most prominent characteristic of the wine is bold, lush, opulent fruit, as opposed to earthiness or other subtle notes such as floral, spicy, and herbaceous.

Can New World Wines Have Terroir?

In every New World wine country, wineries and grape growers have begun to experiment with the idea of terroir, or vineyard-specific character, and how to express it in the bottle. But it is early days. Old World growers' grasp of their vineyards' character and potential was developed over centuries of trial and error. Most New World wineries are still grappling with basic questions, such as, Which grapes grow best in which areas?

In years past, the question of what to plant where was market-driven. Vineyards planted what was selling. But this resulted in some serious mistakes, the most famous of which was the planting of Cabernet Sauvignon in California's Monterey County district. The climate there is usually too cool to successfully ripen Cabernet Sauvignon, as evidenced by some notorious Cabernet flops in the 1970s—"green pepper" was one of the kindest descriptions for their taste. Since then, the region has been replanted largely to Chardonnay and Pinot Noir, both of which thrive in that cool-to-moderate climate.

Retooling a vineyard and then tasting and testing the results takes years. Once the question of what best to plant is settled, it takes more long years to identify and learn to capture in the wine the subtleties of a particular vineyard. Although it may be a long way off, some of the New World's most respected vintners believe that terroir will ultimately have a prominent role in New World winemaking style.

You might have noticed the signs emerging on familiar wine labels. In the Napa Valley, for example, vintners have been closely studying the distinctive characters and grape affinities of particular Napa subsections for about thirty years now. Some consensus is forming. The Carneros subdistrict has become known for characterful Chardonnays and Pinot Noirs. The Rutherford subregions has emerged as a Cabernet Sauvignon mecca. Some of Sonoma County's subregions have developed similar specialty reputations. The Russian River Valley for Pinot Noir and the Dry Creek Valley for Zinfandel are two prominent examples. In my opinion, these regions do offer terrior, and I encourage you to try them side by side with their straight "Napa" and "Sonoma" counterparts to get a handle on their styles.

Having It Both Ways

Some winemakers get the best of both worlds. In the increasingly global marketplace, joint ventures between Old World and New World wineries are a growing phenomenon. The Opus One winery in Napa Valley was one of the first, a joint venture launched in the late 1970s between Robert Mondavi and the Baron Philippe de Rothschild (owner of Bordeaux's Château Mouton-Rothschild), and remains among the most celebrated. Another more recent trend has been the establishment of vineyards in the Southern Hemisphere by Old World wineries. Since the seasons are opposite, they get to work two harvests a year instead of one, and also to make wine from both Old World and New World viewpoints. Chile's Bodegas Torres winery, launched by the famous Spanish winemaker Miguel Torres, was one of the pioneers in this movement. Many other vintners, including some of Bordeaux's best-known winemakers, have followed.

The Old World and the New

If you are thinking that the idea of a wine being subtle or bold is a matter of personal taste, you are right. There is no absolute definition of subtlety or boldness in a wine, but that's okay. These words are used to help us draw distinctions between one wine and another, just as we use them in comparing other things. You might say a Rolls-Royce is subtle and elegant, while a Ferrari is bold, yet both cars could share a subtle feature, say a black color. A lobster bisque is subtle compared to a bold gazpacho, yet chefs would tell you that at their best, both soups rely on *bold* ingredients—an intense lobster stock on the one hand, perfectly ripe tomatoes, onions, and garlic on the other—as well as a *subtle* layering of flavors.

Here are some tastings that will let you explore the subtlety of the Old World and boldness of the New World style yourself. I encourage you to try them all, because the wines are delicious, and the comparisons will add immeasurably to your tasting confidence. A lot of people tell me they can't taste and remember the subtle differences in wines. It is a skill that comes with experience and by now you have plenty, which will allow you to really enjoy these tastings. Before we start, here is a recap of some of the terms we used to compare and contrast Old World and New World wine. You might like to refer to them as you taste, and I will in the notes:

OLD WORLD	NEW WORLD
Subtle, elegant, refined	Bold, lush, opulent
Earthy, terroir	Fruit-driven, fruit-forward
Expresses the character of the vineyard	Expresses the winemaker's signature

Our selections for tasting necessarily start at the mid-price level, because most of the classic Old World wines are, by definition, at least a cut above everyday wines in terms of both quality and price. My recommendations are chosen to ensure you compare wines of comparable quality.

Old World, New World, and the Big Six

From all of our tastings, you have developed a broad frame of reference for the styles of the Big Six grapes, so this is a great place to start our Old World and New World tasting comparisons. Given your tasting experience, I will not remind you in each tasting box to examine the look of the wines against a white background, or to swirl. I am sure both are second nature by now.

Riesling

OLD WORLD RIESLING	NEW WORLD RIESLING
Alsace, France: Trimbach, Hugel, Schlumberger, Albrecht, Josmeyer, Leon Beyer, Weinbach, or your store's suggestion	*New Zealand:* Brancott, Villa Maria *Australia*: Pike's, Grosset, Mt. Horrocks, Penfolds *United States:* Bonny Doon, Kendall-Jackson, Chateau Ste. Michelle, J. Lohr, Jekel, Trefethen, Eroica

THE LOOK

Pale yellow-green	Also yellow-green, but perhaps a touch yellower

THE SMELL

These are subtle scents—lemon, green apple, and very often an earthiness that pro tasters compare, with no intention of being negative, to petroleum (my description is WD-40). For a lot of pros, that marks it as Old World, but if you don't notice that smell, don't worry. The subtlety will show in comparison to the New World wine in this pair.	Quite a bit more exotic. There are peach, apricot, and citrus scents, mandarin orange, tangerine, and melon. You can probably sense that the aroma seems more "fruit-forward."

THE TASTE

Lemony fruit flavor, prominent acidity, overall very subtle.	The vivid fruit flavors echo those in the scent, and the overall taste is juicy, like a fruit salad.

Sauvignon Blanc

OLD WORLD SAUVIGNON BLANC	NEW WORLD SAUVIGNON BLANC
Loire Valley Sancerre: Lucien Crochet, Domaine Thomas, Pascal Jolivet, Château de Sancerre *Loire Valley Pouilly-Fumé:* Ladoucette, Michel Redde, Alphonse Mellot, Jean-Claude Chatelain	*California*: Morgan, Simi, Murphy-Goode, Dry Creek Vineyard, Matanzas Creek, Iron Horse, Kunde Estate, Kenwood, Robert Mondavi Fumé Blanc, Benziger Fumé Blanc, Honig, Ferrari-Carano, Cain Cellars *Chile*: Casa Lapostolle, Veramonte *New Zealand*: Kim Crawford, Babich, Vavasour, Villa Maria, Brancott Reserve

THE LOOK	
Pale yellow-green to straw yellow	Similar to the Old World wine, but perhaps a bit darker

THE SMELL	
In Old World Sauvignon Blancs such as these, the grassy/herbaceous scent is usually a prominent feature. Some tasters also detect a subtle earthiness like the scent of wet gravel, and a fruit character of lime and tart apples.	The fruit character of New World Sauvignon Blanc is sometimes lush and bold enough that it could be mistaken for Chardonnay—melon, pear, and peach come to mind. But you will probably still catch a whiff of the pungency that says "Sauvignon Blanc"—perhaps a touch of grapefruit or lime.

THE TASTE	
The tart and tangy flavors of this wine give it an overall lean character, and there is a bit of gravelly earthiness that is again hard to describe because it is so subtle.	Compared to the Old World wine, this taste is much richer and riper, with flavors echoing the scents—ripe peach and melon with a little streak of pungency.

Chardonnay

OLD WORLD CHARDONNAY	NEW WORLD CHARDONNAY
Mâcon: Jadot, Bouchard, Verget, Duboeuf, Bonhomme, Manciat-Poncet, Drouhin	*California:* Echelon, Robert Mondavi Napa, Estancia Pinnacles, Gallo of Sonoma, Cambria,
Pouilly-Fuissé: Bouchard, Château Fuissé, Jadot	Matanzas Creek, Beringer Napa, St. Francis, Chalk Hill, Stonestreet, Simi
Chablis: Grossot, Laroche, Moreau, Long-Depaquit, William Fevre	*Australia:* Devil's Lair, Rosemount Roxburgh, Leeuwin Estate, Knappstein-Lenswood, Cape
Meursault: Bouchard, Jadot, Matrot, Labouré-Roi, Louis Latour	Mentelle, Scotchman's Hill, Coldstream Hills
Chassagne-Montrachet: Morey, Fontaine-Gagnard (or your store's suggestion)	

THE LOOK	
Very pale, straw yellow	Darker yellow than the Old World Chardonnay

THE SMELL	
Clean, subtle, pure Chardonnay character, appley fruit. French white Burgundy's "earthy" smell is legendary but quite subtle. The words often applied to Chablis and Pouilly-Fuissé are minerally, flinty, chalky, or wet rocks (think of a gravel driveway after the rain). I sometimes get the scent of chamomile tea—brew a cup for reference and you can probably pinpoint the scent.	The increased intensity and ripeness is impossible to miss. "Fruit-forward" is the perfect description for this wine, especially in comparison to the Old World wine.

Crisp and refreshing, and if you concentrate on the aftertaste, you may again sense some earthiness. There is a lot of complexity here, yet it is extremely subtle, lithe, and elegant—a ballet dancer of a wine.

Isn't this a great comparison? It's hard to resist continuing with the dancer analogy: This is a Polynesian dancer—suppler and a little more exotic. As with the scent, this wine is fruit-driven—melon, peach, pineapple.

Pinot Noir

OLD WORLD PINOT NOIR:
FRENCH RED BURGUNDY

NEW WORLD PINOT NOIR:
CALIFORNIA AND OREGON

Mercurey: Perdrix, Faiveley, Juillot, Joblot
Santenay: Belland, Lequin, Olivier Leflaive,
    Jadot, Nicolas Potel
Bourgogne: Bouchard, Groffier, Leroy
Savigny les Beaune: Bouchard, Leroy
Nuits St. Georges: Gouges, Rion, Engel
(or your store's suggestion)

Calera, Acacia, Meridian, Estancia, Gallo of Sonoma, Domaine Carneros, Robert Mondavi Napa, Byron, Saintsbury Carneros, Ramsay, Au Bon Climat, Marimar Torres, Chalone, Iron Horse, Dehlinger, Belle Glos, Cambria, Sanford, Kent Rasmussen, Etude, Morgan, Truchard, Sokol Blosser, Domaine Drouhin, King Estate, Ponzi

THE LOOK

Limpid, pale ruby

Violet-tinged ruby—the color is darker, though still translucent

THE SMELL

Tangy red berries—cranberry, sour cherry. You may notice a family of earthy scents—tea leaves, spice, mushrooms, and a wet forest floor are all commonly used to describe the subtle terroir character of red Burgundy.

This has the riper and more luscious scents of Bing cherries and raspberries, and an overall "sweet" impression in the smell—partly due to riper fruit, and part to the oak aging.

THE TASTE

Tasting this wine requires concentration, because its entire makeup—fruit, body, texture—is understated. The taste echoes the scent, although the earthy qualities may seem less prominent.

You probably notice a plumper feeling in the mouth, and more forward, juicy fruit flavors— ripe summer berries and cherries.

Old World, New World

Cabernet Sauvignon and Merlot

The next two tastings feature Old World selections from Bordeaux, France. The aroma and taste expression of Bordeaux terroir is one of my favorites in the world of wine. It differs from Merlot-based wines to Cabernet-based wines, as you will see from my varied notes with each tasting. Take a moment to cleanse your palate and be prepared to really focus on these wines. I've included some pretty elaborate descriptions to help you appreciate their depth.

Merlot

OLD WORLD MERLOT: FRENCH RED BORDEAUX	NEW WORLD MERLOT: CALIFORNIA AND WASHINGTON
Château La Cardonne, Château Simard, Château Monbousquet, Clos des Jacobins, Château Canon, Château Figeac, Château Beau-Séjour Bécot, Château Belair, Château L'Angelus, or your store's recommendation	Chataeu St. Jean, Gallo of Sonoma, Wente, Truchard, Stonestreet, Havens, Pride Mountain, Newton, Beringer, Robert Mondavi Napa, Franciscan, Markham, L'Ecole No. 41, Woodward Canyon, Chateau Ste. Michelle, Canoe Ridge

THE LOOK

Dark ruby red	Purplish ruby red

THE SMELL

Go back to the glass often, because you will detect something new every time. The fruit character is mostly plum, with lots of extras layered on top: vanilla-oakiness, roasted coffee beans, wet gravel, cocoa powder, pen ink (not a classic Bordeaux description, but that's what it reminds me of). Yet it is all quite subtle—nothing hits you over the head. If you don't get any of these specific scents, or can't put a name to what you are smelling, that's okay. You will definitely see what matters —that it is different from the New World wine.	It smells much sweeter and riper. All of the fruit scents—plum, blackberry, and blueberry—seem almost overripe or sweetened, like a compote or jam. In fact, "jammy" is a common description of the fruit-forward style of New World red wines. The oak character may also seem more prominent to you in this wine. There is complexity, to be sure, but the dominant note is ripe, succulent fruit, not earth.

THE TASTE

The complexity and subtlety carries through to the taste. The wine has much to communicate, but it does it with a soft voice.	Juicy, succulent fruit that tastes and feels richer in the mouth. Almost seems flashy by comparison to the Old World wine. But you can certainly see why Americans love bold, luscious California wines.

Cabernet Sauvignon

OLD WORLD CABERNET SAUVIGNON: FRENCH RED BORDEAUX	NEW WORLD CABERNET SAUVIGNON
Château les Ormes de Pez, Château Meyney, Château Lagrange, Château Langoa-Barton, Cadet de Mouton, Pavillon Rouge de Château Margaux, Château Fourcas-Hosten, Château Poujeaux, Les Forts de la Tour, Château Cantemerle, Château Duhart-Milon Rothschild, or your store's suggestion	*California:* Robert Mondavi Napa, Pine Ridge, Clos du Val, BV Rutherford, Franciscan, Markham, Simi Reserve, Sequoia Grove, J. Lohr, Staglin Family, Mt. Veeder *Washington State:* Chaleur Estate, Chateau Ste. Michelle, Woodward Canyon, Bookwalter *Australia:* Penfold's Bin 707, Wynn's Coonawarra, Cape Mentelle, Katnook

THE LOOK

Dark ruby red	Purplish ruby red

THE SMELL

Bordeaux's Cabernet-based wines were the original style for which the blackcurrant and cassis descriptions were coined. There is, again, earth. (I think of wet leaves in the fall and wet gravel.) There is also a cedary spiciness, vanilla and sometimes a mocha or coffee bean scent caused by the oak aging. "Pencil lead" is another common scent descriptor for this wine style. If you remember manning the crank-style pencil sharpener in grade school, then you may well relate to that description.

Again, I think of the "jammy" description because the juicy, ripe blackberry, blackcurrant, and cassis flavors are so lush and forward. This is the epitome of New World boldness—of fruit, of body and structure, and also of oak. An abundance of sweet, toasty, spicy oak scent is one of the most prominent features in this wine. Some New World bottlings also show a touch of mint or eucalyptus in the scent.

THE TASTE

There is power here, but on a balanced, proportioned frame. No wonder this wine style is so famous. The fruit is there, but well-integrated with the rest of the parts. The tannin is firm but balanced. The aftertaste may be tinged with the oak character, and a hint of the wine's earthiness.

This style is often described as "blockbuster," and now you can see in comparison to what—its Bordeaux counterpart. The plump, jammy fruit, ample tannins, and sweet oak character are really in-your-face. It is easy to see how this wine style gets the attention of wine critics and consumers.

Syrah/Shiraz

The Old World wines in this tasting are all regionally named wines from France's Rhône Valley, so you will not see the grape name listed on their labels. I have given you several appellations from which to choose: Cornas (*Core-NAHSS*), St. Joseph (*San Joe-SEFF*), and Crozes-Hermitage (*Crows Air-mee-TAHJ*) are all typically in the fifteen-to-twenty-dollar national average price range. Hermitage (*Air-mee-TAHJ*) and Côte-Rôtie (*Coat Row-TEE*) are more expensive. The Syrah/Shiraz choices are price-matched accordingly so that you can compare roughly equivalent wines.

OLD WORLD SYRAH: FRENCH RED RHÔNE WINES	NEW WORLD SYRAH/SHIRAZ
Cornas: Auguste Clape, Colombo, Alain Voge, Robert Michel, Alain Juge	*United States:* Qupé, Jade Mountain, Edmunds St. John, Geyser Peak, Andrew Murray, Columbia Red Willow, Cline Cellars, Columbia Crest Grand Estates
Crozes-Hermitage: Graillot, Chapoutier, Jaboulet, Albert Belle, Louis de Vallouit	*Australia:* Rosemount Balmoral, Eileen Hardy, Penfolds Bin 28, Wynn's, d'Arenberg The Dead Arm, Cape Mentelle, Brokenwood, Pike's, Trevor Jones
Hermitage: Jaboulet, Chapoutier, Delas, Chave	
St. Joseph: Chapoutier, Jaboulet, Cuilleron (*Kwee-air-OHN*)	
Côte-Rôtie: Delas, Guigal, Clusel-Roch, Rostaing, Jasmin	

THE LOOK

Dark, nearly opaque ruby red	Inky ruby-purple

THE SMELL

The scent alone makes this one of my favorite wine styles in the world. Most tasters find the resemblance to fresh-ground black pepper uncanny, but there are other spices as well—cumin and cardamom—and other earthy scents—anything from leather to mushroom to wet dirt and rocks. You may sense herbs as well—rosemary, thyme, oregano, or an unspecific herbal presence. The fruit is also rich—raisin, prune, dried fig. You could smell this one for hours and not exhaust your imagination.

The scents here always make me think "overripe" and "wild"—raspberries, boysenberries, and the like in a sweet, concentrated, jammy essence. The oak character gives a sweet, coconut-vanilla overlay to all that fruit, making for an extremely exotic drinking experience. Sometimes the spicy scent of black pepper that you noticed on the Old World wine shows here, too; however, some of the New World versions show a sweeter spice family—cinnamon, clove, and allspice.

I'll bet you couldn't wait to taste it after that scent. The beauty of this wine is that all of the promise of the aroma comes through in the taste. It is an utterly powerful style, yet still everything remains in proportion—the hallmark of an Old World classic wine.

This wine, too, delivers in the taste what the scent promised—bold, exotic flavor saturated with fruit and oak. This wine is not a "gulper" by any means. Frankly, both wines are monumental in scale, but the New World style is more over-the-top.

If they were divas, this one would be Tina Turner to the Old World's Edith Piaf.

Old World and New World, Beyond the Big Six

I urge you not to skip these next tastings. We will be focusing on some delicious wines made from grapes outside the Big Six, which are nonetheless important wines in the buying market, and also great ways to illustrate the Old World and New World style contrasts. We will taste two white grapes that have traveled beyond their Old World home bases: Pinot Gris (*PEE-no GREE*), called Pinot Grigio (*PEE-no GREE-jee-oh*) in Italy, and Viognier (*Vee-own-YAY*).

Pinot Gris/Pinot Grigio

New World winemakers typically use the French spelling of *gris* (meaning gray), rather than the Italian *grigio*. The Italian versions are the quintessential "luncheon" wines—light, crisp, refreshing, and noncerebral. The American versions have more obvious fruit flavor and make a good aperitif at cocktail hour because they taste good without food, but are not heavy.

OLD WORLD PINOT GRIGIO: ITALY	NEW WORLD PINOT GRIS: UNITED STATES
Campanile, Cavit, Zemmer, Zenato, Placido, Ritratti, Lageder, Livio Fellugor or your store's suggestion	King Estate, Ponzi, WillaKenzie, Adelsheim, Estancia, 'J' Wine Co., Argyle, Sokol Blosser
THE LOOK	
Nearly water-clear, tinged with greenish-straw	Very pale yellow-green; slightly darker than the Old World version
THE SMELL	
Italian whites generally are some of the most understated, subtly scented wines in the world. The smell here is clean and refreshing, with faint lemon and apple character, and perhaps faintly minerally, like the scent of mineral supplements from the health food store.	This scent is more obviously fruity, and for me very marked with the scent of ripe pears, peaches, and applesauce.

This taste is refreshing and crisp, not obviously fruity. There are subtle hints of lemon zest, and the prominent acidity gives a mouthwatering quality.

The fruit flavors very much mirror the scents, and the fruit character, though not heavy or exotic, is quite lip-smacking and juicy.

Viognier

This is a wonderfully exotic white grape to explore, traditional to France's Rhône Valley but planted in small quantities elsewhere. You will need to conjure up your floral and spicy vocabulary, but also be prepared for exotic fruit flavor. It may require a search or a special order to acquire some of these wines, and they are not cheap. But it is worth the extra effort and expense to try something this distinctive. Enjoy!

OLD WORLD VIOGNIER (RHÔNE OR SOUTHERN FRANCE)

The Rhône Valley's Condrieu appellation:
    Guigal, Cuilleron, Delas, Georges Vernay, Francois Villard
Southern France: Triennes, George Duboeuf

NEW WORLD VIOGNIER

Joseph Phelps, McDowell, RH Phillips, Arrowood, Edmunds St. John, Calera, Testarossa, Alban, Andrew Murray

THE LOOK

Straw yellow

Darker yellow than the Old World Viognier

THE SMELL

This is one of the most complex-smelling grapes in the world: floral scents (honeysuckle, orange blossom, lavender) are common, as are stone fruits like peach and apricot. Some wines also show subtle earthiness, but the other scents may dominate.

The New World wine's scents really jump from the glass. They are in the same family as the Old World's but more exotic, with floral scents of honeysuckle but also jasmine, gardenia, and other tropical blossoms. The fruit scents are more tropical as well—mango and pineapple.

THE TASTE

The peach and apricot flavors predominate, but the Old World subtlety shows here. The wine is full-bodied but still balanced and in proportion. A mineral character may also show subtly in the taste.

This is a full-blown, exotic wine. The tropical fruit flavors may remind you of an umbrella drink you had on your tropical vacation—coconut, mango, pineapple, with a very full and unctuous texture.

As always, I hope you had fun with these tastings. Now you have a better understanding of the style differences between classic Old and New World wines so you can choose between them to suit your taste and the occasion.

Wine professionals sometimes say that the New World wines, whose bold style tends to steal the show, are best-suited to simple foods—a fine cheese or a meat or fish simply grilled or roasted without fussy preparations—that let the wine shine. When the meal or a special dish are the focus, the subtlety and reserve of the Old World wine style is often thought to better complement the food without overpowering it. Ultimately, that decision is up to your personal taste, which means you must experiment. We will explore that and other wine and food dynamics in Chapter 10.

CHAPTER SIX

France

The Objects of Desire

Ah, Paris. It is the city of romance and food, and the order of priority can change like the wind. Is that Chanel No. 5 perfuming the air, or croissant? Either is enough to drive you to distraction. But in May 1990, cash-poor and flying solo, I barely stopped long enough to sniff the breeze. In fact, I spent a grand total of two hours and seventeen minutes there—the time it took to take the airport bus from Charles de Gaulle Airport to the Gare du Nord train station, for the first train to the town of Reims. For although it was neither love nor lunch, I did have an agenda.

It was wine. My first stop was the Champagne region, less than two hours east of the City of Lights but a world away. The first Champagne cellar I happened upon, just minutes by foot from the train station, remains one of my sentimental and taste favorites—Taittinger. Forty-eight hours later, I had visited seven other Champagne cellars, and was on the train again.

Eight weeks, 7 youth hostels, 650 wines, and 2,200 miles (mostly by train and foot) later, the immersion was complete. I had tasted and breathed and slept Alsace, Bordeaux, Burgundy, Rhône, and Loire Valley wines—all the *classiques*. And as I learned later, in those same weeks I navigated virtually the entire fine-wine world, without ever venturing beyond the borders of France.

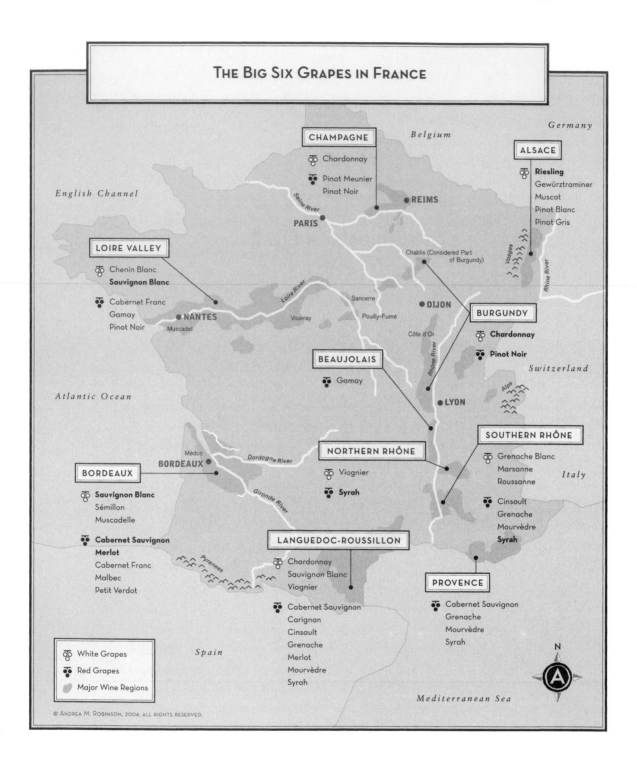

THE BIG SIX GRAPES IN FRANCE

CHAMPAGNE
Chardonnay
Pinot Meunier
Pinot Noir

ALSACE
Riesling
Gewürztraminer
Muscat
Pinot Blanc
Pinot Gris

LOIRE VALLEY
Chenin Blanc
Sauvignon Blanc
Cabernet Franc
Gamay
Pinot Noir

Chablis (Considered Part of Burgundy)

BURGUNDY
Chardonnay
Pinot Noir

BEAUJOLAIS
Gamay

BORDEAUX
Sauvignon Blanc
Sémillon
Muscadelle
Cabernet Sauvignon
Merlot
Cabernet Franc
Malbec
Petit Verdot

NORTHERN RHÔNE
Viognier
Syrah

SOUTHERN RHÔNE
Grenache Blanc
Marsanne
Roussanne
Cinsault
Grenache
Mourvèdre
Syrah

LANGUEDOC-ROUSSILLON
Chardonnay
Sauvignon Blanc
Viognier
Cabernet Sauvignon
Carignan
Cinsault
Grenache
Merlot
Mourvèdre
Syrah

PROVENCE
Cabernet Sauvignon
Grenache
Mourvèdre
Syrah

White Grapes
Red Grapes
Major Wine Regions

English Channel
Atlantic Ocean
Spain
Germany
Belgium
Switzerland
Italy
Mediterranean Sea

PARIS
REIMS
NANTES
Muscadet
DIJON
LYON
BORDEAUX
Médoc

Seine River
Loire River
Rhône River
Dordogne River
Gironde River
Rhine River
Vosges
Alps
Pyrenees

Sancerre
Pouilly-Fumé
Vouvray
Côte d'Or

N

France, the Fashion Leader (in Wine Styles, Too)

In the global world of wine, France is indisputably the headquarters. Most of the wines on the world market, across the quality spectrum from budget to boutique labels, are modeled after a French classic, or paradigm. Although at first it may seem overly simplistic, it is absolutely true. Take, for example, Chardonnay, the world's preeminent white wine. Every bottle made, from Adelaide, Australia, to Yountville, California, and every region in between, is modeled after French white Burgundy. And how about the elite red Cabernet Sauvignon—varietal versions the world over and all the proprietary, Meritage, and Tuscan specialties? All look to red French Bordeaux as their paradigm. There are more of these French archetypal wines, all of which I will share with you in this chapter, but you get the picture. For the buyer, the picture's a rosy one, because it shows the power of the Big Six, which you already know so well. (The map, opposite, lays it out, highlighting the Big Six grapes in bold, in their home base regions: (1) Riesling—Alsace, (2) Sauvignon Blanc—Loire Valley and Bordeaux, (3) Chardonnay—Burgundy, (4) Pinot Noir—Burgundy, (5) Cabernet Sauvignon/Merlot—Bordeaux, and (6) Syrah—Rhône.)

Our tastings will explore the flavors and styles of each of the French classics, but the wonderful truth is that you already explored most of them when tasting the Big Six. This means that we can make quick work of internalizing the two most important things the buyer needs to know about the French paradigm wines: (1) their Big Six varietal connection to the rest of the quality wine world as shown on the map, and (2) their pronunciations (it's hard to buy it if you can't say it).

With these two simple but powerful tools, mastering the wine shop environment, and nine out of ten wine lists, is a completely realistic proposition. Since virtually all of the world's big wines, and most of the rest, are fashioned after a French classic, they are more alike than different. Knowing these style links between the Big Six grapes and the French classic wines, you will be prepared to handle any buying situation, even the dreaded all-French wine list, where the only name you used to know was the wallet-busting Champagne. And you will be able, should you so desire, to use your Flavor Map and Old World/New World knowledge to predict the subtler differences—in body, fruit flavors, and style intensity—between the French classics and the wines from other regions that emulate them.

The Other Cool French Wines

As we explore the classic French wines, we'll also take time to look at two other categories of wines found in France.

Cheap but good In addition to the standard-bearers, France has a wine family that you should definitely get to know—the "little wines." I call them that because the French do—*petits vins*. They are the nifty, noncerebral wines the French drink every day—little in price and prominence but big in flavor and value. You have to remember that in France, wine is first and foremost a peasant drink. We English speakers are the architects of wine elitism. (What were we thinking?) So nearly every major and minor French wine region has these affordable-to-drink-everyday gems. I will give you some of the best readily available styles, and point out some of my favorites for you to try.

One-of-a-kind wines There are some specialty wine styles that are so original and special you must give them a try, too. I will describe them and give some specific recommendations.

FRENCH THE AMERICAN WAY

To help you pronounce the French wine words in this chapter, I will be giving a lot of phonetic spellings. Apologies in advance to native speakers and French language students—my phonetics are "Americanized" to make it a little easier for the average person. I adore the French language, but some of the sounds are tough for the uninitiated. And I do believe that people can say Paris and Champagne as *PAIR-iss* and *Sham-PAIN* (rather than *Pah-REE* and *Shahm-PAHN-yuh*), and still be understood well enough. So you will forgive me, I hope, if I tell you that Chassagne (a town in the Burgundy region) kind of rhymes with lasagne. In my experience, the alternative is that people won't even try to pronounce the wine name. At that rate, the odds are almost zero that they will ever try the wine. And that would be tragic, indeed.

Champagne

Champagne is where my love affair with great wine began more than fifteen years ago. While still on Wall Street, I was doing everything I could to learn about wine and food in hopes of someday making it my career. Weekends, I worked for free as a *plongeur* (that's a dishwasher, *mon cheri*) at a French cooking school, and nights I spent pouring and doing cleanup at a wine school. One fateful evening, an impassioned Frenchman named Rémi Krug came to the school to teach us about Champagne. His ardor for his family's Champagnes was infectious, and it was easy to see why. As I tasted them, I couldn't speak. For days I felt punch-drunk from the memory of those exotic scents, and it seemed as if I could still taste the flavors. When I finally came to my senses, I walked into my boss's office at Morgan Stanley and quit. Within a month, I was in France, armed with a Eurail train pass, a youth hostel card (I still qualified), and a vineyard map (you already know my first stop). So began my graduate school.

My favorite wine is still Champagne. Along with the sensory beauty of it—the glimmer in the glass, the bewitching scents, the nerve-tingling taste—there is a lot to love from a buyer's perspective.

Consistency You can really count on the big brand names for consistent quality, and style. Every house has its signature style, ranging from delicate and elegant, to powerful and exotic (the way I like them). This means that once you pick your style preference, you can buy by brand with confidence.

Price Compared to other world-class wines, Champagne remains quite affordable. No, it is not cheap, but really great Champagne starts at around $25 to $30 a bottle in most cities, and you can get the absolute top of the line for $100 to $150. Even better, the price/value relationship is rock solid. When you pay more, you get more, which is not always the case with other wine categories, particularly the hype-heavy ones like trophy French Bordeaux and California Cabernets.

Instant gratification This is the best part of all. Most people do not have wine cellars for storing great bottles until they are in peak drinking condition. This is not a problem with Champagne, because the wineries literally cellar the wine for you, so Champagne is ready to drink when you buy it.

For fashion mavens, the house of Chanel connotes a certain "look," Yves Saint-Laurent another, and so on. Champagne houses work the same way. Devotees of a particular winery can count on its distinct style to mark every bottle it makes, regardless of type.

But how do you choose? You have to consider your style preference and your budget. The label will guide you to a choice that satisfies both.

Champagne Styles

Champagne style has three parts: (1) House style: Light-, medium-, or full-bodied. (2) Category: classic or specialty. (3) Taste: dry or sweet. Here is how the label answers each of these questions:

BODY STYLES The "house style," as in, light-, medium-, or full-bodied. Luckily, the factor that most affects the body style of a Champagne is also the most prominent feature on its label—the winery—because each takes its own approach to body style. Looking at these three labels, you can clearly see the name of the maker.

CHAMPAGNE CATEGORIES Most Champagne houses make several types. The major ones are, from most common to rarest, nonvintage, vintage, blanc de blancs (*blanc DUH blanc*), rosé (*row-ZAY*), and luxury. Here is what they mean:

Nonvintage In this case it's what is *not* printed on the label that's important. None of the labels shown here lists a vintage year, so all are called nonvintage. Nonvintage refers to the very essence of the Champagne production process: blending. Champagne is nearly always a blend, of vintages (harvest years) and of grapes—the reds Pinot Noir and Pinot Meunier and the white Chardonnay—to maximize its complexity and consistency. Each component in the blend brings distinctive character to the whole in the same way different instruments harmonize to produce beautiful music. The nonvintage is usually the calling card of every Champagne producer, making up the bulk of production and embodying the house style. On wine lists, it is often abbreviated as NV. Some houses use the term *multivintage*, abbreviated as MV.

Vintage In the best years, when the growing season weather produces top-quality grapes, many wineries like to bottle some of the harvest as vintage (rather than blended) Champagne, to show off the characteristics of that particular year. I like it for variety. I don't feel it's necessarily better than nonvintage Champagne, just different, and certainly more expensive because it is rarer.

Blanc de blancs White wine from white grapes, as the name implies. Remember that most of the grapes in Champagne are black (as the industry refers to red wine grapes)—Pinot Noir and Pinot Meunier—so this is a fairly rare specialty style, using only the Chardonnay grape. It is elegant and racy, and one of my favorite Champagnes with food, because it is so versatile. I especially love it with sushi.

Rosé This is another very rare style, made usually by adding a little bit of still (nonbubbly) red Pinot Noir wine for color. For me, the best rosés have the complexity of a red wine without the weight. Try one with dinner, and I bet you'll be converted. Rosés go especially well with duck, salmon, tuna, and pork.

Luxury cuvée Cuvée (*coo-VAY*) means blend, or selection. This style (sometimes called Tête de Cuvée, loosely "cream of the crop") represents the rarest and finest bottling of each house. Examples include Moët's Dom Pérignon, Roederer's Cristal, Krug's Grande Cuvée, and Veuve Clicquot's La Grande Dame. They are often, but not always, vintage-dated. They are considered to be more intense and complex than the other Champagne styles, but the differences are subtle. I think people buy them as much for the prestige as for the taste difference, because it adds to the fun and helps make a special occasion even more distinguished.

SWEET OR DRY TASTE? When "Brut" (rhymes with root) is printed on the label it means the wine is dry, with no sweet taste—the usual style of all the types shown above. The other styles, from least to most sweet, are: extra dry, sec (dry), demi-sec (off-dry), doux (sweet). A lot of people enjoy the touch of sweetness in the extra-dry style as an aperitif. Demi-sec makes a good dessert-style Champagne (the other styles are rarely exported to this country).

THE WINE OF LEGEND

Did the blind monk Dom Pérignon invent Champagne? Probably not. Was the young widow (or Veuve, in French) Clicquot the first modern businesswoman, bringing her late husband's Champagne house to prominence in the czarist courts of Russia? Most definitely. Whether all the stories surrounding it are true, Champagne is the wine of romance and legend, and with every bottle you open you will add to the repertoire.

But if you are eagerly anticipating your next Champagne "occasion," I have three words for you: Get over it. Say this to yourself: "I deserve to open a bottle of bubbly. I do not need an excuse. I do not have to deny myself and wait until some significant 'event' comes along." For me, if the day dawns, that is an occasion for Champagne.

The High Price of French Champagne

Why is French Champagne so much more expensive than other bubblies? There are two reasons for the price premium of Champagne versus other bubblies. The first is supply and demand, which is always a factor in the French paradigm wines. Since the appellation system limits the use of a classic wine name to the produce of its particular growing region, the supply cannot be increased to meet demand. The price reflects this.

The second reason is the production process, called the Méthode Champenoise (*method Shahm-pen-WAHZ*). Getting the bubbles and complexity into Champagne is a major ordeal. Here are the steps:

Blending This is truly an art for which few people have the talent. The blenders take hundreds of different base wines from different years, grapes, and vineyard sites to blend the raw material for each different Champagne type to be made. If you think of how an Impressionist painter synthesizes countless discrete paint dabs into a beautiful and richly textured image, you'll have a sense of the Champagne blender's task.

Second fermentation in the bottle The completed wine blend goes into the bottle with a liqueur of yeast and sugar, and is capped with a crown cap (like that on a beer bottle). The liqueur starts a second fermentation, yielding two by-products—carbon dioxide bubbles and yeast.

Aging Beneath the streets of Reims and Epernay, Champagne's two main towns, are miles of cool corridors burrowed out of the pure chalk subsoil, dug during Roman times. You will see them when you visit, because that is where the bottles lie to ferment the second time and then age. (Bring a sweater. They are the perfect place for wine as they naturally maintain a constant cool temperature and high humidity.) By law, the nonvintage wines must rest there for at least fifteen months, and the vintage wines at least three years. The longer the aging time, the more complex and "yeasty" the wine becomes. Yeasty, bready, biscuity, and nutty are all words that tasters use to describe the wonderful scent and taste that results from this long aging time. The tasting on page 149 will illustrate this flavor.

Disgorging After aging, what remains in the bottle along with the wonderful flavor and bubbles is a sediment of yeast cells left over from the second fermentation. If the sediment stayed in the bottle, the Champagne would be cloudy. To remove it, the wineries twist and shake each bottle, working the sediment into the neck in a process called *remuage* (*reh-moo-AHJ*, or "riddling" in English). The neck of the bottle is then frozen, capturing the sediment in a plug of ice that is popped out by flipping off the crown cap that was put on after blending. The bottle is then topped up, corked, and labeled.

Voilà! The Méthode Champenoise makes the real thing, on which virtually all other quality bubblies in the world are modeled. The lower prices of other sparkling wines can be further explained as follows:

Region of origin Some sparklers are made using the same intensive process as Champagne but come from regions with less notoriety and demand, or where land is more plentiful (which lowers production costs). Cava (*KAH-vuh*) from Spain and many California sparkling wines fit this description. They are good-quality alternatives when French Champagne is not in your budget (big parties, weddings, etc.).

Production process Other sparklers are made with less labor-intensive, more mechanized techniques that result in cost savings. The result is a less complex style that is good for making punches and sparkling wine drinks (mimosa, Bellini, and Kir royale are all classics). If you are going to add ingredients that dominate the flavor anyway, why pay the premium for true French Champagne?

Champagne

Our first tasting will allow you to compare Champagne house styles—light and elegant versus powerful and yeasty—so that you can see the style differences and identify your preference. The second tasting will compare the paradigm, French Champagne, to a California sparkler made with the same style and process. Another nifty tasting that you might want to do (maybe with friends to share the cost) would compare Champagne types—brut nonvintage, vintage, rosé, and luxury, for example—to see the differences. Have fun!

(*Note:* In many of the tastings in this chapter, I will not comment on the appearance unless the comparison is especially noteworthy, since by now you will know roughly what look to expect from most of these wines and can do this tasting step on your own.)

Champagne House-Style Comparison

LIGHT AND ELEGANT BRUT NV CHAMPAGNE	POWERFUL AND YEASTY BRUT NV CHAMPAGNE
Pol Roger Brut NV	Bollinger Special Cuvée Brut NV
Perrier-Jouët Grand Brut NV	Veuve Clicquot Yellow Label Brut NV
Taittinger Brut La Francaise NV	Charles Heidseick Brut NV
Laurent-Perrier Brut NV	Jacquesson Cuvée Prestige NV
	Krug Grande Cuvée MV

THE LOOK

Differences in appearance are negligible—pale, straw yellow color. Very fine bubbles. Some professional tasters use the expression "bead" for bubbles, as in "It has a very fine bead." That is because the fine bubbles often stream up from the bottom of the glass in a continuous line, like beads on a thread. Beautiful!

THE SMELL

Delicate scents of soft, golden apples and fresh cream are common. You may also notice a faint yeastiness—a scent familiar to bread bakers, of the yeast softening in warm water.

Here, the scents are similar, but it is as though the volume is turned up—the apple scent is richer, like a baked apple, and if you frequent a bakery, or have a bread machine, you will surely recognize that yeasty, toasty scent of baking bread.

France

149

THE TASTE

Crisp and refreshing, with soft bubbles of course, and a racy, lacy elegance. It is more about texture than flavor, which is ethereal. There is a lot here, but concentrate. It seduces you back to the glass so you must taste it again and again.

You sense the fuller body, and the more powerful, richer flavor of baked apples, yeast, and perhaps toasted hazelnuts or almonds—yet no heaviness. The length of flavor in the aftertaste is extraordinary.

No wonder this wine is in such demand! There's nothing quite like it. It is delicious and very original.

French Champagne versus California Sparkling Wine

This is a fun comparison, because several Champagne houses also produce California sparkling wines—meaning you could actually compare French versus Californian from the same winemaking "family," so to speak. As you do the tasting, keep in mind the distinction between Old World and New World styles—subtle versus fruit-forward.

AMERICAN BRUT NV SPARKLING WINE	FRENCH BRUT NV CHAMPAGNE
Domaine Chandon Brut Classic NV	Moët et Chandon Brut Imperial NV
Mumm Cuvée Napa Brut NV	Mumm Cordon Rouge Brut NV
Domaine Carneros Brut NV	Taittinger Brut La Francaise NV
Roederer Estate Brut NV	Louis Roederer Brut Premier NV

THE LOOK

Pale, straw yellow color

THE SMELL

Most tasters immediately notice a more vivid, ripe fruity scent—of sweet applesauce, sweet oranges, and marmalade. Why? The grapes get much riper in the California sun, and the flavors reflect this.

This is the telling part of the comparison. Notice the yeasty, creamy, nutty smell of this wine compared to its California cousin, whose scent is dominated more by vibrant fruit.

THE TASTE

Again, ripe, vivid fruit character is the predominant feature, as it was in the scent.

Certainly there is fruit, but the yeasty, nutty character is the most prominent style marker.

Bordeaux

I consider Champagne and Bordeaux to be the "aristocrats" of the French paradigm wines because, in addition to their historical and current status as world quality benchmarks, they have a commanding market presence. The other paradigm regions, by contrast, keep a lower profile, mainly because they are much smaller. Bordeaux claims the distinction of being the largest fine-wine region in the world, and is the model for all wines made from Cabernet Sauvignon and Merlot. (As shown on the Big Six Grapes in France map, page 140, a small part of the Bordeaux production is white wine which, along with the wines Sancerre and Pouilly-Fumé from the Loire Valley, serves as the benchmark for wines made from Sauvignon Blanc.)

Bordeaux Is a Blended Wine, Too

Like Champagne, Bordeaux is nearly always a blended wine—not of years, but of grapes. Depending on the winery, up to five red grapes may be used. The two majors are Merlot (the most widely planted) and Cabernet Sauvignon; the three others sometimes used in small amounts are: Cabernet Franc (*Cabernet FRAHNK*), Malbec (*MAHL-beck*), and Petit Verdot (*Puh-TEET Vair-DOUGH*). The virtues of this varied palette of grapes are several.

Complexity In the same way that the best cooks combine a little of this and a little of that to make the whole dish better than the sum of its

BORDEAUX'S BEST ADDRESSES

Margaux (*Mahr-GO*)
St. Julien (*Saint Joo-lee-YEN*)
Pauillac (*POH-yack*)
Ste. Estephe (*Saint Eh-STEFF*)
St. Émilion (*Saint Eh-mee-lee-YOHN*)
Pomerol (*POM-er-all*)
Pessac-Léognan (*Peh-SACK Lay-ohn-YOHN*)
Sauternes (*Saw-TURN*)

parts, Bordeaux wineries get added complexity in their wine by blending the grapes, each of which contributes its distinctive character to the final wine.

Practicality The grapes ripen at different rates, making it much easier to get the harvest and winemaking work done in stages. If all the grapes ripened at once, picking would be an overwhelming task, and few wineries would have the tank capacity in their fermenting rooms to handle the entire harvest at one time.

Insurance Staggered ripening of the grapes also protects against complete crop loss in years of bad or erratic weather. Take the all-too-common predicament of harvest rain. If it comes early in the picking, the early-ripening Merlot may be ruined, but a good Cabernet crop is still possible if the rain stops. When wine experts speak of certain vintages as being "Merlot years" and others as "Cabernet years," they are referring to this phenomenon.

Flexibility Bordeaux is a very large region, with growing conditions (soil, sun, rainfall, and so on) that vary from one subdistrict or town to the next. With different grapes to choose from, wineries can plant the best choice for their vineyard's particular conditions.

Red Bordeaux—The Classic Styles

Cabernet Sauvignon and Merlot are the two main Bordeaux "ingredients," and knowing that will help you predict the body style and flavor profile of the famous Bordeaux wines. Since you know the body and taste differences of these two grapes, if you know which prevails in a particular section of Bordeaux, then you will have a very good idea of the wine style from there.

The geography of Bordeaux makes this easy, because all of the best wine estates are clustered in just three top vineyard areas, the "left bank," the "right bank," and Graves. To remember where they are located, think of the Bordeaux region as a peace sign, tilted off-balance to the left. Each line in the peace sign is one of Bordeaux's rivers. The long center line is her major river, the Gironde (*Jhee-ROND*). The two forks are tributaries—the Dordogne (*Door-DOHN-yuh*) and Garonne (*Gah-RUN*).

The names are not important, but their blueprint is. The best vineyard zone west (left) of the center line (the Gironde River) is Bordeaux's "left bank." The top zone to the east, near the city of Bordeaux, is called the "right bank." And the land west of the two forks is called Graves (*Grahv*). Although the word *Graves* is found on wine labels, because it is an official

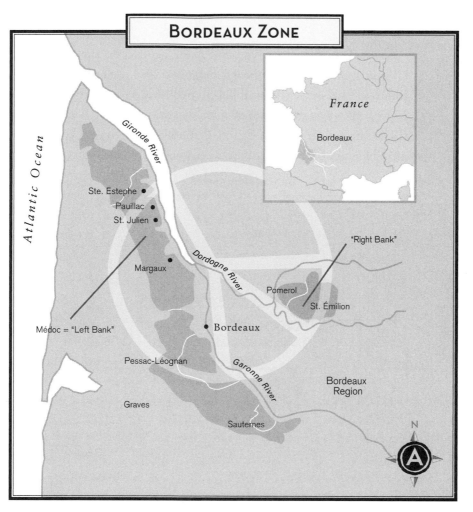

region, you will not see the words *left bank* or *right bank*, which are short-hand terms used in the trade, on the labels of their respective wines. What you *will* see, in addition to the château name, is the name of its town or district. If you know the important town names from each zone—five on the left bank, two on the right bank, and one in Graves—and the dominant grape in each zone, then you can use the town name on the label to help predict the style of all the top Bordeaux wines.

Here they are, matched with the main grape in each:

BORDEAUX ZONE	LEFT BANK	RIGHT BANK	GRAVES
Dominant grape	Cabernet Sauvignon	Merlot	Merlot/Cabernet (roughly equal
Main districts/towns	Médoc (a district name)	St. Émilion, Pomerol	proportions)
shown on label	Towns: Margaux,	(towns)	Graves, Pessac-Léognan
	St. Julien, Pauillac,		(districts)
	Ste. Estephe		

Look at the district or town name printed on the label beneath the château name. Is it on in the left-bank list? If so, Cabernet dominates most likely, so the wine will be fuller-bodied and have more tannin. If it is a right-bank village where Merlot holds sway, the wine will be medium- to full-bodied, with softer tannins. It follows that Graves, commonly a balanced blend of the two, falls between them in terms of body and tannin.

LEFT BANK LABEL	RIGHT BANK LABEL	GRAVES LABEL
Château Latour	Château Figeac	Château La Louvière
Mostly Cabernet	*Mostly Merlot*	*Cabernet and Merlot*
Full-bodied, tannic	*Medium-bodied, medium tannins*	*Medium-bodied, medium tannins*

TOWN
APPELLATION

DISTRICT
APPELLATION

The Châteaus of Bordeaux

Although I rarely hear wine professionals present Bordeaux so simply, the fact is that we all use exactly this logic to swiftly assess the style of selections we do not know, as well as to categorize the famous wines. By "famous wine," I mean the ones whose quality reputation contributed to Bordeaux's world-class status. They are called "château" wines, and you might have heard of some of the legendary ones, such as Château Latour, Château Mouton-Rothschild, Château Lafite-Rothschild, Château Haut-Brion, and Château Margaux. Thomas Jefferson was a fan of the latter two.

Why "château"? It is, in Bordeaux, the traditional name of a wine estate—a vineyard (or several) with winemaking facilities attached. The "château" thereon may be modest or grand (check the label—the grand ones are often pictured). Because each is a single wine estate, and châteaus may not boost their production by buying grapes from other vineyards, supply is limited. As such, château wines rarely come at everyday prices, and the most famous names are some of the highest-priced bottles in the entire wine world.

That is it for understanding famous Bordeaux wines. It may seem simplistic, but this is exactly how the pros deal with Bordeaux, because the alternative is tasting and memorizing the individual château names and styles—all seven thousand of them. This approach makes far better sense,

and it's quite accurate. If you like Bordeaux, you will certainly memorize your favorite château names as time goes on, just as you would memorize the winery names of Merlots and Cabernets that you like from other regions.

Some château wine labels include the term *cru classé* or *grand cru classé*, which translates in English as "classifed growth" or classified estate. This means the estate has been given a quality ranking, which many buyers find

useful. For reference, I include lists of these famous rankings in Appendix A. The left bank list, called the "1855 Classification" because it was drawn up by wine merchants in that year, is very well known. It ranks the sixty-one most famous left-bank (Médoc) châteaus in classes, from first to fifth—referred to as "first growth," "second growth," and so on (Château Haut-Brion, from Graves, was included because of its quality reputation). The Graves list is an official classification of just the top estates from that area, written in 1953. Finally, the right-bank list only includes St. Émilion châteaus, which were classified in 1955, and are periodically reviewed, most recently in 1996. Since Pomerol châteaus have never been classified, I include a list of trade favorites.

THE MINOR LEAGUE *You've just picked up a "château wine" for less than twenty-dollars—where does it fit in?*

You have discovered Bordeaux's "farm league." Not all of Bordeaux's many châteaus make the major leagues (the very top rankings), often because they are located outside of the very best growing areas. Still, for devotees of the Bordeaux style, they make very worthy and affordable choices. In the trade, they are often called petit châteaus, and some are included in an officially ranked group called cru Bourgeois (*croo Buh-JHWAH*). Here are some of my favorites:

Château Larose-Trintaudon (*Lah-ROSE Trent-oh-DOAN*)

Château Greysac (*GRAY-sack*)

Château La Cardonne (*Lah Car-DOAN*)

Château Fourcas-Hosten (*Four-cahs AUS-ten*)

Château Poujeaux (*Poo-JHOE*)

Château d'Angludet (*dahn-glue-DAY*)

Château Meyney (*May-NAY*)

Basic Bordeaux

There are also wines that just say "Bordeaux," with no village name, and many of these have proprietary names like Mouton-Cadet (*Moo-tohn Cuh-DAY*), or even varietal names like Christian Moueix (*Muh-WEX*) Merlot. They bear no resemblance to the château wines, Bordeaux's calling cards. The main reasons are these:

1. They are grown on vineyard sites less suited to top quality (to review the best-quality growing conditions, refer to the "What Is Quality?" section of Chapter 3).

2. The production standards are less strict for nonchâteau wines, especially in the key area of vineyard yield (also explained in Chapter 3). Basic Bordeaux wines are allowed to have higher vineyard yields than château wines, giving wines of less complexity and concentration.

3. Vinification is quite different. Oak marks the style of the top château wines, which are given lengthy aging (eighteen months

on more) in oak barrels after fermentation. The varietal wines that emulate this style use the same technique. By contrast, most of the basic wines see no oak aging, or a very small amount in used barrels that give little oak character.

This does not mean that basic Bordeaux wines are not worthwhile, for the price. What you should know about them includes the following: (1) If no varietal is listed, Merlot usually dominates. (2) In style, they compare to their varietal counterparts from other countries at similar price points. So, for example, Mouton-Cadet at about ten dollars is similar to a ten-dollar Merlot from, you name it—California, Washington, Chile, Australia, and so on.

Just keep in mind the Old World versus New World style differences we explored in the last chapter. On that basis, you would expect the Bordeaux to be a little subtler, and the New World varietal versions more fruit-driven, which is usually the case. As our tasting will illustrate, the same is true for the château wines and the comparable-quality Cabernet and Merlot varietals that emulate them. I have indicated both Merlot- and Cabernet-based château wines in the tasting list, so be sure to compare them to a like varietal wine to get the most out of the tasting.

"Off-vintages" and "Second Labels"

Bordeaux on a Budget . . . Well, sort of. The prices of classified château Bordeaux have gotten so crazy in the last few years that many of my students despair of ever being able to try them. If you shop around, you will see that most of the bottles I've suggested in the tasting that follows are, while not cheap, doable, especially if you share the costs with your tasting buddies. There are two other Bordeaux buying strategies to keep in mind:

"Off Vintages"—This refers to years when the growing season weather was less than perfect. In that case, the best estates still make excellent wine, but no quite top-of-the-top. To the taster, it just means the wine is "ready to drink" sooner, and the prices can often be half that of a stellar vintage. Inquire at a knowledgeable wine shop—you're likely to get some great deals.

"Second Labels"—In the 1970s and 1980s, in pursuit of ever-better quality, most of Bordeaux's top châteaus began producing "second labels." The wine under these la-bels is from the same vineyards, produced with the same care. It is simply a selection of barrels that, after tasting, the winemaker determined weren't quite up to the level of the main wine, called the *grand vin*. The second label gives you a hint of the grand vin's style, at a better price. A good wine shop can steer you to some worthy second labels to try, or look for these:

GRAND VIN	SECOND LABEL
Château Latour	Les Forts de Latour
Château Margaux	Pavillon Rouge de Château Margaux
Château Lafite-Rothschild	Carruades de Lafite
Château Cos d'Estournel	Les Pagodes de Cos
Château Pichon Longueville-Comtesse	Reserve de la Comtesse
Château Palmer	Reserve du General

Comparing Red Bordeaux, and Varietal Merlot and Cabernet Sauvignon

One note on costs: You might have noticed that the wines in our tastings are becoming costly. This is to be expected since we are exploring very upscale wine categories. If you want to skip this tasting, feel free. But if you are a buyer of classic Bordeaux and/or pricey varietal wines made in the Bordeaux style, this exercise will give you an excellent frame of reference.

FRENCH RED BORDEAUX

Merlot-based: Château Simard, Château Beau-Séjour Bécot, Château Petit-Village, Château Pavie, Château Monbousquet, Château Figeac, Château De Sales
Cabernet-based: Château Lynch-Bages, Château Pontet-Canet, Château Gruaud-Larose, Château Pichon-Longueville-Baron, Château Talbot, Château Meyney, Château de Pez, Château Lagrange

VARIETAL MERLOT AND CABERNET SAUVIGNON

(You may also refer to our previous Merlot and Cabernet tastings for suggestions.)
Merlot: Franciscan, Frog's Leap, Chateau Souverain, L'Ecole No. 41, Stonestreet, Pine Ridge
Cabernet Sauvignon: Mt. Veeder, Newton, Cakebread Cellars, Jordan, Joseph Phelps, Gallo Estate, Frog's Leap, Robert Mondavi Reserve

THE SMELL

The Merlot-based Bordeaux show the fruit character of their main grape—plum and dark berries, often accented with more earthy scents of coffee bean and damp leaves. The Cabernet-based wines show blackcurrant and cassis character, often with vanilla and scents of cedar from the oak, and sometimes the earthy scent of wet gravel or autumn leaves.

The Merlots here are exotically ripe, showing rich scents of plum compote and blueberry preserves. The oak is also very exotic and sweet-smelling. The Cabernets show typical blackberry and cassis fruit, but also ripe fig, and sometimes scents of mint and eucalyptus. The oak gives vanilla and a sweet spice character (cinnamon, clove).

THE TASTE

These wines show their fruit flavor in an understated way, woven harmoniously with the other components of earth, oak, tannin, and alcohol. Sometimes the tannin in Bordeaux is quite firm, making the wines seem more austere than their emulators; however, the Bordeaux style has evolved toward softer tannins, so the wines may seem more similar than different.

This may remind you of the Old World/New World tasting. In comparison to their Bordeaux models, these wines display more intense, in-your-face fruit and oak character, and often higher alcohol.

France

159

The Bordeaux Whites

As with the red wines, there are essentially two groups of Bordeaux white wines: the basic, inexpensive whites labeled as "Bordeaux," often with a proprietary name like Mouton-Cadet; and famous château wines, mainly from the Graves area (whose most famous subsection is Pessac-Léognan). Some of the best wines in this latter group come from estates that are famous for their red wine as well, and are included in the Graves ranking in Appendix A. These wines are the model for a particular style of Sauvignon Blanc wine that is, outside of Bordeaux, most common and successful in California. It is typically a fuller-bodied style for two reasons. First, Sémillon (*Sem-ee-YOHN*), a grape that adds a creamy scent, rich fruit flavor, and juicy texture, is usually blended in (and may be the dominant percentage). Second, the wines are usually aged in oak barrels, adding further body and intensity. Here is how they taste.

Comparing White Bordeaux and Oak-aged California Sauvignon Blanc

FRENCH WHITE BORDEAUX	OAK-AGED CALIFORNIA SAUVIGNON BLANC
Château La Louvière, Château Rahoul, Château Carbonnieux, Château Smith-Haut-Lafitte, Blanc de Lynch Bages, Pavillon Blanc de Château Margaux, Château Olivier	Matanzas Creek, Robert Mondavi Reserve Fumé–Blanc, Ferrari-Carano Fumé Blanc, Iron Horse, Simi, Babcock Cellars, Rochioli, Dry Creek Reserve

THE SMELL

The slightly grassy, herbaceous character comes through; however, the Sémillon adds some rich notes that remind me of honey and fig. The oak aging usually shows as a sweet, vanilla scent.	Here, the grassiness may be less prominent because the grape-growing climate is warmer. The Sauvignon character often comes through more as a citrus smell (lime and lemon candy), and you may notice riper fruit smells of melon and peach. The oak character is similar to the Bordeaux version.

THE TASTE

I love this flavor, because the tangy herbaceousness with the honeyed Sémillon taste and the sweet oak make very interesting layers of flavor that last into the finish. It is a great wine for crab cakes.	As you would expect, this is a less herbaceous, more succulent, fruit-driven style marked more by peach and melon and by the oak taste. You see the family resemblance, though.

For barrel-formented-Chardonnay fans, both of these styles provide an alternative with similiar body and richness, but something new in terms of fragrance and flavor.

France

161

Other parts of the wine world also emulate the Bordeaux style of Sauvignon Blanc, notably Washington State, Australia, and Chile. Italy also makes some worthy versions, but they are rare.

Sauternes: Bordeaux's One-of-a-Kind Dessert Wine

Sauternes (*Saw-TURN*) is truly one of the world's great wines—I can comfortably say imitated but never duplicated. True, other regions grow the same grapes as Sauternes—Sauvignon Blanc and Sémillon as in the adjacent Graves region, plus a bit of a beautifully scented grape called Muscadelle. And they may also use the same vinification style—barrel fermentation and aging. But they rarely achieve the unique harvest condition that creates the Sauternes style—rot.

In most regions, rot at harvest is a bad thing. But the rot in Sauternes, called botrytis (*bow-TRY-tiss*), is a benevolent one (the French call it *pourriture noble*—noble rot). As mentioned in Chapter 2, it shrivels and shrinks the grapes, concentrating their sugar and flavor, so that the final wine is a honeyed, heavenly nectar—rare and expensive but worth every penny in my opinion. Because of their richness, these wines are often sold in half-bottles—a very good idea. A classification of the famous Sauternes chateaus is included in Appendix A. Some California wines that emulate this style are Dolce (by Napa's Far Niente winery), Beringer Nightingale, and Chalk Hill Late Harvest Sémillon from Sonoma. Australia's late-harvest Sémillons are also made in this style. Petaluma and Peter Lehmann are two names to look for.

The Loire Valley

The Loire Valley is home to the other classic paradigms for Sauvignon Blanc—the regionally named wines Sancerre (*Sahn-SAIR*) and Pouilly-Fumé (*Poo-EE Foo-MAY*). They are quite a different style from the Bordeaux model. First, their taste is more tangy and tart because the region is farther north and cooler than Bordeaux, so the wines have higher acidity. Second, they are not usually oaky. The wineries use either stainless-steel tanks or big oak vats that give no wood taste to the wine, thus allowing the pure, vibrant Sauvignon Blanc flavor to come through. Finally, they are pure Sauvignon Blanc, with no Sémillon blended in. The outstanding Sauvignon Blancs from New Zealand, South Africa, and Austria, which are getting quite a bit of attention in the wine trade, are modeled on this style, as are some from the United States, Chile, and Italy. You tasted Loire-style Sauvignon Blanc quite a bit in previous chapters, so I will

not present detailed tasting notes here; however, I have recommended some great ones, along with their similarly styled counterparts, so that you can do a comparative tasting. It would also be interesting to choose a wine from either the Sancerre or Pouilly-Fumé list to taste and compare alongside one of the Bordeaux whites from the previous tasting.

Loire Valley Sancerre and Pouilly-Fumé	Loire-style Sauvignon Blanc from the New World
Sancerre:	*New Zealand:*
Michel Redde	Cloudy Bay
Domaine Lucien Thomas	Villa Maria
Bailly-Reverdy	Brancott Reserve
(*Bye-YEE Ruh-vair-dee*)	Nobilo
Crochet (*crow-SHAY*)	Vavasour
Jolivet (*Jhoe-lee-VAY*)	Babich
Cotat (*Coe-TAH*)	*South Africa:*
Alphonse Mellot (*Muh-LOW*)	Mulderbosch
Pouilly-Fumé:	Thelema
Daguenau (*DAG-uh-know*)	Brampton
Jean-Claude Chatelain	*United States:*
(*Shah-tuh-LANE*)	Frog's Leap
	Silverado
	Babcock
	Flora Springs Soliloquy

Cheap but Good—Loire Valley Muscadet

Muscadet (*Moo-scuh-day*) is a light, crisp, fun little white wine from the Loire Valley, but far downriver from Sancerre and Pouilly-Fumé, near France's Atlantic coast. The grape is Muscadet (also called Melon). Muscadet is famous as an accompaniment to fresh oysters, and is a regular on the Parisian bistro scene as the *vin blanc* carafe wine. "Sur Lie" on the label means the wine was aged on the lees—the solids that settle to the bottom of the fermentation tank—to give it a lively freshness and sometimes a little spritz. It is a noncerebral, drink-it-young wine.

Chenin Blanc—The Loire Valley's One-of-a-Kind Wine

From Wall Street, I had taken the fast track to wine. In 1993, scarcely three years after leaving the world of interest rate swaps and currency options, I had graduated from interested to immersed, from tasting blindly to blind tasting. And there I sat, head bent, peering intently at an anonymous glass of white wine, swirling, smelling, willing it to reveal something of its identity to me. There were thirty of us in that room, "working" that same wine under the supervision of a team of famous British wine-tasting experts— the concentration was so thick you could cut it with a knife. Finally it came time to "commit" to an answer. Grape? Region? "Chenin Blanc, Loire Valley" someone boldly offered. Bingo! Year? None of the guesses strayed far from the rest—1990, 1988, 1985. The Brits chuckled, prompting us all to return to the pale straw liquid in the glass, looking for clues.

It was a 1953—forty years old! The fact is that the age-worthiness of Loire Valley white wines made from the Chenin Blanc grape is legendary, though little known to American wine drinkers. I think they are some of the world's great white wines, and that is why I include mention of them among France's one-of-a-kind offerings. They cannot be ranked with the French paradigms, because Chenin Blanc grown elsewhere in the world (notably California and South Africa, where it is called Steen) makes quite ordinary wine, never seeming to achieve or even attempt the eminence of the Loire Valley versions. They are sold under the following regional names —Vouvray (*Voo-VRAY*), Savennières (*Sah-venn-YAIR*), and Coteaux du Layon (*Coh-TOE duh Lay-OHN*), and you must try them.

Here are some of my favorite wineries from each region:

Savennières Domaine des Baumard (*Domain day Bow-MARR*), Nicolas Joly (*Jhoh-LEE*)

Vouvray Champalou (*Shahm-puh-LOO*), Prince Poniatowski (*Prince Pahn-uh-TOW-ski*) Bourillon-d'Orleans (*Boor-ee-YOHN Door-lay-OHN*), Huet (*Hugh-AY*), Philippe Foreau (*For-OH*), Benoit Gautier (*Go-tee-AY*)

Coteaux du Layon Château Bellerive, Château de Fesle (*duh FELL*), Domaine Godineau (*Goh-duh-NO*), Moulin Touchais (*Moo-LAHN Too-SHAY*), Domaine Ogereau (*Oh-jhuh-ROW*), Domaine Cady (*Cah-DEE*), Beaumards (*Bow-MARR*)

SUBTLE BUT SPECTACULAR Using your Flavor Map and Old World/New World reference points, you already have a sense for the character of these wines—apple/pear fruit-flavor profile; light and elegant body and structure; overall subtlety. What makes them spectacular? You must taste for yourself, but it is the virtue that all classic wines share—complexity. Their scents and flavors, and especially the aftertaste or finish, will command your attention and keep you coming back to the glass for more. Expert tasters often refer to scents of beeswax (like a candle), apple, and honey, but if you don't relate to these specifics, it doesn't matter. You will still love the wines. There are dry, off-dry, and sweet styles of Loire Valley Chenin Blanc. The sweet styles are usually made, like Sauternes, from grapes concentrated by noble rot. Here is how to use the label to determine which is which:

Region name (appellation)	Style(s)
Savennières	Always dry
Vouvray	If the label says *sec*—dry
	If the label says *demi-sec*—off-dry
	If the label says *moelleux* (Moy-YUH) —sweet dessert-style
Coteaux du Layon	Always sweet

The Loire wines I have covered here are great ones, and there are other worthy Loire Valley wines, including some tasty reds and rosés, but their availability in the United States is quite limited. If you happen upon a restaurant or shop that takes special interest in Loire Valley wines, let them help you choose some to try. Compared to other regions and countries, value for the money is excellent.

Alsace—France's Classic Varietal Wines

Shielded from storms by the Vosges Mountains, Alsace (*Al-ZASS*) has some of the sunniest and most reliable growing-season weather of all of France's classic wine regions. The abundance of great food matches the weather. The Alsatian (*Al-SAY-shen*) larder groans with spectacular fruits and vegetables, extraordinary bread and pastry, the famous choucroute (*shoo-KROOT*, or meat-braised sauerkraut), world-class sausages, the real Muenster cheese, and wonderful freshwater fish. Only Paris has more three-star Michelin restaurants.

And more to the point, Alsace has great wines. Americans should feel right at home with the wines of Alsace, because it is the only classic French wine region to consistently use varietal labeling. But if the grape name on the label of an Alsace wine makes us comfortable, the bottle shape does not. It is the elongated, flute-shaped bottle that immediately makes Americans think "sweet" and "no thanks." Both things—the use of varietal names and the tall, thin bottle—are a product of Alsace's history as a political jump-ball in the border games between France and Germany. The winery names—Trimbach, Hugel, and so on—are indeed Germanic. The noted grapes—Riesling and Gewürztraminer—are, too. But the dominant wine style is quintessentially French, bone dry, with a complexity so subtle it sneaks up on you. To those tasters who discovered, after the Toolbox Tastings in Chapter 2, that they aren't wowed by oakiness: These wines are for you, because Alsace wines aren't oaky.

The Grapes

To wine lovers looking for signs of life beyond the varietal world of Chardonnay, Alsace offers a whole new galaxy to explore. The great wines are all whites. Choosing one to buy is as simple as choosing which grape style you would like. Four are known as Alsace's noble grapes, and each is distinctive, as our tasting will show:

Riesling

Gewürztraminer

Pinot Gris—formerly called Tokay d'Alsace or Tokay Pinot Gris, but the European Community's wine committee thought this might be confused with Hungary's famous Tokaji (*Toe-KYE*) dessert wine

Muscat (*MUSS-cat*)

Other, more everyday, white varieties are planted for blending and making sparkling wine, as is a tiny bit of red Pinot Noir.

With the grape listed front and center, it is easy to use the label to figure out the wine style. The climate, cool but very sunny, would suggest fruit flavors from the cool to moderate zone of the Flavor Map—ripe apple, pear, citrus, and peach—which is spot on for these wines. And as you may remember from Chapter 2, two of these grapes have an exotic flair—the spicy Gewürztraminer and the floral Muscat.

Here is a tasting comparison to familiarize you with the different grape styles. In previous chapters, we've tasted most of these already, so this tasting is really a review for all but the Pinot Gris.

The Grapes of Alsace

ALSACE RIESLING	ALSACE PINOT GRIS	ALSACE MUSCAT	ALSACE GEWÜRZTRAMINER
Trimbach	Hugel	Blanck	Blanck
Albrecht	Blanck	Mittnacht-Klack	Mittnacht-Klack
Schlumberger	Dirler	Zind-Humbrecht	Sparr
Weinbach	Zind-Humbrecht	Weinbach	Hugel
Deiss	Schlumberger	Ernst Brun	Leon Beyer
Zind-Humbrecht	Josmeyer	Trimbach	Schlumberger
Albert Boxler			Zind-Humbrecht
Kientzler			Muré
Schoffit			Deiss

THE SCENT

Classic Riesling—clean, apple and lemon scents, and the whiff of the oily petroleum scent you have encountered before.	Pinot Gris's scent is similar to, but richer than, Riesling. Quince, marmalade, and candied fruits are common scents.	Floral! Honeysuckle, orange blossom, and tropical flowers are abundant here, as well as fruit scents like tangerine and apricot.	Here is our spicy wine— lychee nuts, allspice, clove, rose petal potpourri, and plenty of apricot and candied apple fruit.

THE TASTE

Forget your notions of Liebfraumilch. This is bone dry and austere. Tasters often get a sense of minerally earthiness with the apple/lemon fruit, and the vivid acidity carries the finish on and on. Don't hurry with this one.	After the Riesling, this feels almost "fat" and exotic in texture. The fruit tastes echo those in the scent, and the aftertaste goes on and on. It is hard to believe that this is the same grape as the Pinot Grigio of Italy.	After the pretty, perfumed scent, a lot of tasters expect sweetness, but this wine is bone dry. Still, you get the exotic flavors of apricot and marmalade—a great example of how a wine can be both dry *and* fruity.	This has a "fat" texture similar to the Pinot Gris, but the flavor is classic Gewürztraminer—lychee, apricot, quince, candied ginger, pineapple.

Something Special—Alsace Grand Cru and the One-of-a-Kind Sweet Wines

Once you fall in love with the wines of Alsace, you may wish to trade up to her specialty wines, which are more expensive (but not outrageous), and quite distinctive. There are three label designations to look for:

Alsace Grand Cru Grand Cru (*Grahn* CROO) translates roughly as "top-class vineyard," and there are about fifty that are so designated, based on having the best location and soil for growing quality grapes. Use of the Grand Cru name also obligates a winery to reduce vineyard yields. As we learned in Chapter 3, lower yields make for more concentrated grapes and wine.

Vendange Tardive This translates as late harvest, meaning the grapes were picked later than normal to let them get much riper. Vendange Tardive (*Vahn-DAHNJH Tar-DEEV*) wines are usually very full-bodied and rich, and sometimes a bit sweet.

Selection de Grains Nobles Literally, "noble berry selection"—this means a wine made from grapes picked berry by berry so as to select only those fully infected with noble rot. Labor intensive? Absolutely. Like other nobly rotten wines (it still sounds funny to say this) that we have talked about, these are expensive, sweet, original, and mind-bendingly exotic.

Cheap but Good

It doesn't rank with the noble grapes, but Alsace Pinot Blanc is a delicious, refreshing, and inexpensive little wine that you can afford to keep around and drink often with simple meals, takeout, leftovers, picnics, or when your significant other isn't around and you'd feel guilty opening something a little more expensive. Some of my favorites include Schlumberger (*Shlum-ber-JHAY*), Lucien Albrecht (*Loo-SYEN ALL-breckt*), Hugel (*Hue-GELL*), Marcel Deiss (*Dice*), Dirler (*DEER-ler*), Pierre Sparr, Blanck (*Blahnk*), and Josmeyer (*JOCE-meyer*). This is often a worthy budget bet on French wine lists.

Burgundy—Two Grapes, Hundreds of Wines

If imitation is the sincerest form of flattery, then Burgundy surely takes the prize for the most adoring fans. White Burgundy, under the grape name Chardonnay, is the most imitated wine in the world. And, as we learned in Chapter 4, Pinot Noir, the classic red grape of Burgundy, is the winemaking pinnacle that vintners seek to conquer. And the accolade they covet is not "complex," "monumental," or even "delicious." It is "Burgundian."

By now you know Chardonnay and Pinot Noir quite well. It's powerful knowledge, because you can look at any Burgundy wine, red or white, and have a basic idea of the style. Even so, it isn't always easy when you try to buy Burgundy wine. The enormous range in price makes it quite clear that this isn't a question of just two grapes.

There are three other major variables to consider—geography, wine type, and producer—each of which I will explain here in simple terms. Whether you are a devoted fan or just an occasional buyer, Burgundy is an expensive wine category. This section will help demystify the dizzying array of labels and prices, let you know when and why premiums are charged, and when they are worth paying. It will also give you some sound strategies to find good quality and the best values. We'll start from the ground up.

JUG "BURGUNDY"

As with any coveted commodity, there are "Burgundy" imposters sold in boxes or big screw-cap jugs. You may find generic "chablis" (a borrowed name from one of Burgundy's most famous regional white wines) and "burgundy," but these are mass-market beverages bearing absolutely no relationship to the real thing. Enough said.

Burgundy—It's the Address That Counts

When it comes to the price and style of Burgundy wines, geography is the defining element. In Burgundy, wines are defined by their "neighborhood" (vineyard area) in terms of both price and flavor:

PRICE AND QUALITY The price and quality potential of the wine depends on the quality and prestige of the neighborhood (vineyard area). This is nothing new, really. From tony Park Avenue to hip Greenwich Village in New York City, every neighborhood has an unofficial status, but Burgundy's vineyards are ranked officially. The ranking, which also defines the regional appellation names, runs from most basic to most prestigious, in the following order:

Village Wine Label

Premier Cru Label

    Regional These are the basic-level wines, labeled Bourgogne (Burgundy). This rank encompasses all the vineyards in the region, including the comparatively less prestigious "fringe" spots.

    District This rank is restricted to wines from vineyards within one of several large but good-quality subdistricts, for which the wine will be named. Two good ones are Côte de Nuits-Villages (*Coat duh* NWEE *Vill-AHJH*) and Côte de Beaune-Villages (*Coat duh* BONE *Vill-AHJH*).

    Village This rank applies to wines from vineyards within a single village. The village name will be used as the wine name on the label. Examples are Gevrey-Chambertin (*Jhev-ray Shahm-bear-TAN*), Morey Saint Denis (*More-AY San-duh-NEE*), Pommard (*Poh-MARD*), Puligny-Montrachet (*Poo-leen-YEE Mohn-rah-SHAY*), and Meursault (*Muhr-SEW*).

    Premier Cru This translates roughly as "first-class vineyard," and refers to vineyard sites whose quality potential earns this rank. The village name, plus either the vineyard name or the words *premier cru* (abbreviated to 1er cru), will be used as the wine name on the label. An example is Puligny-Montrachet Folatieres (*Foe-lah-tee-AIR*). In this example, Puligny-Montrachet is the village, and Folatieres is the premier cru vineyard.

Grand Cru This is the top of the line and, as in Alsace, roughly translates as "top-class vineyard." There are thirty-two vineyards so ranked in Burgundy's main district, the Côte d'Or (read on for more on this). Examples include Clos de Vougeot (*Cloe duh Voo-JHOE*), usually a red, and Le Montrachet (*Luh Mohn-rah-SHAY*), a white.

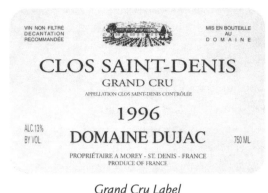

Grand Cru Label

What does all this mean? It is just like the real estate market: The most exclusive addresses cost the most. In the Burgundian equivalent, wines from the best vineyard sites are the most expensive, due both to quality potential and to supply and demand. As you move up the ranks, from the general rank for the whole region, to the top class for just thirty-two individual vineyards (in the main Burgundy district), the quantity of wine available goes down as the quality potential goes up. What makes one vineyard site better than another? Above all, it is location, the best spots being those that get the most sun. Generally, these are the east-facing slopes, which get the first morning sun, and thus have maximum ripening potential. Specifically, they are often at the slope's middle part, with the best drainage and soil.

To help this make sense, consider the layout of a side of beef. The meat for your hamburger represents the most generic of beef "real estate." The filet mignon, or tenderloin, is the most specific, finest, and most limited, as reflected in the price—generic to grand cru, so to speak. Then there are short rib, sirloin, and all the other cuts in between, each with varied quantity and quality potential, and also a different flavor style, depending on their location. Burgundy is similar, as our next point will show.

FLAVOR STYLES Burgundy's flavor styles vary according to the "neighborhood" (vineyard area). Now we are talking not status but the *personality* of each vineyard area. As shown on the map on the opposite page, there are five such vineyard areas, or subdistricts — the Côte d'Or (*Coat DOOR*), Chablis, the Côte Chalonnaise (*Coat Sha-luh-NEZZ*), the Mâconnais (*Mah-coh-NAY*), and Beaujolais—whose wines vary quite a bit from one to the next. Most people find this amazing considering how small the growing areas are. For instance, the most famous section of Burgundy, called the Côte

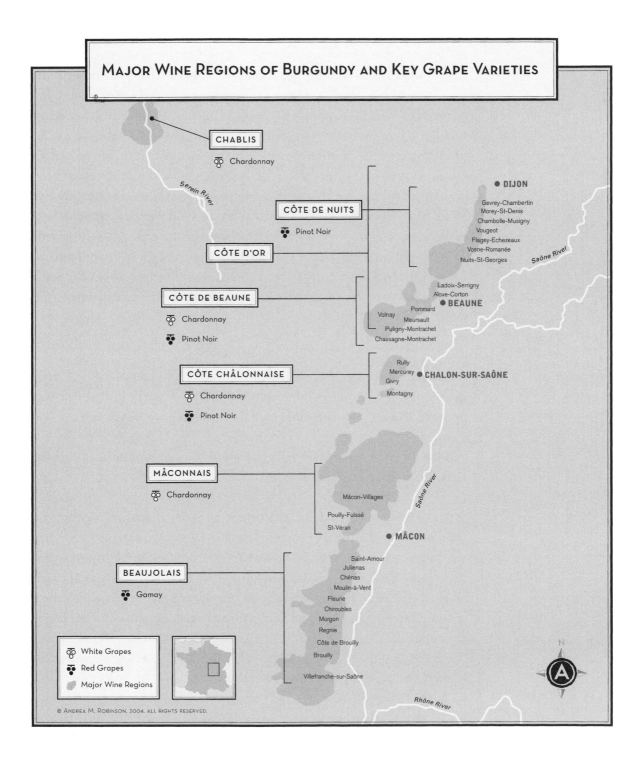

Major Wine Regions of Burgundy and Key Grape Varieties

CHABLIS
Chardonnay

Serein River

CÔTE DE NUITS
Pinot Noir

● DIJON

Gevrey-Chambertin
Morey-St-Denis
Chambolle-Musigny
Vougeot
Flagey-Echezeaux
Vosne-Romanée
Nuits-St-Georges

Saône River

CÔTE D'OR

CÔTE DE BEAUNE
Chardonnay
Pinot Noir

Ladoix-Serrigny
Aloxe-Corton
Pommard ● BEAUNE
Volnay
Meursault
Puligny-Montrachet
Chassagne-Montrachet

CÔTE CHÂLONNAISE
Chardonnay
Pinot Noir

Rully
Mercurey
Givry ● CHALON-SUR-SAÔNE
Montagny

MÂCONNAIS
Chardonnay

Saône River

Mâcon-Villages
Pouilly-Fuissé
St-Véran

● MÂCON

BEAUJOLAIS
Gamay

Saint-Amour
Julienas
Chénas
Moulin-à-Vent
Fleurie
Chiroubles
Morgon
Regnie
Côte de Brouilly
Brouilly
Villefranche-sur-Saône

Rhône River

White Grapes
Red Grapes
Major Wine Regions

N

d'Or, is just thirty miles long—easily biked in a leisurely afternoon, to the joy of its many visitors.

It's pretty neat how all this variation happened. I have a Master Sommelier friend who studied geology and maintains a zeal for it equal to his passion for wine. He explains that over the passing of millennia, successive geologic layers have been stacked one on top of the other, creating a kind of giant layer cake of different soils. During tectonic shifts of the earth's crust, the Alps to the northeast and the Pyrenees to the southwest of Burgundy rose up and cut this cake, serving up a neat slice with the different layers laid bare at the earth's surface. That is the Burgundy vineyard—just two grapes, yes, but every layer, every variation of soil type, gives wines with a slightly different character. Lovers of Burgundy might tell you that they *feel* the earth move when tasting and comparing their favorite appellations, because at their best, these wines can be among the most seductive in the world.

Wine Types

In teaching waiters about Burgundy, I have found that it is easiest to understand if you divide the wines into two groups—the classics and the rest —according to the subdistrict of Burgundy from which they come. As you will see, these two groups dovetail nicely with the appellation and vineyard ranking system we covered above.

THE CLASSICS Burgundy's classic wines come from two areas within the whole—the Côte d'Or and Chablis. They are the classic areas because they are home to most of the top-ranked appellations of Burgundy—the Premier and Grand Cru ranked vineyards. *Côte d'Or* translates as "golden slope," a reference to the east-facing slope at its heart, where all the best vineyards are found. It further divides into two halves, named for the major town in each. The north half is the Côte de Nuits (*Coat duh* NWEE), named for the town of Nuits St. Georges, and the south half is the Côte de Beaune (*Coat duh* BONE), named for the town of Beaune.

The Côte de Nuits gives us the most famous Pinot Noir red wines in the world. The wines are worthy at all three top-quality ranks—village, premier cru, and grand cru. Chances are you have heard of some of the famous appellations before. They are:

Village-Ranked Appellation	Premier Cru–Ranked Appellation	Grand Cru–Ranked Appellation
The village name is on the label. Grapes can come from anywhere in the village.	The village, plus the specific premier cru vineyard name, or the words *premier cru*, are on the label. Grapes can come only from premier cru–ranked vineyards within the named village.	Just the grand cru vineyard name is on the label. Grapes must come exclusively from the named grand cru vineyard.
VILLAGE NAMES (FROM NORTH TO SOUTH)	SOME PREMIER CRU NAMES	SOME GRAND CRU NAMES
Gevrey-Chambertin (*Jhev-RAY Shahm-bear-TAN*)	Aux Combottes (*Oh Cohm-BOHT*) Clos St. Jacques (*Cloe Saint JHAHK*)	Le Chambertin (*Luh Shahm-bear-TAN*) Chapelle-Chambertin (*Shah-PELL Shahm bear TAN*)
Morey-St-Denis (*More-AY Saint Duh-NEE*)	Les Genevrières (*Lay Jhen-uh-vree-AIR*) Clos Bussières (*Cloe Boo-see-AIR*)	Clos St. Denis (*Cloe Saint Duh-NEE*) Bonnes Mares (*Bun MAR*) (part is in Chambolle-Musigny)
Chambolle-Musigny (*Shahm-bowl Moo-seen-YEE*)	Les Amoureuses (*Lays Ah-mor-ROOZ*) Charmes (*Shahrm*)	Le Musigny Bonnes Mares
Vougeot (*Voo-JHOE*)	None	Clos de Vougeot
Flagey-Echezeaux (*FLAH-jhay ESH-uh-ZOE*)	None	Echezeaux Grands-Echezeaux (*Grahnz-ESH-uh-ZOE*)
Vosne-Romanée (*Vone-Row-mah-NAY*)	Beaux-Monts (*Boe MOHN*) Malconsorts (*Mal-con-SORE*)	La Romanée La Tache (*la TAHSH*)
Nuits-St.-Georges	Les St. Georges Vaucrains (*Voe-CRAN*)	None

*Tiny quantities of white are produced in a handful of Côte de Nuits vineyards.

Although the Côte de Beaune grows mostly Pinot Noir red wines, it is most famous for its great white wines made from Chardonnay. They are:

Village-Ranked Appellation
The village name is on the label. Grapes can come from anywhere in the village.

Premier Cru–Ranked Appellation
The village, plus the specific premier cru vineyard name, or the words *premier cru*, are on the label. Grapes can come only from premier cru–ranked vineyards within the named village.

Grand Cru–Ranked Appellation
Just the grand cru vineyard name is on the label. Grapes must come exclusively from the named grand cru vineyard.

VILLAGE NAMES (FROM NORTH TO SOUTH)	SOME PREMIER CRU NAMES	SOME GRAND CRU NAMES
Aloxe-Corton* (*Ah-LUX Core-TOHN*) Beaune (*Bone*)	Les Chaillots (*lay Shay-OH*) Clos des Mouches (*Cloe day MOOSH*)	Corton-Charlemagne (*Core-TOHN Shahr-luh-MAIN*) None
Meursault*	Perrières (*Pear-ee-AIR*) Charmes* (*Sharhm*)	None
Puligny-Montrachet	Pucelles (*Pue-SELL*) Folatières (*Foe-lah-tee-YAIR*)	Montrachet Chevalier-Montrachet (*Shuh-vall-YAY*) Bâtard-Montrachet (*Bah-TAHR*)
Chassagne-Montrachet* (*Shah-SAHN-yuh Mohn-rah-SHAY*)	Morgeot (*More-JHOE*) Cailleret (*Kye-uh-RAY*)	Montrachet Bâtard-Montrachet Criots-Bâtard-Montrachet (*Cree-OH*)

*Some red wines are also produced under these appellations.

And here are the famous Côte de Beaune red appellations:

Village-Ranked Appellation
The village name is on the label. Grapes can come from anywhere in the village.

Premier Cru–Ranked Appellation
The village, plus the specific premier cru vineyard name, or the words *premier cru*, are on the label. Grapes can come only from premier cru–ranked vineyards within the named village.

Grand Cru–Ranked Appellation
Just the grand cru vineyard name is on the label. Grapes must come exclusively from the named grand cru vineyard.

VILLAGE NAMES	SOME PREMIER CRU NAMES	SOME GRAND CRU NAMES
Aloxe-Corton	Les Chaillots (*lay Shay-OH*)	Le Corton Corton-Pougets (*Poo-JHAY*) Corton-Grancey (*Grahn-SAY*)
Beaune (*Bone*)	Les Grèves (*lay GREV*) Marconnets (*Mahr-cuh-NAY*)	None
Pommard	Rugiens (*Roo-jhee-YENN*) Épenots (*Epp-uh-NOE*)	None
Volnay (*Vole-NAY*)	Champans (*Shahm-PAHN*) Cailleret (*Kye-uh-RAY*)	None

The final classic Burgundy type comes from the Chablis region. Here are its appellations:

CHABLIS APPELLATIONS (ALL WHITE)		
Village-Ranked Appellation Just the name Chablis is on the label. Grapes can come from anywhere in the Chablis region.	*Premier Cru–Ranked Appellation* Chablis, plus the specific premier cru vineyard name, or the words *premier cru*, are on the label. Grapes must come from the named premier cru vineyard or, if no specific vineyard is listed, may be a blend from several premier cru vineyards. *Some examples:* Montmains (*Mohn-MAN*) Fourchaume (*Foor-SHOME*) Vaillons (*Vye-YOHN*)	*Grand Cru–Ranked Appellation* The words Chablis Grand Cru, and the specific grand cru vineyard from which the grapes are sourced, are on the label. There are seven Chablis Grand Crus: Blanchots (*Blahn-SHOW*) Bougros (*Boo-grow*) Clos Grenouilles (*Gruh-NWEE*) Preuses (*Prewz*) Valmur (*Val-MURE*) Vaudesir (*Voe-day-ZEER*)

These classic Pinot Noir and Chardonnay wines are the benchmarks against which all other Pinot Noirs and Chardonnays made worldwide are measured—high standards, indeed. What are they like? While it is true that the flavor styles of these wines vary from one village and vineyard to the next, sorting through these subtleties isn't necessary for you to buy and enjoy Burgundy (although Burgundy fanatics think it is fun to do exactly that). The overall styles are:

Reds All of the Côte d'Or's classic Pinot Noir wines are aged in oak barrels, with more oak—longer aging and newer barrels—applied to the best (premier cru and grand cru) vineyards. The greater oakiness builds on the intensity (and cost) of the wines as you move up the appellation rankings. The Côte de Nuits reds from the northern half of the Côte d'Or are generally fuller-bodied and more powerful than their Côte de Beaune cousins grown farther south.

Whites Chablis whites are lighter-bodied than their Côte de Beaune white wine counterparts. This is partly because the Chablis district is cooler, giving less ripeness and body. The comparative coolness also gives them higher acidity. Chablis is often described as lean and racy. The final factor in the body equation is oak. Although there are exceptions, Chablis is traditionally not aged in oak barrels. Côte de Beaune whites, on the other hand, are usually both barrel fermented and barrel aged, which makes them taste richer and much more intense and full-bodied—the model for so many blockbuster Chardonnays from California, Australia, and the rest of the wine world.

Finally, there is the effect of the appellation rank on style. As you go up the rankings in status (and price), the quality potential increases. This is due in part to the vineyard itself (a better site can grow better-quality grapes), and in part to the crop yield, which by law has to be lower for the higher appellation rankings. To the taster, all of this typically translates as fuller body and more complexity in the wine.

What It Means to Be Classic "Burgundian"

We know that Chardonnay and Pinot Noir are modeled after the classic white and red Burgundy wines, but are they "Burgundian"? In my experience, the answer is: rarely. This is because at the center of any discussion of Burgundy and "Burgundian" style are our old friends earthiness and terroir. We discussed these in Chapter 5, in our exploration of the style comparison between Old World and New World wines.

To review, earthiness in wine refers to traces of aromas and tastes in the earthy family that are interwoven with the fruit and other style components. The earth words most often used in wine descriptions are dusty, flinty, minerally, chalky, mushroom, truffle (the fungus, not the candy), forest floor, humus, wet leaves, tea leaves, barnyard, and manure—a pretty amazing list. Closely related to the earthiness notion is terroir—the idea that the *particular* earthiness associated with a specific vineyard can be expressed year after year in its wines. And no wine region is more emblematic of these two concepts—earthiness and terroir—than Burgundy.

To the uninitiated, this style can seem strange, or even off-putting. Yet it is an almost cultlike devotion to this style that unites Burgundy lovers. Once, at a friend's birthday party, one of the guests approached me with a glass of red wine. He pointed to some of my former colleagues from the Windows on the World wine cellar and said, "They think this wine may be no good, but we want another opinion." I took a whiff, and my synapses went into overdrive: fruit yes, but also truffles, leather, mushrooms, and cow pasture on a hot day (aka manure)—the scent was utterly bewitching. "What do you think?" he asked.

"Funky," I answered. "Where can I get a glass?" We became fast friends. "Funk" is neither a technical nor trade term, but it is my word for classic Burgundy's greatest virtue.

And funk is what most of Burgundy's varietal emulators are missing. They often compensate with fruit intensity, which is seductive in its own way. Think back to our Old World versus New World Chardonnay and Pinot Noir comparisons. You may even wish to repeat them, as they illustrated the fundamental difference between varietal Chardonnay and Pinot Noir, and their Burgundy benchmarks. The varietals express *what they are*, as in the grape; the Burgundies express *where they come from*. There are exceptions, but they're rare. Not that winemakers aren't trying. They continue to seek the right combination of vineyard and grape to achieve a similar singularity in their wines, and I have every reason to believe they will succeed. Burgundy is several centuries ahead of the aspiring winemakers and regions in terms of doing just that. In fact, the first Burgundy winemakers were monks, whose approach to winemaking was very detailed. They were the first to observe and exploit the subtle differences in vineyard sites, laying the groundwork for what is planted where in Burgundy today and for the Village, Premier Cru, and Grand Cru vineyard rankings. If you visit Burgundy's famous walled vineyard, the Clos de Vougeot (*Cloe duh Voo-JHOE—clos* means enclosure), you can still see one of their ancient and enormous wooden grape presses inside the castle. It is fabulous.

The Rest of Burgundy

Even without her jewels, the classic wines of Chablis and the Côte d'Or, Burgundy is a soulful beauty, offering some delicious selections, and excellent values, from other parts of the region—the group of wines that I call the rest of Burgundy. These are the regions and wines that are the most affordable in stores and restaurants because they are made in greater quantities and are grown in areas that, though less prestigious than the classic zones, have both good quality potential and more acreage.

Compared to their classic cousins, both reds and whites are usually less full-bodied and less complex. Some professional tasters say they are more "rustic" in style and taste, versus the classics' more "refined" style. This is an obscure description to try to understand unless you taste the wines a lot. A good analogy might be a country biscuit versus a croissant.

Both are good, but they are quite different, and the description of rustic versus refined makes some sense. One thing to keep in mind is that the rustic wine (and the biscuit) has less ambitious aspirations than its refined counterpart, because it doesn't have that classic reputation to uphold. Finally, these districts are generally considered to be less distinctive and expressive of a particular earthiness or terroir. Here are two of the "rest of Burgundy" key areas to look for. (The third, Burgundy's cheap-but-good Beaujolais zone, will be covered separately because it uses a different grape.)

Mâconnais Although you may not have heard of this zone, you have probably heard of its most famous wine appellations. In ascending order of quality they are Mâcon-Villages (*Mah-COHN Vee-LAHJH*), St. Veran (*Saint Veh-RAHN*), and Pouilly-Fuissé (*Poo-YEE Fwee-SAY*). All are light- to medium-bodied Chardonnay whites, usually with little if any oak aging. I love selling them in restaurants because they are major crowd-pleasers and are very food-versatile. With a few exceptions, I think the first two offer better value for the money. With the extra notoriety of the Pouilly-Fuissé name, the prices are sometimes higher than they should be for the quality.

Côte Chalonnaise This region, just south of the Côte d'Or, makes Pinot Noir reds and Chardonnay whites styled like their Côte d'Or cousins, but not quite of the same classic pedigree. To me, these are some of Burgundy's great values. The village names to look for are Rully (*Roo-YEE*), Mercurey (*Mare-cure-RAY*), Givry (*Jhee-VREE*), and Montagny (*Mohn-tan-YEE*), and there are both village- and premier cru–ranked vineyards. Don't miss them.

The Producer

Just one major variable remains in the Burgundy-buying equation—the producer. Some wine professionals say that this should really be the first and last factor that Burgundy buyers consider, because it can help to simplify the process. The idea of buying by producer is that you can focus on the quality reputation of the winery rather than on all the fine details (like terroir, winemaking style, and vineyard rank) for each appellation. Frankly, it is the way most wine professionals approach buying Burgundy, because it is a major time-saver.

BURGUNDY'S WINERIES—ESTATE BOTTLERS AND SHIPPERS There are two types of Burgundy producers—estate bottlers and shippers. Estate bottlers, called *domaines* in French, are wineries that grow the grapes and make the wine sold under their name. In contrast, *negociants* (*neh-GO-see-ants*), the French word for wine shippers, sell wine under their label made in one of two ways. Either they make the wine themselves using grapes or juice bought from independent growers, or they buy finished wine, which they then age and bottle. Most well-known negociants do both, and may also produce some estate-bottled wines from vineyards they own. A good comparison is orange juice in this country—most of it is marketed by a branded company such as Tropicana, which may own some orchards but buys a lot of its juice or fruit from cooperative or independent growers.

Which is better, negociant or domaine? The wine trade loves to debate this topic. I say neither is better; they are just different. Here is how they compare:

Size Negociants are typically bigger. Since they buy grapes and/or wine from many sources, their wines are more readily available because the quantity is greater. By contrast, buying domaine wines is catch-as-catch-can. Because they are generally much smaller, you cannot count on regularly finding particular wines and wineries in stores and restaurants. And when you do find one you like, the store or restaurant may be sold out of it when you return, and unable to reorder more.

Quality Some experts say negociants offer greater quality potential because their practice of blending grapes and wines from many sources

KNOWING YOUR BURGUNDY

For those who would like to probe further into these wineries and learn about others, there are entire books on the subject—worthy investments if you plan to buy a lot of Burgundy. My favorite current such title is *Côte d'Or* by Clive Coates, MW. (MW refers to the very prestigious Master of Wine credential. It means you know a whole, *whole lot* about wine.)

evens out variations. They also have a bigger market presence that compels them to maintain quality to protect their brand name. Others insist that domaines have higher quality potential because they control every part of the production process, from the vineyard to the bottle. Their small size allows a more hands-on, detail-oriented approach to grape growing and winemaking.

But I use the term *quality potential*, because fulfilling that promise takes both skill and commitment. Whether negociant or domaine, some producers have it and some don't. Below is a list of quality-minded negociants and domaines that I have found offer consistently good-to-great quality for the money. Exclusion from this list does not necessarily constitute a thumbs-down. Rather, this is my personal list of Burgundy's benchmark wineries — quality-minded producers that have had an ongoing presence on my wine lists, have been well-received by customers, and are priced well for the quality. I have also listed some specific wines to buy from the appellations for which each producer is best known.

NEGOCIANT/GROWERS CÔTE D'OR		
NEGOCIANT/GROWERS	WHITE WINES THEY'RE KNOWN FOR (LEAST TO MOST EXPENSIVE)	RED WINES THEY'RE KNOWN FOR (LEAST TO MOST EXPENSIVE)
Bouchard (*Boo-SHAHR*)	Pouilly-Fuissé (from Mâconnais) Meursault Corton-Charlemagne GC*	Savigny-les-Beaune Les Lavières 1er* Beaune-Grèves (*Bone-GREV*) 1er
Maison Louis Latour (*May-ZOHN Loo-ee Lah-TOUR*)	Mâcon-Villages (from Mâconnais) Meursault Corton-Charlemagne GC	Corton
Maison Louis Jadot (*May-ZOHN Loo-ee Jhah-DOUGH*)	Pouilly-Fuissé Santenay Meursault Chassagne-Montrachet	Beaujolais-Villages Morgon (cru from Beaujolais) Santenay Clos de Malte 1er Nuits-St.-Georges 1er Clos de Vougeot GC
Faiveley (*FAVE-lee*)	Mercurey Meursault	Mercurey 1er Gevrey-Chambertin Corton Clos des Corton GC
Ampeau (*ahm-PO*)	Puligny-Montrachet les Combettes 1er	Pommard Volnay Santenots 1er

*GC = Grand Cru / 1er = Premier Cru

NEGOCIANT/GROWERS	WHITE WINES THEY'RE KNOWN FOR	RED WINES THEY'RE KNOWN FOR
Maison Leroy (*Luh-WAH*)	Auxey-Duresses (*Aux-SAY Duh-RESS*) Chevalier-Montrachet GC*	Savigny-les-Beaune Vosne-Romanée, Gevrey-Chambertin
Joseph Drouhin (*droo-AHN*)	Beaune Clos des Mouches (*Cloe dey MOOSH*) Chassagne-Montrachet Marquis de Laguiche (*Mahr-KEE duh Lah-GEESH*) ᵉʳ	Chambolle-Musigny Les Amoureuses ᵉʳ Beaune Clos des Mouches ᵉʳ* (both colors are made)
Olivier Leflaive (*Luh-FLEV*)	Meursault Puligny-Montrachet Chassagne-Montrachet	Corton-Charlemagne GC

DOMAINES BY VILLAGE (NORTH TO SOUTH)	DOMAINE NAME	WINES THEY'RE KNOWN FOR
Gevrey-Chambertin	Roty (*Row-TEE*) Armand Rousseau	Charmes-Chambertin GC* Chambertin GC & Charmes-Chambertin GC
	Serafin (*SAIR-uh-fan*) Philippe LeClerc Dugat (*Doo-GAH*)	Gevrey-Chambertin Old Vines Gevrey-Chambertin Les Cazetiers ᵉʳ Charmes- and Griottes-Chambertin GC
Morey-St-Denis	Domaine Dujac (*Doo-JHAHK*) Ponsot (*Pon-SEW*)	Clos de la Roche GC, Morey St Denis Clos de la Roche GC, Gevrey-Chambertin
Chambolle-Musigny	Georges Roumier (*ROO-mee-ay*)	Morey St. Denis Clos de la Bussières ᵉʳ Bonne Mares GC
	Comte de Vogüé (*Comt duh VOE-gway*)	Le Musigny GC, Chambolle-Musigny
Vougeot	Hudelot-Noëllat (*Hue-duh-LOW No-eh-LAH*)	Richebourg GC Vosne-Romanée Les Suchots ᵉʳ (*lay Soo-SHOW*)
Vosne-Romanée	Robert Arnoux (*Ahr-NOO*) René Engel (*Ahn-JHELL*) Leroy (negociant/domaine)	Vosne-Romanée Les Suchots ᵉʳ Vosne-Romanée (various ᵉʳ crus) Chambertin GC Vosne-Romanée Les Beaux-Monts ᵉʳ (*lay Bow-MOHN*)

*GC = Grand Cru / ᵉʳ = Premier Cru

DOMAINES BY VILLAGE	DOMAINE NAME	WINES THEY'RE KNOWN FOR
Nuits-St.-Georges	Henri Gouges (*GOOJH*)	Nuits-St-Georges (various 1er*)
	Daniel Rion	Clos de Vougeot GC*
		Nuits-St-Georges (various 1er)
Aloxe-Corton	Louis Latour (negociant/domaine)	(see above in negociant section)
Beaune	Bouchard (negociant/domaine)	(see above in negociant section)
	Joseph Drouhin (negociant/domaine)	(see above in negociant section)
Pommard	Comte Armand (*Comt Ahr-MAHND*)	Pommard Clos des Epenaux 1er (*Epp-uh-NO*)
	Domaine de Courcel	Pommard les Rugiens 1er (*roo-jhee-YEN*)
		Volnay Fremiets 1er (*Fruh-mee-AY*)
	Gaunoux	Pommard les Rugiens 1er
Volnay	Marquis d'Angerville (*DAHN-jhehr-veel*)	Volnay (various 1er)
	Michel Lafarge (*Luh-FAHRJH*)	Volnay Clos des Chenes 1er
	Hubert de Montille (*duh Mohn-TEE*)	Volnay (various 1er)
Meursault	Coche-Dury (*Coshe-duh-REE*)	Meursault-Perrieres 1er
		Corton-Charlemagne GC
	Henri Germain (*Jhehr-MAN*)	Meursault-Charmes 1er
	Patrick Javillier	Meursault, Meursault-Charmes 1er
	Francois Jobard (*Jhoh-BAHR*)	Meursault (various 1er)
Puligny-Montrachet	Louis Carillon (*Carry-OHN*)	Puligny-Montrachet (various 1er)
	Domaine Leflaive (*Luh-FLEV*)	Chevalier & Batard-Montrachet GCs
	Étienne Sauzet (*Sew-ZAY*)	Bâtard-Montrachet GC
		Puligny-Montrachet (various 1er)
Chassagne-Montrachet	Michel Colin-Deleger (*Coe-LAN Deh-luh-JHAY*)	St. Aubin Les Combes 1er
		Chassagne & Puligny-Montrachet (various 1er)
	Jean-Noel Gagnard (*Gan-YAHR*)	Bâtard-Montrachet, Chassagne-Montrachet (various 1er)
	Michel Niellon (*Nee-eh-LOHN*)	Chevalier- & Bâtard-Montrachet GCs
	Ramonet (*Rah-moh-NAY*)	Chassagne-Montrachet (various 1er)
		Bâtard-Montrachet & Le Montrachet GC

*GC = Grand Cru / 1er = Premier Cru

NEGOCIANT/DOMAINES

William Fèvre (*FEV*)
Moreau, Grossot (*Grow-SEW*)
Brocard, Michel Laroche
Long-Depaquit (*Long Duh-pah-KEE*)
Vocoret (*Vo-cohr-AY*)

DOMAINES

Jean Dauvissat (*Doe-vuh-SOT*)
René et Vincent Dauvissat
Francois Raveneau (*Rav-uh-NO*)

MÂCONNAIS PRODUCERS

Verget
André Bonhomme (*Bohn-UMM*)
JJ Vincent (Château Fuissé)

CÔTE CHALONNAISE PRODUCERS

Rodet (*Row-DAY*)
Joblot (*Jhoh-BLOW*)
Juillot (*Jhwee-YO*)

Cheap but Good—Beaujolais

There are really three grapes in Burgundy, when you add in the red Gamay (*Gah-MAY*) used in Beaujolais. It's one of Burgundy's most famous wines thanks to the notoriety of Beaujolais Nouveau. And every November you see, riding the coattails of the nouveau hype, a raft of imitators, notably Gamay nouveau from American and French wineries, and Italian *novello* wines (same word, different language). In that sense it is a paradigm, not as a wine style but as a business model. A wine that gets picked, processed, and sold within about three weeks, start to finish, adds up to serious cash flow. As they say, it ages on the boat.

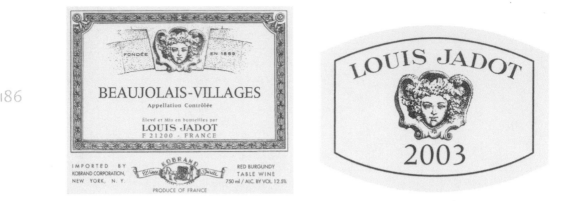

You can have fun with Beaujolais Nouveau, but don't skip the real stuff. Beaujolais is one of the world's few inexpensive wines that offers real character. Beaujolais' signature is a juicy, grapey fruit scent and succulent texture. The smooth as silk feel gives it immediate appeal. You may also detect a slight bit of earthy "Frenchness" thrown in. It reminds me of raking leaves in the fall. You'll notice that Beaujolais is much cheaper than Burgundy's Pinot Noir reds. This is because the Gamay grape itself is easier to grow than Pinot Noir, and perhaps more to the point, there's a lot more of it—Beaujolais represents about two-thirds of the total Burgundy volume.

There are three major appellation ranks in the region: Beaujolais, Beaujolais-Villages, and Beaujolais Cru, and the latter two are the best to buy. For the top level, Beaujolais Cru, the wine is named and labeled for one of ten specific crus (vineyard areas) given this official top rank. My favorites among them are Brouilly (*Broo-YEE*), Morgon (*More-GOHN*), Moulin-à-Vent (*Moo-lan-ah-VAHNT*), Fleurie (*Fluh-REE*), and Julienas (*Jhoo-lee-yeh-NASS*). Among the Beaujolais-Villages wines my favorites are Duboeuf (*Duh-BUFF*) flower label, Jadot, and Jaffelin (*Jhah-FLAHN*). And some of my favorite cru Beaujolais are Morgon from Duboeuf, Brouilly from the Château de la Chaize, and Moulin-à-Vent from either Jadot or Janodet.

Buy any cru Beaujolais or Beaujolais-Villages that you can find from the following producers: Michel Tête (*TETT*), Trenel (*Truh-NELL*), and Janodet (*JHAH-no-day*).

Burgundy

Now that you have a lifetime supply of Burgundy wines to choose from, it is time to taste and compare a few of them so that you become familiar with the different styles. I am presenting three separate tastings, each with a different purpose. The first tasting focuses on the values of Burgundy, from the Mâconnais, Beaujolais, and Côte Chalonnaise. The next two tastings feature wines from the classic regions, Chablis and the Côte d'Or. First, a white Burgundy tasting will let you compare the style of Chablis versus a white wine from the Côte de Beaune to see the difference, which is quite marked. Finally, a red Côte d'Or Burgundy tasting will compare two different vineyard rankings so that you can assess their quality and style differences firsthand.

Classic White Burgundies

It is ironic that the classic French wine name Chablis was the one lifted by America's jug wine producers, when you consider that most Chardonnays made these days emulate the other classic Burgundy white wine style from the Côte de Beaune. Its famous wines—Corton-Charlemagne, Meursault, Puligny-Montrachet, and Chassagne-Montrachet—are all in the barrel-fermented and -aged style so widely copied the world over. Now you will be able to see, in the case of Chablis, what the real thing is; and in the case of the Côte de Beaune whites, the world benchmark for Chardonnay today. You owe it to yourself to compare these two wine styles just to taste where that powerful influence came from. In my *Complete Wine Course* DVD, I take this tasting a step further, to include both a California and an Australian Chardonnay modeled after this style.

FRENCH CHABLIS	FRENCH CÔTE DE BEAUNE WHITE
THE LOOK	
It is not uncommon for the Côte de Beaune white to be slightly deeper and more golden in color, due mostly to its contact with oak barrels during fermentation and aging.	
THE SCENT	
The fruit flavors are definitely as you would expect—Chardonnay flavors in the cool family of the Flavor Map, such as tart apples and	In the fruit, there is greater richness—baked apples or applesauce rather than the tart, crisp apple character of the Chablis. You will also notice the

citrus peel. Chablis often strongly shows its terroir, or distinctive character, in the scent, because there is little or no oak character to obscure it. The classic descriptions are minerally, flinty, and chalky—to me, like a rain-wet gravel road. It is subtle, though. If you don't quite relate, don't worry. You will definitely sense how it differs from the next wine, and that is the point.

oak smell—slightly sweet and toasty—which gives the scent more intensity and volume than that of the Chablis. Finally, there is a sense of terroir here, too, but a bit hard to pick up in the presence of the the oak character. Again, tasters often describe it as mineral or wet gravel. The scent I get quite often from this style is chamomile tea.

THE TASTE

Concentrate on how the two compare, and how those differences might influence your buying choice for a particular situation or meal.

You will be struck by the vivid acidity of this wine—it is a very racy style. The flavors are clean, pure Chardonnay—elegant and light-bodied as Chardonnays go. A distinctive style that is very understated—not the style most wine drinkers have in mind when they order a "Chardonnay." For that, look at the next wine.

There is still bright acidity, but the fruit flavors and texture here are more voluptuous, in part because the grapes get riper in this more southerly area, and partly due to the barrel fermentation and aging. Pay close attention to the aftertaste. White Burgundies, though much subtler than their New World emulators, are known for a very long finish.

Classic Red Burgundies

Here we will compare a village-ranked Côte de Nuits red to a premier cru– or grand cru–ranked wine, so that you can see how they differ. Remember that by law, vineyard yields are lower for the higher rankings, so you may notice increased concentration or intensity in the second wine. You may also notice more oaky character; winemakers often use more oak to match the increased fruit intensity from their higher-ranked vineyards. I have given specific wine suggestions from the Côte de Beaune and the Côte de Nuits. For the best comparison, make sure that you stick with one zone or the other for both wines. Go to a store specializing in fine wines, and if you cannot find these specific ones, let them assist you in finding the two levels to compare.

VILLAGE-RANKED CÔTE DE NUITS RED	PREMIER CRU– OR GRAND CRU–RANKED CÔTE DE NUITS RED
Côte de Beaune	*Côte de Beaune*
Aloxe-Corton: Tollot-Beaut	Corton-Grancey (Grahn-SAY): Louis Latour
Beaune: Bouchard	Corton-Pougets (Poo-JHAY): Jadot
Pommard: Ampeau, Gaunoux, Courcel	Corton: Tollot-Beaut (Toe-low BOW)
Volnay: d'Angerville, Lafarge	Corton Clos des Corton (Cloe day Core-TOHN): Faiveley

Côte de Nuits
: Gevrey-Chambertin: Jadot, Philippe LeClerc
: Morey-St-Denis: Groffier, Dujac
: Chambolle-Musigny: Roumier
: Vosne-Romanée: Rion, Perrot-Minot,
:: Mongeard-Mugneret
: Nuits-St-Georges: Gouges, René Engel,
: A & F Gros

Côte de Beaune (continued)
: Beaune-Grèves: Bouchard
: Beaune Clos des Mouches: Drouhin
: Volnay Premier Cru: d'Angerville

Côte de Nuits
: Clos de Vougeot: Gouges, Jadot,
:: Mongeard-Mugneret
: Echezeaux: Bouchard, Mongeard-Mugneret

THE LOOK

They are typical of Pinot Noir, ruby red that you can see through, but the color of the higher-ranked vineyard may be slightly deeper or more intense.

THE SCENT

Typical Pinot Noir scents from the cool zone of the flavor map—cherry and cranberry. A very soft, vanilla-like sweetness from the oak is there, as well as some terroir—earthy, smoky scents.

Here, the smell is more intense—riper, darker cherries or cherry pie. The oak is also more evident—vanilla and sweet spices (I often notice cinnamon). Many tasters get a licorice character, especially on Côte de Nuits reds, and there is earth. You may notice hints of mushrooms, dead leaves, smoke, sometimes even a "gamy" or "bacon fat" smell, or a scent of potatoes or roasted beets.

THE TASTE

Focus on the differences in texture and concentration.

Soft, red cherry fruit, a touch of tannin, vivid acidity, and some earthiness. It's very subtle. With all the tasting you have done by now, I'm sure you wouldn't mistake this understated style for a New World wine.

There is more fruit richness and intensity here, the oak character is more noticeable, and the tannins are more aggressive. These are wines that, despite their Pinot Noir delicacy (you'd never mistake this for Cabernet Sauvignon), harmonize and improve with some bottle age. You can get an idea of the effect if you cork the unfinished contents of this bottle and taste it again tomorrow. The seductive earthiness will show more then, too.

France

189

The Rest of Burgundy

Burgundy's entries in the value category are not the wine world's cheapest, but if you go with a good producer, they do reward the slight price premium with character. Here, we will taste two Mâconnais whites—the basic Mâcon-Villages level and the famous Pouilly-Fuissé, as well as a Pinot Noir from the Côte Chalonnaise. The Côte Chalonnaise Pinot Noir will show you a more rustic cousin to the classic red Burgundy names.

      The whites are both made without oak, so the comparison is strictly appellation status—a basic versus a more prestigious appellation. Will the quality difference justify the price difference? That's something the buyer must decide.

MÂCON-VILLAGES	POUILLY-FUISSÉ	CÔTE CHALONNAISE RED
Jadot, Bouchard, Verget, Bonhomme, Manciat-Poncet, or Louis Latour	Jadot, Bouchard, Château Fuissé, Louis Latour, or Verget (or your store's suggestion)	Givry: Joblot Mercurey: Rodet, Faiveley, or Juillot
THE SCENT		
Light, delicate, pure Chardonnay fruit. You have tasted this style many times.	Similar to the Mâcon-Villages but with greater intensity. The scent may also show some terroir character—to me, a chalky or wet ravel smell.	There is definitely earthiness here, along with Pinot Noir fruits from the Flavor Map's cool zone—cranberry and sour cherry—and some light spice.
THE TASTE		
This is a clean, soft, simple, and refreshing style of Chardonnay—a crowd-pleaser. The next wine is similar, but a step up. Concentrate on the differences.	Compared to the previous wine, this is slightly fuller-bodied, with more concentrated flavor and a longerfinish. Decide if the increased intensity is worth the price difference to you.	This wine shows the Pinot Noir's light body and tannin in the Old World way—subtle, understated, and slightly earthy versus the more fruit-forward, New World examples we have tasted in other chapters.

The Rhône Valley

I started this chapter with Champagne, my favorite French wine. I'm ending it with my other favorite French wine region—the Rhône Valley. (With all the wines you've tasted by now, you know that choosing a single favorite is impossible.) Rhône wines are full of intensity, generosity, and character; many say this is due to the unique and unusual growing conditions—the vines alternately bake in the Mediterranean sun and cower against the knifelike wind called the Mistral that whips through the valley.

Like so many classic wine regions, the Rhône is named for the river that runs through it. Its soil is a crazy quilt of wildly different blocks and patches that were upended, folded, and tossed about when the Alps emerged, then were eroded, layered, and repositioned by the river's flow, which was once quite powerful.

The easiest way to understand the Rhône is in halves, as shown on the map on page 192—the Northern Rhône and the Southern Rhône—because they differ in a key way. The Northern Rhône's paradigm wines are based on just two grapes—the red Syrah and the white Viognier (both of which you tasted in the last chapter). Like Burgundy, they are regionally labeled in the French tradition, but they could just as well be varietals. By contrast, the Southern Rhône's famous wines in all three colors (red, rosé, and white, all regionally named) are traditionally blends of many different local grapes.

The Northern Rhône

REDS The red wines from the Northern Rhône—all based on the mighty Syrah grape—are full-bodied, intense, and tannic. They are the paradigm wines for New World varietal wines Syrah and Shiraz (the spelling used most often in Australia). You may want to repeat the comparative tasting of these from the last chapter. All of them are oak aged for some period of time—usually in large, old oak casks, although small oak barrels like those used in Bordeaux and Burgundy are increasingly employed. This adds to the full, powerful style of the wines. There is not an official "cru" ranking as in Burgundy (although there are crus whose superior status is acknowledged in the trade), but the top appellations, which I have listed first, come

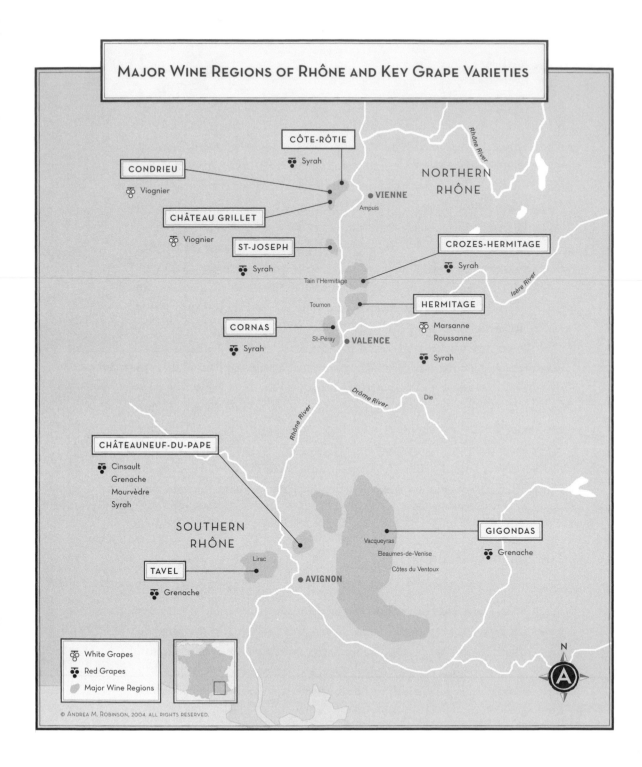

Major Wine Regions of Rhône and Key Grape Varieties

CÔTE-RÔTIE
Syrah

CONDRIEU
Viognier

NORTHERN RHÔNE

VIENNE
Ampuis

CHÂTEAU GRILLET
Viognier

ST-JOSEPH
Syrah

CROZES-HERMITAGE
Syrah

Tain l'Hermitage

HERMITAGE
Marsanne
Roussanne
Syrah

Tournon

CORNAS
Syrah

St-Péray

VALENCE

Rhône River

Drôme River

Die

CHÂTEAUNEUF-DU-PAPE
Cinsault
Grenache
Mourvèdre
Syrah

SOUTHERN RHÔNE

Lirac

GIGONDAS
Grenache

Vacqueyras
Beaumes-de-Venise
Côtes du Ventoux

TAVEL
Grenache

AVIGNON

Rhône River

Isère River

White Grapes
Red Grapes
Major Wine Regions

N

from the best vineyard areas, and yields are kept lower by law. The top appellations usually have the most oak character.

Hermitage (*air-mee-TAHJH*) and Côte-Rôtie (*coat row-TEE*) The top of the line. These are powerful, brawny wines with lots of plummy, raisiny fruit flavor and a peppery, spicy, smoky aroma. These wines have the alcohol, tannin, and fruit concentration to age and improve for many years, so if you see older ones on a restaurant wine list and feel like splurging, they are a great bet. You will be impressed with the exotic character they develop after bottle age—leather, chocolate, spice, smoke, earth, tobacco—yummy stuff.

Cornas (*Core-NASS*) St. Joseph (*San-Jo-SEFF*), and Crozes-Hermitage (*Crows air-mee-TAHJH*) A step down the ladder, although some Cornas are of a quality equal to Hermitage and Côte-Rôtie. Professional tasters call Crozes-Hermitage "Crozes" for short, and refer to the style as "baby" Hermitage. It has a similar flavor, but with less body, tannin, and intensity. Most of the Hermitage wineries make this appellation, too.

The best producers are:

Hermitage: Chapoutier (*Shuh-POO-tee-ay*) and Chave (*Shahv*) are the most famous. Jaboulet (*Jah-boo-LAY*) are the makers of the famous Hermitage La Chapelle (*lah Shah-PELL*), a single vineyard Hermitage named for the tiny thirteenth-century chapel that still stands there. Sorrel (*Soh-RELL*), Vidal-Fleury (*Vee-DAHL Fluh-REE*), and Delas (*Duh-LAHSS*) are other good names.

Côte-Rôtie: Guigal (*Ghee-GAL*) is the standard-bearer. Gentaz (*Jhahn-TAHZ*), Dervieux (*Dehr-vee-YOU*), Rostaing (*Row-STANG*), and Jasmin (*Jhahz-MAN*) are excellent, too.

Cornas: Auguste Clape (*CLAHP*) is the best producer, and Jean-Luc Colombo is

another excellent name. Many of the Hermitage and Côte-Rôtie wineries above also make Cornas.

St. Joseph: Chapoutier and Jaboulet have the biggest market presence.

Crozes-Hermitage: The most famous Crozes producer is Alain Graillot (*Grye-OH*). The biggest Hermitage and Côte-Rôtie wineries listed above also produce Crozes.

WHITES The Northern Rhône's white wine production is tiny but interesting. Around the Côte-Rôtie district, the white Viognier grape, which we tasted in the last chapter, makes exotic, floral wines in two appellations—Condrieu (*Cohn-dree-YOU*) and Château Grillet (*Gree-YAY*). They are rare and thus expensive, but interesting to try if you find them. They are also the model for varietal Viognier wines from California and other New World sources.

In the Hermitage district, two white grapes are planted—Marsanne (*Mahr-ZANN*) and Roussanne (*Roo-sahn*). The two are blended to make a small quantity of white Hermitage—the paradigm for the tiny quantities of Marsanne and Roussanne wines from New World regions (mostly California). The St. Joseph and Crozes-Hermitage appellations also produce tiny quantities of white wine, worth trying if you find them.

The Southern Rhône

"Didn't I just see you on the road?" The words were spoken in French, and I had been there so long I could actually detect the French version of a southern drawl. It was Henri Brunier of the Domaine du Vieux Télégraphe (*View Teh-luh-GRAFF*), a top winery in the Southern Rhône's famous Châteauneuf-du-Pape (*Shah-toe-NUFF duh Pop*) district. As I had just learned, it is a pretty big district. Being on a shoestring budget I had settled at the Avignon youth hostel, then hopped a bus to the famously named village.

But the famous Châteauneuf (the shorter nickname pros use) wineries that I had planned to visit were several miles out of town, so I walked. I was embarrassed, but there was no hiding the thick dust on my shoes. "You will have lunch with us," he said. I joined a couple of generations of Bruniers at the kitchen table for cold chicken (which was delicious; French chickens aren't like the tasteless industrial birds we have here) and wine, and they explained to me the different vineyards I had passed on my trek.

Although a total of thirteen grapes (white and red) are approved for use in Châteauneuf-du-Pape, in practice the best reds are blended mainly from four grapes: Syrah, Grenache (*Gruh-NAHSH*—called Garnacha in Spain, and the world's most widely planted red grape), Cinsault (*San-SEW*), and Mourvèdre (*More-VED-ruh*). Their style is full-bodied, rich, raisiny, spicy, and powerful, and like the Northern Rhône wines, they are capable of long aging. The best producers, in addition to Vieux Télégraphe, are Château de Beaucastel (*Bow-cass-TELL*) and Château Rayas (*Ray-AHSS*), which is such a collector wine that you are unlikely to see it in stores. Other good ones are Château Fortia (*FORE-shuh*), Mont-Redon (*Mohn Ruh-DOHN*), Château la Nerthe (*lah NAIRTH*), Clos du Mont Olivet (*Cloe duh Mohnt Oh-lee-VAY*), Vieux Donjon (*View Dohn-JHOHN*), Clos des Papes (*Cloe day POP*), and Domaine des Cailloux (*Domain day Kye-YOU*). Jaboulet and Chapoutier from the Northern Rhône also make good Châteauneuf-du-Pape.

A small quantity of white Châteauneuf is also made from Roussanne, white Grenache (like the Pinots Blanc and Noir, Grenache comes in a white and red version), and other grapes. It is exotic, delicious, and expensive.

The Rhône Rangers and Australia

These Southern Rhône wines, along with the Northern Rhône's offerings, were the inspiration for a group of California winemakers who branched out from Cabernet Sauvignon and Merlot to experiment with the Rhône's indigenous grapes in California vineyards. They were dubbed "Rhône Rangers" by the wine press, and many of the wines have been successful and popular. The pioneers in this movement were the Bonny Doon Vineyard, Joseph Phelps Vineyard, McDowell Valley Vineyards, Cline Cellars, RH Phillips, and Sanford Winery, among others. Some restaurants now even have entire Rhône Rangers sections on their wine lists, because the wines go so well with popular food styles such as Mediterranean, Pan Latin, and California cuisine.

Long before the Rhône Ranger era in California, Australia had its widespread and well-established tradition of making varietal Shiraz (Syrah), and of blending traditional Rhône varietals. The most famous of all Australian Shiraz wines is the famous Penfolds Grange, truly a collector's item and worthy of its world-class status. Other top Australian Shiraz producers include Hardy's, Henschke, Mount Mary, Brokenwood, Dalwhinnie, St. Hallett, Jasper Hill, Mount Langi Ghiran, Rosemount, Elderton, and d'Arenberg. Then there are the multigrape blends modeled on Southern Rhône wines. They sometimes have proprietary names, but often the list of varietals, and their percentages in the blend, is included right on the label. Rosemount, Jim Barry, Cape Mentelle, Penfolds, d'Arenberg, Hardy's, Hill of Content, and Yarra Yering make some of my favorites in this style. There is a "crossover" style of Australian wine that is also outstanding—blends of Cabernet Sauvignon and Shiraz, which, as you would expect, resemble a cross between French Bordeaux and Northern Rhône reds. They are oak aged, full-bodied, and intense. Many age very well. Penfolds Bin 389 is my favorite of these.

Cheap but Good—Côtes du Rhône

Côtes du Rhône is the name of the overall regional appellation for the Rhône (the classic regions of Châteauneuf-du-Pape, Hermitage, and so on, are its subdistricts just as Chablis and Gevrey-Chambertin are high-quality subdistricts within the larger Burgundy region). Production is mostly red wine, but I think that Côtes du Rhône wines in all three colors—red, rosé, and white—are some of the best-value wines for everyday drinking in the entire wine world. They are loaded with fruit and flavor—the reds spicy, the whites and rosés juicy and refreshing—and good ones often cost less than ten dollars. The big Northern and Southern Rhône wineries listed above all make good Côtes du Rhône. Some of personal favorites are Guigal, Perrin, d'Aigueville, Duboeuf, Jean-Luc Colombo, Jaboulet, and Chapoutier. But Côtes du Rhône is a safe wine to "gamble" on in a store or restaurant even if you have not heard of the winery name—I truly have never encountered a bad one. Also look for wines from the related appellation Côtes du Rhône-Villages, whose grapes come from the top sixteen villages in the area. They are a step up in quality and price.

One of a Kind

Muscat Beaumes de Venise (*Muss-cat Bohm duh Vuh-NEEZ*) is a very distinctive dessert wine that you see a lot on restaurant wine lists, and often available by the glass, for good reason. It is wonderful and not very expensive. You'll recall our "floral" tasting in Chapter 3, which featured the exotic Muscat grape. We also tasted the dry version from Alsace earlier in this chapter. Here it is in a sweeter, fuller-bodied version. That's because it belongs in a category of French dessert wines called *vins doux naturel* (*van doo nah-tuh-RELL*), fortified sweet wines. They are made from grapes dried into raisins to concentrate their sugar. Before fermentation is complete, the wines are fortified with the addition of neutral alcohol. This stops the fermentation, leaving residual sugar and thus sweetness. It is a beautiful wine with, or as, dessert. There are other French *vins doux naturel* from other regions that are worth trying if you see them in stores and restaurants. The most famous, Banyuls (*Bahn-YOOL*), is made from the red Grenache grape and is similar to Port (more on this in Chapter 9).

Rhône Wines

All of the Rhône wines I have mentioned here are worth exploring. This tasting will focus on a basic red Côtes du Rhône, in comparison to one of the classic paradigm wines. A Muscat Beaumes-de-Venise dessert wine, for fun, completes the tasting.

CÔTES DU RHÔNE	CHÂTEAUNEUF-DU-PAPE	MUSCAT BEAUMES-DE-VENISE
Select from the "Cheap but Good" producers listed above.	Select from the producers listed above.	Vidal-Fleury Coyeaux (*Kwah-YUH*) Beaumalric (*Bow-mahl-REEK*) Durban (*Duhr-BAHN*) Chapoutier (*shuh-POO-tee-yay*)

THE SCENT

Juicy fruit scents from the moderate-to-warm zones of the Flavor Map—plums, berries, and figs—but also a mouthwatering spicy character.	In addition to the rich, intense, raisiny fruit, there are savory spice scents like black pepper and cumin. There is also earthiness, and sometimes a slightly "wild" note—gamy or leathery. Wow.	Scents of orange blossom, honeysuckle, and tropical fruit are the signature of this wine. It is beautiful.

THE TASTE

The flavors echo the scents—juicy ripe fruit with a touch of spice. It is a very crowd-pleasing style. You may notice some soft tannin, too.	This is a powerful, mouth-filling, intense wine with fruit flavors of raisins and dried figs. The spice, tobacco, and earthy notes also come through in the flavor. The high alcohol makes it very full-bodied, and the finish lingers a long time.	This wine is full-bodied and unctuous—almost a syrupy texture due to the sweetness and added alcohol. The flavors mingle luscious fruit and sweetness, reminding me of apricot jam, orange marmalade, and peach preserves.

France—Wine Headquarters of the World

We've covered a lot of ground. This is the book's longest chapter—emblematic of the enormous influence of France and French wines on the rest of the wine world. Here is a chart to sum it all up.

FRENCH WINES BY REGION		
CLASSIC WINES	WINES THEY INFLUENCE/ BIG SIX GRAPE PARADIGM	CHEAP BUT GOOD/ONE OF A KIND
CHAMPAGNE		
Champagne (Brut NV, Rosé, Blanc de Blancs, prestige, etc.)	All sparkling wines, but notably classic-method sparklers from quality regions (California, Italy, Spain, and others)	
BORDEAUX		
White château wines from Graves	Barrel-fermented varietal **Sauvignon Blancs** (mainly from California and Chile)	*Cheap but Good:* basic Bordeaux appellation varietal Merlots and Cabernets; "petit château" and Cru Bourgeois reds
Red château wines from the left bank (Médoc, Pauillac, Margaux, St. Julien, Ste. Estephe), right bank (St. Émilion, Pomerol), and Graves (Pessac-Léognan)	Varietal **Cabernet Sauvignon** and **Merlot**, some super-Tuscan red wines	*One of a Kind:* Sauternes late-harvest botrytis dessert wine
LOIRE		
Sancerre and Pouilly-Fumé	Stainless-steel-fermented varietal **Sauvignon Blancs** from New Zealand, Chile, and the United States	*Cheap but Good:* Muscadet whites

One of a Kind: Chenin Blanc appellation wines: Savennières (dry), Vouvray (dry to sweet), Côteaux du Layon (sweet) |

CLASSIC WINES	WINES THEY INFLUENCE/ BIG SIX GRAPE PARADIGM	CHEAP BUT GOOD/ONE OF A KIND
ALSACE		
Dry white varietal wines: Riesling, Gewürztraminer, Pinot Gris, Muscat	**Riesling** and other corresponding dry varietals from the United States, Australia, Italy, and other countries	*Cheap but Good:* Pinot Blanc whites *One of a Kind:* Vendange Tardive (late harvest) and Sélection de Grains Nobles (sweet botrytis wines)
BURGUNDY		
Chablis and Côte de Beaune whites (e.g., Meursault, Chassagne-Montrachet, Puligny-Montrachet, Corton-Charlemagne)	All varietal **Chardonnays**	*Cheap but Good:* Gamay reds from Beaujolais-Villages and Beaujolais Crus (Morgon, Moulin-à-Vent, Brouilly, etc.)
Côte d'Or reds (e.g., Vosne-Romanée, Pommard, Clos de Vougeot)	All varietal **Pinot Noirs**	
RHÔNE		
Hermitage and Côte-Rôtie reds	Varietal **Syrah** and **Shiraz**	*Cheap but Good:* Côtes du Rhône red, rosé, and white wines
Châteauneuf-du-Pape reds	"Rhône Rangers" red blends in the United States and Australia	*One of a Kind:* Muscat Beaumes de Venise white dessert wine
Condrieu whites	Varietal Viognier whites	
Châteauneuf-du-Pape whites	Varietal Marsanne and Roussanne, and blends of the two	

CHAPTER SEVEN

A Little Italy

"Ahn-drayyy-ah," the voice said, calling my name across the table in that lilting singsong that makes a simple conversation with an Italian man feel like a serenade. Mesmerized, I put down the pen I'd been using to take tasting notes and looked up.

"Don't think. *Drink.*"

At that moment, in those words, I learned the true meaning of wine. In pursuit of "wine knowledge," my three-month pilgrimage had taken me to every classic wine region of Spain and France. Now it had led me here, to Cantina Vietti, one of the Piedmont region's great wineries, to the terrace of Luciana and Alfredo Currado's umpteenth-generation family home—to dinner, of course, because this was Italy. Throughout the meal, I had been scribbling furiously in my notepad, determined to take it all in and somehow convert that collection of notes into expertise.

The entire table (a few generations of family and other hangers-on like me, because that, too, is Italy) stared in silence while I picked up my glass as directed. Then they burst into gales of laughter. It has been more than ten years since that lesson from Alfredo, but I have never forgotten. The real purpose of wine is not about the snobbery, the fancy labels, the big bucks, and status symbols that are supposedly going to make you look and feel sophisticated. Its real purpose is simple: Wine is a *lube for life*.

Even great winemakers like Alfredo, who pour their heart and soul into making the elite Italian wines, know that when all is said and done, the wine is just an enhancement to living. It is the life part that matters—the occasion, the lover, the meal, whatever. Now, *that* is real wine knowledge.

And you should keep that in mind as you dive into the world of Italian wines, because it is vast. Many find it intimidating, so I always suggest that people think about learning Italian wines in the same way they'd think about learning to cook. Most people never worry about acquiring the refined culinary skills and knowledge of a great chef. They just live a perfectly tasty life by mastering a few basic techniques (roasting, sautéing, and boiling) that work for most foods. That, mixed with regional and family traditions, defines the stock of home-cooking standards for most of us.

But if you keep an open mind about new foods and tastes, then you are likely to try new things when you eat at restaurants or in friends' homes. Sometimes a new dish, ingredient, or technique will strike your fancy enough to be added to your repertoire. So you ask the chef for the recipe, watch a cooking show, help out in your friend's kitchen, or pick up a book to learn the new stuff. When I was working at the Sea Grill, a famous New York City seafood restaurant overlooking the Rockefeller Center skating rink, I became so enamored with the food that whenever I could, I spent time in the kitchen, watching and talking with Ed Brown, the chef. Ultimately, I became fairly accomplished at cooking fish and seafood.

I suggest taking a similar approach to learning and drinking Italian wines, and that's what we will do in this chapter. Through tasting, we will learn the "basics" of Italian wines, which are in two categories. The first category includes the classic wine styles from Italy's two most famous regions—Tuscany and Piedmont. The second category is made up of her widely available, cheap-but-good offerings (Italy is a treasure trove of these). These two groups are all you need to know to choose enjoyable wines in any restaurant or wine shop setting. For fun, I'll also introduce you, through tasting, to some of Italy's most interesting and delicious one-of-a-kind wines that I think are too original and delicious to miss. Some of them are so unforgettable that their names will easily stick in your wine consciousness. And if you are completely *sedutto* by Italian wines (I wouldn't be at all surprised if that happens), I will give you a surefire buying tip for jumping off into the world of adventure beyond these two basic groups.

Finally, aside from the wine styles, there are two other very exciting things that we'll begin to explore in this chapter: how food can change the taste of wine, and how aging affects the taste of wine. And don't forget that all-important lesson for ultimate enjoyment: Don't think (well, not too much). Drink. *Andiamo!*

The Label

Italian Wine Names

You may have noticed that Italy's wines, like her people, are often beautifully dressed. That Italian flair that you see in cars, clothes, and architecture often carries over to wine in beautiful bottles and stylish labels. The labels are lovely to look at, but people often get confused by the content, because there are several different ways Italian wines can be named:

> A regional name The equivalent of appellation wines in France, these are named for the village or district where the grapes are grown, for example, Chianti or Soave (*SWAH-vay*).

> A grape name plus a regional name Some examples: Barbera d'Alba (*Bar-BEAR-uh DAHL-buh*), the Barbera grape from the Alba region in Piedmont; Pinot Grigio del Veneto (*VENN-uh-toe*), the Pinot Grigio grape from the Veneto district, and so on.

> A proprietary (brand) name Basically, a made-up name—Sassicaia (*Sass-uh-KYE-uh*), a famous wine from Tuscany, and Corvo Rosso and Bianco (red and white) from Sicily are some well-known examples.

The Appellation System

Italy regulates the use of regional wine names (with and without a specified grape) in much the same way France does with its *Appellation d'Origine Controlée (AOC)* system. Italy's place-naming system is called *Denominazione di Origine Controllata*, or controlled denomination of origin—obviously, another great candidate for abbreviation, as DOC. Like the French system, the DOC law seeks to ensure the style authenticity of wines sold under the famous regional names by regulating the same grape-growing and winemaking factors we covered previously—permitted grapes, growing area, maximum vineyard yield, minimum alcohol content, viticultural practices (like pruning and irrigation), and vinification techniques. In this last respect, Italy's laws go quite a bit farther than France's, specifying minimum oak-barrel and bottle-aging times for a lot of the wines.

There is also another, even stricter, appellation rank called DOCG (*Denominazione di Origine Controllata e Garantita*). Regional wines with the *garantita*, or guaranteed, status have the strictest yield limitations, longer minimum aging times, and other controls intended to ensure the best quality potential. Many famous DOC wines have applied for an upgrade to DOCG status. On page 206 is a list of DOCG appellations, and the region they come from, to date.

More About the Label

The Italian wine label has a lot of other words that offer clues to the wine style:

Riserva Reserve in English, but unlike American wine labels, the Italian use has a legal meaning. Riserva attached to an appellation (for example, Chianti Riserva) indicates additional aging in the barrel and bottle beyond the basic (non-riserva) requirements for that particular place-name or DOCG appellation, the length of which varies by appellation. It may also mean a higher minimum alcohol content (and thus riper grapes at harvest) and stricter yield control. Although riserva is not a guarantee, all of these factors should add up to higher quality in skilled winemaking hands.

Classico A geographical term referring to the historic heart and quality center of a particular growing region—such as Chianti Classico and Soave Classico.

Classico Superiore This implies grapes from the classico zone *and* a higher minimum alcohol content.

Fattoria (*Fah-toh-REE-uh*), **Tenuta** (*Teh-NOO-tuh*), **Podere** (*POH-deh-reh*), and **Azienda Agricola** (*Ah-zee-END-uh Ah-GREE-coh-luh*) These are words to describe estates that both grow grapes and make wine.

Cantina This is the Italian word for winery.

Vigna, Vigneto (*VEEN-yuh, Veen-YETT-oh*) These are words for vineyard, and are often seen on labels to designate a single-vineyard wine, meaning the grapes all came from one special vineyard plot, rather than many blended together, which is more common in Italy.

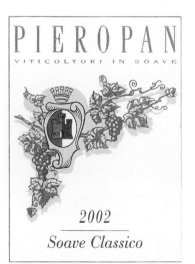

PIEROPAN
VITICOLTORI IN SOAVE

2002
Soave Classico

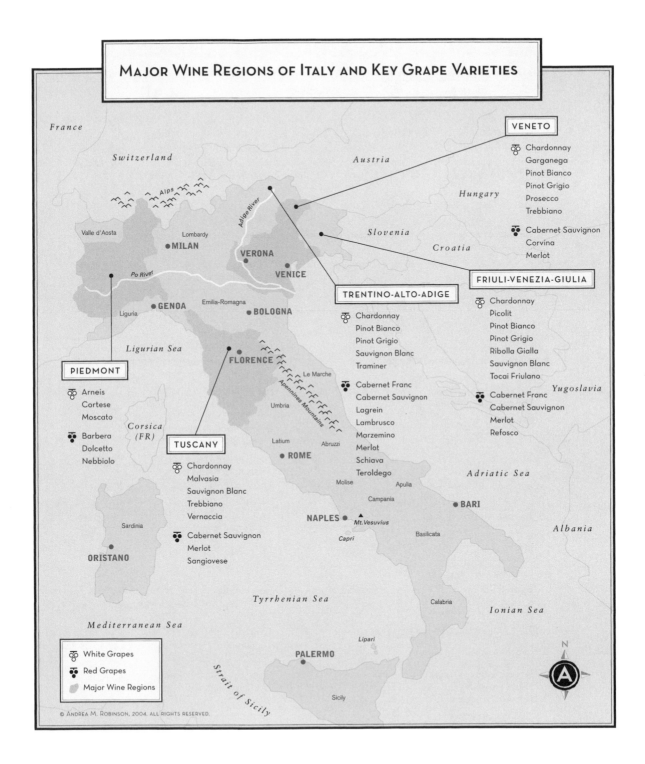

MAJOR WINE REGIONS OF ITALY AND KEY GRAPE VARIETIES

France

Switzerland

Austria

Alps

Hungary

VENETO

- ⚇ Chardonnay
  Garganega
  Pinot Bianco
  Pinot Grigio
  Prosecco
  Trebbiano
- ⚇ Cabernet Sauvignon
  Corvina
  Merlot

Slovenia

Croatia

Valle d'Aosta

Lombardy

● MILAN

VERONA

Adige River

Po River

VENICE

FRIULI-VENEZIA-GIULIA

- ⚇ Chardonnay
  Picolit
  Pinot Bianco
  Pinot Grigio
  Ribolla Gialla
  Sauvignon Blanc
  Tocai Friulano
- ⚇ Cabernet Franc
  Cabernet Sauvignon
  Merlot
  Refosco

Yugoslavia

TRENTINO-ALTO-ADIGE

- ⚇ Chardonnay
  Pinot Bianco
  Pinot Grigio
  Sauvignon Blanc
  Traminer
- ⚇ Cabernet Franc
  Cabernet Sauvignon
  Lagrein
  Lambrusco
  Marzemino
  Merlot
  Schiava
  Teroldego

Emilia-Romagna

● GENOA

Liguria

● BOLOGNA

Ligurian Sea

FLORENCE

Apennines Mountains

Le Marche

Umbria

PIEDMONT

- ⚇ Arneis
  Cortese
  Moscato
- ⚇ Barbera
  Dolcetto
  Nebbiolo

Corsica (FR)

TUSCANY

- ⚇ Chardonnay
  Malvasia
  Sauvignon Blanc
  Trebbiano
  Vernaccia
- ⚇ Cabernet Sauvignon
  Merlot
  Sangiovese

Latium

Abruzzi

● ROME

NAPLES ● ▲ *Mt. Vesuvius*

Molise

Apulia

Campania

● BARI

Adriatic Sea

Albania

Sardinia

Capri

Basilicata

ORISTANO

Tyrrhenian Sea

Calabria

Ionian Sea

Mediterranean Sea

Lipari

PALERMO ●

Strait of Sicily

Sicily

N

- ⚇ White Grapes
- ⚇ Red Grapes
- Major Wine Regions

ITALIAN DOCGS			
NAME	**NAME TYPE**	**WINE STYLE**	**WINE REGION**
Albana di Romagna (*All-BAH-nuh dee Row-MAHN-yuh*)	Grape (Albana) plus place	White	Emilia-Romagna
Asti-Moscato d'Asti/ Asti Spumante	Grape (Moscato) plus place	Lightly sparkling to fully sparkling; both off-dry	Piedmont
Barbaresco (*Bar-buh-RESS-coe*)	Regional name	Full, dry red from the Nebbiolo (*Neh-bee-OH-loe*) grape	Piedmont
Barolo (*Buh-ROW-loe*)	Regional name	Full, dry red from the Nebbiolo grape	Piedmont
Brachetto d'Acqui (*Brah-KETT-oh DOCK-we*)	Grape (Brachetto) plus place	Sparkling, slightly sweet red	Piedmont
Brunello di Montalcino (*Broo-NELL-oh dee Mohn-tall-CHEE-no*)	Grape (Brunello) plus place	Full, dry red from the Brunello grape, which is a type of Sangiovese (*San-joe-VAY-zeh*)	Tuscany
Carmignano (*Car-meen-YAH-no*)	Regional name	Full, dry red from chiefly Sangiovese and Cabernet Sauvignon grapes	Tuscany
Chianti/Chianti Classico	Regional name	Full, dry red from chiefly the Sangiovese grape	Tuscany
Franciacorta Spumante (*Frahn-chuh-CORE-tuh*)	Regional name	Sparkling white (modeled on Champagne), from similar grapes (Chardonnay, Pinot Nero, Pinot Bianco)	Lombardy
Gattinara (*Gah-tee-NAH-rah*)	Regional name	Full, dry red from the Nebbiolo grape	Piedmont
Gavi or Cortese di Gavi	Regional name or grape plus place	Dry white wine from the Cortese grape	Piedmont
Ghemme	Regional name	Full dry red from the Nebbiolo grape	Piedmont
Montefalco Sagrantino (*Mohn-teh-FALL-coe Sah-grahn-TEE-no*)	Grape (Sagrantino) plus place	Dry or sweet red	Umbria
Recioto di Soave	Regional name	Sweet white dessert wine from chiefly the Garganega grape	Veneto
Taurasi (*Taw-RAH-zee*)	Regional name	Full, dry red from the Aglianico (*Ah-lee-AH-nee-coe*) grape	Campania (where the ancient city of Pompeii is located)
Torgiano Rosso Riserva (*Tore-jee-AH-no ROH-so Ruh-ZUR-vuh*)	Regional name	Full, dry red from the Sangiovese grape	Umbria
Valtellina Superiore	Regional name	Medium to full, dry red from the Nebbiolo grape	Piedmont
Vermentino di Gallura (*Vuhr-men-TEE-no dee Guh-LUR-uh*)	Grape (Vermentino) plus place	Dry white	Sardinia

NAME	NAME TYPE	WINE STYLE	WINE REGION
Vernaccia di San Gimignano (*Vuhr-NAH-chee-uh dee San jee-meen-YAH-no*)	Grape (Vernaccia) plus place	Dry white	Tuscany
Vino Nobile di Montepulciano (*VEE-no NO-bee-lay dee Mohn-teh-pool-CHAH-no*)	Regional name (Montepulciano); *vino nobile* is a romanticized reference to the Sangiovese grape	Full, dry red from Prugnolo Gentile, a variant of Sangiovese grape	Tuscany

Confusing Wine Labels

You are familiar by now with the idea of place-names and appellation systems. So why, even within the parameters of the DOC system, do Italian wines and wine labels seem so inscrutable? My answer to the question is elaborate, because I have several theories, and I think all are accurate depending on the wine or region in question. Here they are:

Italians are fierce individualists. This alone explains a lot, such as why there are *twenty* separate wine regions, many of them often dramatically different from neighboring ones, in this very small country. And why, despite the commercial evidence that just a few grapes (the Big Six among them) rule the wine world in sales, there are literally hundreds of different grapes planted, most of which no one has ever heard of outside of Italy. For variety, it's great. Anyone who has ever traveled to Italy has experienced the joy of discovering the local wine—after getting over the shock of not always

20 ITALIAN WINE REGIONS

1. Abruzzo	8. Liguria	15. Sicily
2. Basilicata	9. Lombardia	16. Trentino-Alto-Adige
3. Calabria	10. Marche	17. Tuscany
4. Campania	11. Molise	18. Umbria
5. Emilia-Romagna	12. Piedmont	19. Valle d'Aosta
6. Friuli-Venezia-Giulia	13. Puglia	20. Veneto
7. Latium	14. Sardegna	

A Little Italy

finding what they thought were Italian standards (Chianti, Soave, and the like). Unfortunately, you can forget ever finding these local wines outside their home bases. Think of them as good excuses to go back to Italy!

Italians are an improvisational culture. Italian food is the ultimate example of this. The signature dish, pasta, adapts to what's in season—tomatoes and basil in summer, mushrooms in fall, garlic and olive oil when you can't think of (or afford) anything else. But you also see it in nearly every other aspect of Italian life. From speed limits to the business hours at the post office, to wine labeling laws, the attitude is . . . flexible.

Although it might be a problem when you're trying to buy stamps, this approach to life makes for interesting wines. For although Italians are staunch supporters of their classic wine styles, they also like to experiment and try new things. Often that means playing a little loose with the rules. This can lead to classic regional wine names made with unusual grapes or in styles outside the regulatory norm; or famous wineries in classic regions growing utterly atypical grapes, making completely unexpected wine styles or "out there" blends, and so on. And of course, many of these improvised wines have improvised names, as the next point shows.

Italians are the masters of the fantasy wine name. For many wineries, the urge to improvise extends to wine names. I guess it's only natural that stepping beyond the winemaking strictures of your appellation would open the door to creativity in naming your wine, too. The trend began in the 1970s with names such as Cella (as in "chilling a . . .") and Riunite ("on ice, that's nice"), and really picked up steam in the 1980s and 1990s. Today there is a raft of proprietary super-Tuscan wine names (more on this below), and Italy's passion for fantasy names continues. Libaio (*Lee-BYE-oh*), Luce (*Loo-chay*), and Sassicaia are all proprietary wines, but the names could just as easily be fashion designers or opera singers. And nothing about the name tells you the style of the wine, so there is no choice but to taste them one by one, and memorize the names of the ones you like. Well, things could be worse.

Italians had to respond to adversity. Everyone remembers those straw-covered Chianti bottles that made such quaint candleholders in the 1970s. You may even remember the wine, too, but probably not very fondly. Those were the dark days of Italian winemaking, when quantity-over-quality-minded producers used such poor farming and winemaking prac-tices that the quality of Chianti (and some other classic Italian wines) hit rock bottom. (You might say in hindsight that the straw bottle, called a *fiasco* in Italian, was aptly named.)

Fiercely proud, Chianti vintners responded to the crisis creatively, in the Italian improvisational spirit. They planted foreign grapes (usually French, such as Chardonnay, Cabernet Sauvignon, and Merlot), often blending them with the locals to upgrade the resulting wine, or using them to produce the varietal wines so popular with American consumers. They also "reinterpreted" the weakest winemaking and grape-growing laws, eliminating sloppy practices, developing improved ones, and sharing with other wine countries to cull their best practices. The most prominent result of all this was the emergence of so-called super-Tuscan wines, a luxury wine category combining the best of local traditions (such as the Sangiovese grape) and newly imported ones (including the Cabernet grape, and the use of new French oak barrels for aging rather than the large, Slavonian oak barrels traditional to Italy). The results sent many of Italy's top wines back to world-class status and premium prices. The super-Tuscan wines remain some of Italy's most famous, regularly trading in the same league with the French classics at wine auctions.

"Old Style" and "New Style" Winemaking

All of this experimentation and cross-pollination of ideas with other famous wine regions also launched a "new style" of winemaking in some of the most traditional regions. Winemakers working in the new style are careful to avoid oxidation of the grape juice at harvest so as to preserve the fresh fruit flavor and youthful, vivid color. They see to it that the grape skins are handled more gently during crushing and pressing in order to get softer, suppler tannins in the reds. Often, they use small, new French oak barrels to give a prominent, sweet oakiness to the wine (in the style of classic Bordeaux and top California Cabernets). Critics of the new style say it robs the traditional wines of their individuality and character, and the wine world of some welcome diversity. They also say these new-style techniques are used more to gain critics' attention than to make great wine (you may remember our discussion of how an oaky scent and taste can sometimes make a wine stand out in a critic's blind wine tasting). Proponents of the new style say it often produces better-quality wines that are "ready to drink" (meaning pleasant to the taster) sooner, and thus more commercially viable.

The Modern Italian Wine Law

Gradually, the government reacted to all of this change, creating the DOCG category to upgrade winemaking standards in Chianti and other traditional wine zones, and writing into law some of the better (but unauthorized at the time) winemaking practices that launched the super-Tuscan movement. In addition, in 1992, a new category was created—*Indicazione Geografica Tipica (IGT)* indicating a wine or style that is typical of its region. Its purpose was to try to bring the untraditional blends and varietal wines into the wine law system. Doing this is helpful (presumably) to the government in fulfilling the European Community mandate to upgrade the overall standard and prices of member countries' wines by phasing out the production of table wines outside the quality wine regulation system. It is still too soon to tell whether the IGT category will become meaningful (and therefore useful) to the buyer, but for now I have to say that it is not. It is most often seen on varietal wines in this country, usually basic styles that buyers choose by grape and winery brand, rather than by geography.

All of which brings us back to our basic strategy: Get comfortable with the two famous regions, get a handle on the cheap-but-good stuff, dabble with the one-of-a-kinds, and then remember my secret weapon buying rule for when you are out of your league (see below).

Rosso, Bianco, and Rosato

We need to spend a moment on color. Serious Italian wine, and there is certainly plenty of it, is red. The Italians, with extremely rare exception, just do not care about white wine. Not that plenty of it isn't made, but much is for export and for cheap, refreshing drinking during seaside holidays in Italy's stunningly beautiful coastal towns. The rest is meant to employ gallons of mediocre-quality juice from vineyards whose output used to go into Italy's famous reds (to their detriment) before the recent quality revolution. So you mainly need to know that most Italian whites are refreshing but basic, and the prices should be, too. Rosato (rosé in Italian), on the other hand, can be fun. Nearly every region makes it from whatever red grape reigns locally. They are inexpensive and tasty—definitely worth trying, slightly chilled, in summer, or any time with spicy food.

Tuscany

Getting to Know Tuscan Classic Reds

The cedar, the olive, and the vine—these icons define the Tuscan countryside just as the Duomo in Florence and the Piazza del Campo in Siena define her two major metropolises. Although Tuscany is a major center of experimentation in Italian winemaking, it remains a headquarters for Italian classic reds, all based on the Sangiovese grape. Their other common theme is that all are oak aged by law, although the minimum oak-aging time varies according to the DOCG, with Brunello the longest of all.

The dichotomy between old and new styles exists here, although it seems that many wineries have solved the debate by doing a bit of both. It is not uncommon for one winery to have multiple bottlings—a "new style" wine, either as a proprietary blend or an appellation wine, using perhaps Cabernet Sauvignon or small French oak barrels, or both; and an "old style" wine made of Sangiovese and other local grapes, aged in the traditional large Slavonian oak barrels. This lets them cater to fans of either style.

CHIANTI DOCG This wine has come a long way since the days of the kitschy straw-covered bottle—although these are still produced, and you should avoid them. Nowadays, the Chianti worth your attention ranges from solid everyday drinking wines with some character, to serious, complex, age-worthy wines of world-class status. Unfortunately, the DOCG rank applies equally to the entire range of the region's wines, making it difficult to predict the quality of any given wine, and thus generally holding the Chianti DOCG's image at an average level. Here's a little more information on the zones that are consistently worthy of the DOCG ranking.

Chianti Classico is the hilly center and historic heart of the Chianti zone between Florence and Siena, generally yielding some of the best-quality Chiantis. Yield limits here are the strictest of all the Chianti subdistricts. Recent changes in the law now allow the use of 100 percent San-giovese (previously, inclusion of lesser grapes, including some whites, was mandatory), as well as the inclusion of small proportions of untraditional grapes such as Cabernet Sauvignon. Those are powerful changes. On the taste side, with white grapes eliminated, and Cabernet sometimes blended in, you'll find a deeper, richer, more powerful version of Chianti than you might remember from the straw-bottle days. Indeed, they are serious wines, and they have prices to match. Serious wines can cost serious money. I think many of the best ones are worth it, but our tasting will let you decide for yourself. Other Chianti zones worth trying are Chianti Rufina (*Roo-fee-nuh*) and Chianti Montalbano (*Mohn-tall-BAH-no*). Some producers to look for: Chianti Rufina: Selvapiana (*Sell-vuh-pee-AH-nuh*) and Frescobaldi (*Fress-coh-BALL-dee*); and Chianti Montalbano: Cappezzana (*Cah-pett-SAH-nuh*).

Chianti Classico: There are a lot of great producers. Not all of the wineries that charge luxury prices for Chianti make wine that justifies the high price. I only list here those wineries I think are worth the (sometimes very high) premium, and I've defined a separate "splurge" category below to identify those in the upper price tier:

PREMIUM Volpaia (*Vol-PIE-uh*), Fonterutoli (*Fohn-teh-ROO-toh-lee*), Querciabella (*Kwehr-chuh-BELL-uh*), Dievole (*Dee-EH-voe-lay*), Brolio (*BROE-lee-oh*), Ricasoli (*Ree-CAH-zoh-lee*), Castello di Gabbiano (*Cah-STELL-oh dee Gah-bee-AH-no*), Badia a Coltibuono (*Bah-DEE-uh ah Cole-tee-BWOH-no*), Melini (*Muh-LEE-nee*), Rocca delle Macie (*ROH-cuh deh-luh Mah-CHEE-ay*), Terrabianca (*Tear-uh-bee-AHN-cuh*), Castellare di Castellina (*Cass-teh-LAR-eh dee Cass-teh-LEE-nuh*), Castell'in Villa (*Cass-tell in VEE-luh*), Querceto (*Kwair-CHETT-oh*), Castello dei Rampolla (*Cass-TELL-oh day RAHM-poh-luh*), Uggiano (*Ooh-jee-AH-no*).

SPLURGE Among the splurge wines are Castello di Ama (*Cass-TELL-oh dee AH-muh*), Fontodi (*Fohn-TOE-dee*), Felsina Berardenga (*FELL-see-nuh Bear-ahr-DEN-guh*), Ruffino Riserva Ducale (*Doo-CAH-leh*), Isole e Olena (*Ee-SOH-leh eh Oh-LEH-nuh*), Monsanto Il Poggio (*Mohn-SAHN-toe eel PO-joe*), and Antinori (*Ann-tee-NOH-ree*).

Outside of these pedigreed subzones, here are a few good basic

Chiantis—refer to them for the Tuscan wine tasting below: Alaura (*Ah-LAUW-ruh*) from Monsanto, and Cetamura (*Chett-uh-MUHR-uh*) from Badia a Coltibuono. Brolio, Frescobaldi, and Ricasoli also make good basic Chianti.

CARMIGNANO DOCG This is a small vineyard zone northwest of Florence. Here the red wine is mostly Sangiovese and other local grapes, with up to 10 percent Cabernet Sauvignon, giving a medium- to full-bodied, elegant style of wine. Producers to try are Capezzana, Fattoria di Ambra, and Fattoria Il Poggiolo (*eel Poh-JOE-loh*).

VINO NOBILE DI MONTEPULCIANO DOCG If you visit Florence, rent a car and go see the fabulous hilltop town of Montepulciano. You will have to park on the outskirts, because the tiny streets within the stone walls are too narrow for any but foot traffic. They've been doing the winemaking thing here for a long time. On my visit to the most famous producer, Avignonesi (*Ah-veen-yo-NAY-zee*), they took me to the ruins of an ancient Etruscan wine cellar beneath their offices—on the floor of which still lay fragments of their clay amphora-like wine "bottles." But in spite of its long history, the wine enjoys far less attention than its sister Tuscan DOCGs, although a comeback appears to be in the making. It is made from a high-quality type of Sangiovese called Prugnolo Gentile (*Prune-yo-lo Jen-TEE-lay*), plus some other blending grapes. Rosso di Montepulciano DOC is a sort of "baby" Vino Nobile made from grapes that don't quite reach the quality level appropriate for the top wine. These may be grapes from young, recently planted vines, or from the main vineyards in weak harvest years.

Among the best producers are Avignonesi, Boscarelli (*Boh-scah-RELL-ee*), Poliziano (*Poh-leet-see-AH-no*), Fattoria de Cerro (*deh CHAIR-oh*), and Tenuta Trerose (*Tray-ROSE-eh*).

BRUNELLO DI MONTALCINO DOCG Biondi-Santi (*Bee-YOHN-dee SAHN-tee*), one of the most famous wineries and wine families, is credited with inventing this wine because they were the first to isolate the Brunello (also called Sangiovese Grosso), an especially high quality version of the Sangiovese grape (*grosso* means big). The small growing area surrounds the hilltop town of Montalcino, southwest of Siena. The very full-bodied, powerful wines rank with Barolo as Italy's longest agers (and in fact usually

need some bottle aging to taste good). How long? The day I visited the Biondi-Santi estate, a "recorking" was under way, in which clients brought their oldest bottles to be topped up and closed with a fresh cork, so they could continue to age under a tight seal. The youngest wines there were thirty years old.

Rosso di Montalcino DOC is "baby Brunello" (like Rosso di Montepulciano is a "baby" Vino Nobile), a good wine to drink while you are

waiting for the real thing to age in the cellar. Good producers of both Brunello and Rosso di Montalcino include Altesino (*All-teh-ZEE-no*), Costanti (*Coh-STAN-tee*), Castelgiocondo (*Cass-tell-joe-COHN-doe*), Il Poggione (*eel Poh-jee-OH-neh*), Lisini (*Lee-SEE-nee*), Val di Suga (*Val* dee *Soo-guh*), Col d'Orcia (*Cole DOOR-chuh*), Barbi (*BAHR-bee*), Caparzo (*Cuh-PART-so*), and Poggio Antico (*POH-joe Ahn-TEE-coh*). Castello Banfi (*BAHN-fee*) makes an excellent Brunello.

New on the Tuscan Horizon

BOLGHERI DOC (*BOHL-gare-ee*) This region on the western coast of Tuscany became famous for Cabernet Sauvignon–based super-Tuscan wines like Sassicaia, Ornellaia (*ORE-nuh-LYE-uh*), and others, all of which are expensive, collector wines. Watch for more from this region, including Tuscany's up-and-coming white grape, Vermentino.

VARIETAL SANGIOVESE With prices of even the most basic Chiantis pushing fourteen dollars and up, Italian wineries have launched a category of soft and simple Sangiovese to compete in the ten-dollar and under price range. I am not too excited about the trend, because I think it mostly provides an excuse to raise the basic Chianti prices without necessarily boosting quality. But there are a couple of good ones, including Antinori's Santa Cristina, Capezzana's Conti Contini (*COHN-tee Cohn-TEE-nee*), and Ruffino's Fonte al Sole (*FOHN-teh all SOH-leh*).

Tuscan Red Wines

This is a really fun and eye-opening tasting, because it compares several variations on a common theme, the Sangiovese grape, and shows you how each variation affects the end result. One of the variations on the theme is *quality level*. We compare a basic Chianti, a Chianti Classico Riserva, and a Brunello di Montalcino. The quality comparison encompasses several aspects of the wine. First, there is *vineyard quality*—comparing Chianti, whose grapes can come from anywhere in the zone, to the hilly Classico zone, the center part that is considered to have the best soil for grape growing, to a wine from the even more exclusive Montalcino zone. Second, there is *grape quality*, comparing the fruit quality of basic Chianti to a Riserva (for which most wineries use their very best lots of grapes), to a Brunello, made from a superior strain of Sangiovese grapes. Then we'll consider oak and bottle aging, with basic Chianti aged the least amount of time, Chianti Classico Riserva aged longer, and Brunello the longest. You already know that oak aging affects the aroma, flavor, and body of a wine, so you know to expect increasing intensity as you go up the scale. Finally, I have included one of the "new-wave" Tuscan Sangioveses with Cabernet Sauvignon blended in, so you'll know what this tastes like.

Before we begin, let me give you a practical suggestion for this tasting. Italian wines are really made for food, and tasting them without it can be difficult and can shortchange your appreciation of the wines. I recommend that you try the wines in sequence so that your palate can taste their styles undistracted. But then go back and try them with either some aged cheese (Tuscan Pecorino, Parmigiano Reggiano, or Spanish Manchego are the best) or crusty bread dipped in high-quality olive oil. You will be amazed at the difference. Come to think of it, you may just want to have dinner ready at that point, because once you see how great these wines are with food, you'll be hungry.

For this tasting, refer to the appellation sections above for wine suggestions. (See Chapter 9 for meal suggestions.) Here are some suggestions for the "new-wave" Tuscans (blends of Sangiovese and Cabernet Sauvignon), all with proprietary names:

WINERY	PROPRIETARY WINE NAME
Terrabianca	Campaccio (*Cahm-PAH-chee-oh*)
Ornellaia	Le Volte (*leh VOLL- teh*)
Melini	I Coltri (*ee COLE-tree*)
Altesino	Alte d'Altesi (*All-teh Dall-TEH-zee*)
Antinori	Tignanello (*Teen-yuh-NELL-oh*)
Caparzo	Ca' del Pazzo (*Cah dell POT-soe*)
Monsanto	Tinscvil (*TINKS-vill*)
Querciabella	Camartina (*Cah-mahr-TEE-nuh*)
Volpaia	Balifico (*Bal-ee-FEE-coh*)

CHIANTI   CHIANTI CLASSICO RISERVA   BRUNELLO DI MONTALCINO   SANGIOVESE/CABERNET

THE LOOK

You will notice a gradual deepening in color from the basic Chianti, up the quality scale to the Sangiovese/Cabernet blend.

THE SCENT

Given that Tuscany is in the moderate zone of the Flavor Map, you would expect berry fruit—I find basic Chianti's fruit scent is like strawberries. The Sangiovese grape is also a bit spicy.

This is much more complex —spicier, with maybe an earthy hint of meat or leather. I once had a great but unusual salad—very ripe strawberries with balsamic vinegar and black pepper. The same smell is in this wine.

This is much "bigger"—your nose can feel the alcohol vapors, and the spiciness is quite prominent. The fruit smell also may seem richer and riper, more toward plum or even dried fruits like prunes.

From all of our tastings, you know the smell of Cabernet well. I usually find that I can sense the cassis character of Cabernet, here, but it's overlaid with the spice of the Sangiovese. It's a great combination.

THE TASTE

This is soft, simple, and a little rustic. There is some nice berry flavor, a little bit of spice, a soft texture, and, notably, a nice "cut"of acidity. This is a signature of Sangiovese that makes it really shine with food.

There is clearly more body and tannin in this wine, and more richness, ripeness, and complexity to the fruit flavor. The finish—spice, fruit, and earthy flavors— lingers quite a long time.

Serious vino. The tannin and body are dominant, so you can see that the wine would benefit from aging. You can mimic that effect somewhat by pouring a glass, letting it aerate for a while, and then tasting again later.

Remember the velvety texture from the Cabernet tasting for tannin? You may feel that here, too. It is the best of both worlds —Cabernet's rich fruit flavors and tannins with Sangiovese's spice and great acidity.

White Wine in Tuscany

Vernaccia di San Gimignano, now a DOCG, is named for the grape (Vernaccia) plus the place (the hilltop town of San Gimignano, with its many stone towers, is beautiful). The wine is, like other Italian whites, crisp and refreshing—look for Falchini (*Fall-KEE-nee*) and Teruzzi e Puthod (*Tear-OOT-see eh POO-thoad*). Galestro is a brand name of an inexpensive but pleasant white named for a distinctive soil type in the Chianti Classico district. The famous Antinori family, who have been making wine in Tuscany for more than five hundred years, invented this wine when the blending of white grapes into (red) Chianti was phased out, leaving them with white grapes on their hands. Galestro has been commercially successful. Most of the other well-known Tuscan whites are brand names rather than DOCs, but Italian wine experts are paying close attention to the rise of Vermentino, the white grape from Bolgheri mentioned above.

One of a Kind—Tuscan Vin Santo

Vin Santo (*Veen SAHN-toe*, "wine of the saints") is in a category we have mentioned before called dried-grape wines, known as *passito* (*Pah-SEE-toe*) wines in Italian. This refers to the practice of drying the grapes into raisins before pressing and fermentation so as to concentrate their sugar. In Tuscany, they hang them or spread them out on tiered mats, in a place with good ventilation to speed the drying. After pressing, the juice goes into very small oak barrels with a "mother" yeast that is continually nursed and fed like a good sourdough bread starter. In the barrels, the wine ferments and oxidizes (to encourage this, the barrel isn't filled to the top). The resulting wine is rich and slightly sweet, with a tawny-gold color and nutty character from the oxidation. The Italians serve it with crisp biscotti cookies to dunk in the wine. It's a terrific wine and I urge you to try it. Good producers include Antinori, Avignonesi, Volpaia, and Villa la Selva.

Piedmont

Tuscany, with its burnt siena–colored, vine- and olive-cloaked landscape, walled hilltop towns, and extraordinary Florentine architecture takes the trophy for visual delights. But for tastes and smells there is no contest—for me, it is Piedmont. In fact, to this day I feel practically naughty when I recall the decadence of my days there during the summer of 1990. I still remember the taste of the *raza nobile* ("noble race")—a Piedmontese veal that was as sweet as dessert, figs fresh off the tree, fresh hand-cut tagliatelle with butter and sage, and truffles—on veal carpaccio, with pasta and butter, with eggs and butter, with polenta and butter. The dazzling richness of the food makes the word *obscene* come to mind. And then you throw the wonderful wines into the mix and, well … let's get right into it.

The Grapes of Piedmont

We are still in Italy, so of course the important wines are red. Piedmont grows chiefly three red grapes:

Dolcetto (*Dohl-chett-oh*, "little sweet one") A grape that makes light-bodied, uncomplicated reds for everyday drinking.

Barbera The region's most widely planted red grape. Barbera was the wine we were drinking on Alfredo Currado's terrace when he reminded me to "chill out, it's just wine." And indeed it used to be an everyday quaff, the workhorse of the Piedmontese table. Nowadays, though, many winemakers are giving the grape more serious winemaking attention, and using expensive techniques like French oak-barrel aging to make more ambitious, and expensive, styles.

Nebbiolo The prized vine behind the region's most famous wines, the DOCGs Barbaresco, which reigns as queen to the king, Barolo, historically called "wine of kings, and king of wines." Barolo and Barbaresco are truly majestic, powerful wines capable of long aging and amazing complexity.

This often prompts my wine students to ask, "If Nebbiolo is so great, why do they bother with the other two?" Certainly a fair question, and the answer is "survival." Piedmont, which translates as "foot of the mountain," is a cluster of Alpine foothills. It's a marginal climate for the Nebbiolo grape, which struggles to ripen there. Dolcetto and Barbera both ripen earlier, ensuring there will be at least some wine crop even in years of bad growing weather. The terrain itself also plays a part. The hills curve and scrunch like folds of cloth. Nebbiolo is planted where it gets the most sun, on the hills' outer crests. These crests are so important there are words for them in the local dialect: bricco (*BREE-co*) and sori (*SORE-ee*). Specific ones are sometimes even cited on the wine label. For example, the Ceretto winery's top Barolo wine is grown on the Bricco Rocche (*ROW-keh*), and Angelo Gaja's most famous Barbaresco wines are grown on the Sori San Lorenzo and Sori Tildin. Dolcetto and Barbera fill in the rest of the spaces on the hills, so not a single inch of potential vineyard is wasted.

The Piedmont Classics—Barolo and Barbaresco

BAROLO DOCG Barolo is named for one of the towns in the growing region, which spreads over several other villages as well. It is a rich and powerful, dry red wine that, in the best years, is ideal for long aging, in part because the Nebbiolo grape is known for high tannin and acidity. The Riserva and Riserva Speciale designations refer to increasingly longer minimum aging requirements, in wood barrels and then in the bottle, before the wine can be sold.

Barolo producers to try: Elio Altare (*EH-lee-oh All-TAR-ay*), Azelia (*Ah-ZEH-lee-uh*), Ceretto (*Cheh-RETT-oh*), Clerico (*CLAIR-ee-coh*), Aldo Conterno (*ALL-doh Cohn-TEAR-no*), Giacomo Conterno (*JAH-coh-moe Cohn-TEAR-no*), Franco Fiorina (*FRAHN-coe Fee-oh-REE-nuh*), Marcarini (*Mahr-cuh-REE-nee*), Mascarello (*Mahss-cuh-RELL-oh*), Alfredo Prunotto (*Proo-NOH-toe*), Luciano Sandrone (*Sahn-DROH-neh*), Vietti (*Vee-ETT-ee*), Roberto Voerzio (*Voe-AIRTS-ee-oh*), and Marchesi di Barolo (*Mahr-KAY-zee dee Buh-ROW-loe*).

BARBARESCO DOCG This wine is also named for the region. It is slightly smoother and less tannic in youth than Barolo. "Tar and roses" is the classic description for the bouquet of this wine. Riserva again refers to longer minimum barrel and bottle aging. Angelo Gaja (*AHN-jell-oh GUY-uh*) is the most famous producer. Other Barbaresco producers to try: Ceretto, Pio Cesare (*PEE-oh CHEZZ-uh-ray*), Bruno Giacoso (*Jah-COE-suh*), Marchesi di Gresy (*Mahr-KAY-zee dee GRAY-zee*), Moccagatta (*Moe-kuh-GAH-tuh*), Prunotto (*Proo-NO-toe*), and Produttori del Barbaresco (*Pro-doo-TOR-ee dell Bahr-buh-RESS-coe*).

When young, both Barolo and Barbaresco can seem kind of hard, tough, and short on fruit, especially to American palates weaned on fruit-forward Merlots and Cabernets. It is after some years of bottle age that the grandeur of the wines emerges, in scents of tobacco, truffle, chocolate, licorice, and cherry, and a powerful flavor and texture that seems to build in the mouth as you drink the wine—worth the wait. But under these circumstances, it is perhaps understandable that Piedmont is a hotbed of debate between old style traditional winemakers, and the new style vintners seeking to make wines that require less patience on the part of the wine-drinking public.

Other Nebbiolo-based wines from Piedmont, all of them far less prestigious than the King Barolo and Queen Barbaresco, include two regionally named wines—Ghemme (*GEMM-ay*, hard *g*) and Gattinara (*Gah-tee-NAH-ruh*) (both now DOCGs)—as well as Nebbiolo delle Langhe (*Neh-bee-OH-lo deh-leh LAHN-gay*), with a grape-plus-place name. Langhe is the name for the hills in the heart of the Piedmont region.

Dolcetto and Barbera

Just a few short years ago, I probably would have put Dolcetto and Barbera under a "cheap but good" subheading. These days, though, the lowest-priced examples are not cheap, and some of the wines, thanks to luxurious winemaking touches like aging in French oak barrels, are quite expensive. Still, though they are not what they used to be, some at the lower price points are fun, and the more ambitious ones can be quite special. The main appellations for Dolcetto and Barbera follow the "grape plus place" labeling protocol. The best known are Dolcetto d'Alba, Barbera d'Alba, and Barbera d'Asti, near the towns of Alba and Asti, although between Dolcetto and Barbera, there are more than a dozen grape plus place DOCs. In general, Dolcetto is considered the lighter style of the two. I often find it a little earthy and simple in all but the greatest vintages. Barbera has soft tannin and higher acidity, which I like, because it makes the wine a great partner for food—any kind, not just Italian, in my experience. Some good ones to try are:

> Barbera d'Alba Pio Cesare (*Pee-oh CHEZZ-uh-ray*), Clerico (*CLAIR-ee-coh*), Aldo Conterno, Giacomo Conterno (*JAH-cuh-moe*), Elio Grasso, Prunotto (*Proo-NOH-toe*), and Vietti.

> Barbera d'Asti Michele Chiarlo (*Mee-KELL-eh Kee-AHR-loe*), Coppo (*KOH-poe*), and Zonin (*ZONE-in*).

Dolcetto d'Alba Elio Altare, Azelia (*Ah-ZEH-lee-uh*), Ceretto (*Cheh-RETT-oh*), Elio Grasso, and Mascarello (*MAHSS-cuh-RELL-oh*).

White Wine in Piedmont

This category, led by the dry, crisp wine called Gavi (*GAH-vee*) doesn't excite me, except for Piedmont's one-of-a-kind white, *Moscato d'Asti/Asti Spumante DOCG.* It caused quite a sensation when the Asti appellation was elevated to DOCG status a few years ago, with wine experts guffawing at the memory of the annoying, singsongy Martini & Rossi Asti Spumante voice-overs in the 1970s commercials. Maybe DOCG status is overkill, but I think this is a fun wine category. Spumante is the Italian word for a wine that's fully sparkling (about 90 psi—a lot higher than the pressure in your car tires), so that is what you can expect from Asti Spumante. Moscato d'Asti, on the other hand, is semi-sparkling, what the Italians call *frizzante* (*free-ZAHN-teh*), and the French *petillant* (*peh-tee-YAHNT*). It is a wonderful, fragrant, slightly sweet wine (you tried it in Chapter 3's "floral" tasting). It is lower in alcohol than most wines, around 8 or 9 percent, and not very expensive, making it perfect for brunch. Some good producers: Paolo Saracco (*POW-low Suh-RAH-coe*), Nivole (*NEE-voh-leh*, "clouds") by Michele Chiarlo, Rivetti La Spinetta (*Spee-NETT-uh*), Vietti, Marco Negria, and Bruno Giacosa.

Piedmont Wines

Since we already tasted Moscato d'Asti, I will not repeat that here, but you may want to do so. It would make a great palate refresher after tasting these big red wines—Dolcetto, Barbera, and one from the Piedmontese dynamic duo of Barbaresco and Barolo. Choose from the recommendations above, or, if you buy from a good wine shop, ask for their suggestions. As with the Tuscan tasting, add bread and olive oil or cheese to your tasting after you have first tried the wines au naturel. It is even more important to have some food with these wines, to help tame their acidity and tannin.

DOLCETTO	BARBERA	BARBARESCO OR BAROLO
THE LOOK: Be sure to compare all three against a white background.		
Medium ruby-red, that you can probably just see through.	Barbera is usually pretty deeply-colored and often tinged with purple.	Considering all its intensity and tannin, the Nebbiolo grape's color may seem surprisingly pale–usually limpid ruby and sometimes even a little garnet or orange at the rim.
THE SCENT: Again, go back and forth among the wines to compare them—all are quite different.		
This wine smells so "Italian" to me: a little earthy, light sour cherry fruit scents, simple and rustic.	Barbera's fruit character is a touch richer than Dolcetto's—more toward plums. It also has a distinctive mineral smell that reminds me of pen ink. You can also detect the faintly sour smell of the acidity.	I love this scent—sweet dark cherries, licorice, smoke or tar, and often sweet spices like cinnamon. The aroma is complex, so keep returning to it and you'll pick up something new every time. I sometimes get a scent that reminds me of wilted rose petals.
THE TASTE: Concentrate especially on the texture, body, and finish of the wines.		
Echoing the scent, there is a tart cherry flavor and a definite rustic earthiness, along with a little tug of gritty tannin. This style needs food to put its best foot forward.	Since the tannin is softer, I think Barbera tastes better on its own than Dolcetto. It's kind of juicy, plummy, and soft. On the other hand, it has such lovely acidity that I have yet to find a food that it doesn't taste great with.	Pow! Right in the kisser. This wine has serious tannin. Depending on the year you are tasting, the tannin may dry your tongue right out (cheese or olive oil will solve that). The flavors are of earth, smoke, pure cherry fruit, and maybe a little licorice or chocolate. Very complex.

The Rest of Italy

Besides Piedmont and Tuscan wines, there are a few other wine types that you'll likely see in stores and restaurants, either because they are big sellers or because they are the distinctive styles that have contributed positively to Italy's reputation in the global wine market. We'll look over the major ones.

The Veneto Region

The Veneto region, with Venice as its historic heart, for the most part isn't a quality leader, despite Verona being the headquarters of "Vinitaly," the huge annual trade show for Italian wines. However, it was once the source of Italy's top export wine—Soave from the Bolla winery, along with its neighboring red, Valpolicella (both are regional names). I don't put either wine in the "cheap but good" category, because I still think the overall standard is weak. However, there are some good producers. For Soave, made from the local white grapes Trebbiano (*Trebb-ee-AH-no*) and Garganega (*Gahr-GAH-neh-gah*)—the wines from Anselmi (*Ann-SELL-me*), Gini (*JEE-nee*), and Pieropan (*Pee-AIR-oh-pahn*) are all worth trying. In Valpolicella, made from local red grapes—mainly Corvina—look for Allegrini (*Al-uh-GREE-nee*), Guerrieri-Rizzardi (*GWEAR-ee-air-ee Ree-ZAHR-dee*), and Quintarelli (*Quin-tuh-RELL-ee*).

CHEAP BUT GOOD—SPARKLING PROSECCO This inexpensive, usually dry sparkler is named for the grape Prosecco (*Pro-SECK-oh*), often attached to one of the two best regional village names, Conegliano (*Coh-nell-ee-AH-no*) or Valdobbiadene (*Val-doe-bee-AH-duh-neh*). Given these pronunciations, most people just say Prosecco. This is the sparkler traditionally mixed with peach puree to make the famous Bellini cocktail, invented at Harry's Bar in Venice.

RECIOTO AND AMARONE DELLA VALPOLICELLA—THE VENETO'S ONE-OF-A-KIND REDS Recioto (*Reh-chee-OH-toe*) is a kind of bittersweet, rich, almost Port-like red wine made from grapes grown in the Valpolicella vineyards. The best quality and ripest grapes are dried to concentrate the flavor and sugar according to the *passito* method, as for Vin Santo. Amarone is made the same way, but fermented to dryness or near dryness, so that it's very strong and full-bodied. Both are amazing, distinctive styles when skillfully made. Look for the following producers: Quintarelli, Allegrini, Bertani (*Bear-TAH-nee*), Tommasi (*Toe-MAH-see*), Masi (*MAH-zee*), and Pasqua (*PAHSS-quah*).

The One-of-a-Kind Wines— Vin Santo and Amarone

You really must do this exciting tasting, for two reasons. Most important, there is an excellent lesson to be learned from it, because this is our first opportunity to taste the effect bottle age has on a wine. I think you'll be amazed. These two wines are particularly suited to the lesson because, although they are not cheap, they remain quite affordable compared to the classic wines that improve with bottle age—Bordeaux, top California Cabernet, and so on. In addition, you can actually find them, aged, in stores, which is rarely the case with the classics. What does aging do to a wine? A lot.

The color of age Aging dramatically affects a wine's color. As we discussed at the beginning of this book, think what happens when you cut an apple in half and expose the flesh to air. It turns brown. Similarly, white wines darken and turn brown as they age, and red wines fade and turn brown as *they* age, due to the oxidation that takes place.

The scent of age Aging also dramatically affects a wine's scent. Over time, the fresh, ripe fruit flavors change and evolve, fading from those pure, farm-fresh fruit scents into the smell of dried fruits. But in addition, all kinds of new scents emerge that would seem to have nothing at all to do with fruit—scents of spices, nuts, sassafras, chocolate, dried flowers, pastry, caramel, toffee, honey, molasses, brown sugar, and countless other exotica will emerge depending on the particular wine. When you start to taste these, it becomes easy to see why some people get so gah-gah over older wines. (But remember that this applies to the minority of wines that are built for, and will improve with, aging. Most wines just lose their fruit flavor and will ultimately taste of vinegar with age.)

The taste of age Often, the flavors of aged wines echo the scents described above. In addition, the texture of older wines mellows and softens, in two ways. First, the acidity in both white and red wines tones down and becomes less vivid and tangy, which gives the wine a softer texture in your mouth. Second, the tannin in red wines softens a lot, and may actually settle out of the wine altogether, forming a sediment in the bottom of the bottle. This softening is what drinkers of the big "Killer B" red wines like Barolo, Barbaresco, Brunello, Bordeaux, and Burgundy are waiting for as they age the wines in their cellars.

But right now, we can't wait. We're going to taste a Tuscan Vin Santo and an Amarone from the Valpolicella region in the Veneto. On the Vin Santo, the effects of age are exaggerated by the fact that the wine is allowed to oxidize as it ages in barrels. Amarone is classically aged for a long time at the winery before release, so, unlike most wines, it comes to market with extra age. As a reminder, both are *passito* wines, meaning their grapes are dried into raisins before pressing and fermentation, so both wines, though different, share a common trait—*very* concentrated flavor. I know you'll love them. The wines are quite strong, so I suggest doing this tasting with friends. Get some biscotti for dipping into the Vin Santo, and a nice block of aged Parmigiano Reggiano or a similar cheese to go with the Amarone, and make an evening of it.

That's the second reason to do this tasting—it's really fun.

VIN SANTO	AMARONE

Choose from the producers listed previously (pages 218 and 225), or your store's suggestion.

THE LOOK

The color is quite dark—a golden, burnished, coppery-butterscotch color.	This is also very dark in color, but look at the shade of color, especially at the rim where it starts to fade. Instead of a purple hue, you will see the orange-brown tinge of aging and oxidation.

THE SCENT

You will really want to pay attention to the scent, because age affects it so markedly.

Toasted almonds, hazelnuts, caramel . . . it's not overly fruity, but it is beautiful. There is some dried apple, but nothing like the fresh fruit smell of a young wine.	Chocolate, truffles, earth, licorice, coffee, smoke, mocha—we could go on and on. There is a dried fruit scent of raisins.

THE TASTE

Concentrate on the texture in addition to the flavors.

You will notice the mouth-filling texture that is extra smooth because the acidity is so muted, and a bit of sweetness. The flavors echo the scents of nuts, caramel, dried apples—bring on the biscotti.	The texture is pure, plush velvet, so full-bodied and intense that you are reminded immediately that the wine started as raisins. The flavor, though dry, is raisiny-rich and has a distinctive note of bitterness similar to that in bitter chocolate. The depth and complexity continue into the finish—smoke, earth, chocolate, and dried figs.

Trentino-Alto-Adige and Friuli

These two regions in Italy's northeast quadrant produce some distinctive wines, but quantities are small. Most are varietals, some familiar (Merlot, Chardonnay, etc.), and some unique to the region, such as Friuli's (*Free-OOH-lee*) delicious dry white Tocai and Trentino's distinct dry red, Teroldego (*Tear-OHL-deh-go*). But the main presence of these regions in the American market comes in the form of Pinot Grigio.

PINOT GRIGIO—ITALY'S ULTIMATE "CHEAP BUT GOOD" OFFERING To me, the crisp, dry, refreshing white Pinot Grigio is one of Italy's great commercial wine achievements. It joins Chardonnay, Merlot, and Champagne as one of the handful of wine words that has instant meaning to most people—the words *Pinot Grigio* connote, quite accurately, "dry white wine." How many other wine names can lay claim to an identity that is so well known? It is also one of the most consistent wines on the globe. Most bottles I have ever tasted were perfectly pleasant, and I cannot ever remember an awful one. I can't say that about any other wine category.

Even better, Pinot Grigio prices have, with a few exceptions, held at a decent level—but I have a few words to say about pricing. Pinot Grigio's virtues are familiarity and reliablity, but the wine rarely goes beyond that. Offhand, I can only think of one winery, Jermann (*YAIR-mahn*), that makes a "special" Pinot Grigio. Considering these circumstances, *it makes no sense whatsoever to pay extra for a household-name-brand Pinot Grigio. You get absolutely nothing for the premium.* If you're sure a particular brand will impress your date or client, that's a different story. But keep in mind that it's the label you're paying for, not a better wine. That said, here are some good, reasonably priced Pinot Grigios: Livio Felluga, Scarbolo, Lageder, Zenato (*Zen-AH-toe*), Zemmer (*ZEMM-er*), Zonin (*ZONE-in*), Campanile (*Camp-uh-NEE-leh*), and Cavit.

Southern Italy

TAURASI DOCG, THE CAMPANIA REGION'S ONE-OF-A-KIND DRY RED This region near Naples, and in the shadow of the famous volcano Mt. Vesuvius, grows the Aglianico (*Ah-lee-AH-nee-coe*) grape, whose origins are said to be in ancient Greece. The wine, called Taurasi, is full-bodied, powerful, and tannic, needing lots of bottle age to shed its toughness. Mastroberardino (*Mass-tro-bear-ahr-DEE-no*) is the famous producer. Another wine from the area, Lacryma Christi (tears of Christ), white and red, has a famous name but that's all. The wine is nothing special.

If You Want More Than a Little Italy

While we've tasted the best of Italy, we've nonetheless just scratched the surface of Italian wine. What about all those other labels you noticed on your trips to the wine shop to buy the wines for our tastings? I have been doing the wine thing for a long time, and I'm still amazed by how much more there is for me to learn about Italian wines. But that is what keeps the wine world so exciting. If your curiosity is piqued, and you would like to go on, there are two things you should do. The obvious one is to continue reading. *Vino Italiano*, by Joseph Bastianich and David Lynch, of Babbo Restaurant in New York City, is one of the most comprehensive titles on the subject. Second, keep your corkscrew handy and keep tasting. For *what* to taste when you're in uncharted territory, read on. In the next chapter, I'll give you a strategy for choosing those wines, too.

CHAPTER EIGHT

The Rest of the Wine World

Consider how far we've come. You hoped to learn to consistently find wines that tasted good for a decent price, but that's become almost second nature. You've tasted a lot of wines and learned a great deal about what you like and don't like. With your understanding of the Big Six grapes and their styles, the classic European wine regions and their styles, the New and Old World differences, and the Flavor Map, you have more than enough knowledge to find a good bottle in any wine shop or restaurant wine list. What's more, you're comfortable doing it.

And you're probably finding that's no longer enough.

If you are the curious type, you want to keep trying new things. You are the kind of person who's always in step with the latest thing—from foods to books to compact discs, you love variety, and that applies to your repertoire of wine tasting experiences, too. Variety was my mission when I was studying intensively to compete in the sommelier world championship, the 1998 Concours Mondiale, where absolutely any wine (or spirit, for that matter) was fair game in the blind tasting. To help out, friends and colleagues from all over the country sent me wines, the weirdest and most obscure grapes, regions, and blends they could find, including Mavrud, a red grape from Romania, and Xynomavro, a red grape from Greece. In case you were wondering, the competition tasting included an Austrian Gumpoldskirchner (a white wine) and Martini & Rossi sweet vermouth. (For the record, I didn't win.)

Other people prefer to specialize. Having found a wine style they like, either grape or region, they want to probe it in-depth. My husband, John, has been exploring the Pinot Noir grape (his favorite, too), trying to "lock in" to his taste memory how the styles differ depending on the growing region. It was while working at the Sea Grill restaurant a few years ago that I discovered *my* passion for Pinot Noir. The chef, Ed Brown, shared that passion, so we decided to probe the possibilities of Pinot Noir with all his fish and seafood dishes. I no longer work there, but my obsession with Pinot continues. And I am not alone. Every year, about five hundred of us Pinot pilgrims converge on McMinnville, Oregon, for the International Pinot Noir Celebration—forty-eight hours of intense devotion to this grape (several thousand more Pinot-philes get turned away for lack of space). To date, I have tried every Pinot I could find from Australia, Austria, Bulgaria, New York, Oregon, Canada, California, Rhode Island, Chile, Australia, New Zealand, and South Africa—and the tasting goes on. They have ranged from great to god-awful, but that's part of the fun of exploring a wine in depth.

Navigating the Rest of the Wine World

Whether you want to specialize or branch out, you're in great shape because we still have before us the whole rest of the wine world. It's a vast flavor frontier, I assure you. And with what you know now, you will be able to navigate it via any route you choose—express stops on the main drag, the quirky backroad locales, or a little bit of both. We will go by country and I'll show you how to dabble a little to expand your taste horizons, as well as how to probe the specialties of each area in-depth if you care to. I have two buying strategies to make this easy:

> Buy by grape variety. This is a very easy approach, because with your Big Six, Old World/New World, and Flavor Map experience, you can predict the varietal style of wines from Australia, Chile, New Zealand, South Africa, Argentina, and of course the United States (all of them chiefly varietal wine producers) as well as upstart regions in the Old World wine countries. For each country, I will give a quick-reference breakdown of the grapes and styles for which they are known; this way you will know where to focus your attention for the best and most exciting wines.

It's not what you know, it's who you know. You know a lot about wine labels. From vintages and grapes to naming protocol, back label descriptions, quality ranks, and more, we have covered the gamut. Yet some imported wine labels still defy interpretation by even the most zealous wine geeks. For those, forget the front label and look for the importer label, either on the back or as a strip label adjacent to the main label. Buying from the best importers is almost like getting a wine insurance policy, especially handy when you are considering unusual or unfamiliar wine choices. That helps us cover the rest of the fine wine world—Italy beyond the dynamic duo of Tuscany and Piedmont, France outside the classic zones, plus Spain, Germany, and Austria. For each area, I give a who's who of the best importers and the wine types they represent.

With this information, you're golden, because for each of these wine sources, there are a few truly great importers. Their virtues are twofold. First, they have an uncanny talent for uncovering the great wines and wine-makers of the countries in which they specialize. Second, they are uncompromising in their quality standards, so every winery they represent is among the best in its region or category. These importer names are well worth memorizing, because from everyday-priced wines to collector's items, their label on the bottle is as good as a Wall Street stock whiz's "buy" recommendation.

Getting to Know the New World

Our survey of the New World countries (United States, Chile, Argentina, Australia, New Zealand, South Africa) focuses on their common link—varietal wines. For the intrepid taster, I will tell you about each country's interesting offerings beyond the Big Six—their body styles, flavors, and some good ones to try. For the specialist, we will focus on the signature wine styles from each country, and the best regions for each to help you target your buying. My wine recommendations don't include numerical scores or definitive lists—there are many credible sources to go to for those. Rather, these are just the favorites that I have been writing about, showcasing on my TV show, and selling for years in my restaurants, and would not want you to miss.

The United States—The Lay of the Land

American appellations (place-names) are called Approved Viticultural Areas, abbreviated AVAs. They don't compare to the European appellations because they only regulate the boundaries of the growing area. Everything else—grapes planted, winemaking techniques, vineyard yield, and so on—is left up to the winery. This makes choosing American wines a question not of appellation style and winery reputation, as in Europe, but rather about *varietal* style and winery reputation. By now you know varietal styles and many of the top-quality winery names. But what about the many winery names you're not familiar with?

Branching out doesn't just have to be for gamblers. In Chapter 5's terroir discussion, I mentioned that American wineries, in pursuit of ever-better quality, have been experimenting with what grapes grow best in each AVA region. In the process, they have established what are called sub-AVAs —smaller subsections of the famous regions like Napa and Sonoma that were given a separate AVA name in recognition of their distinct growing conditions—*and have learned what grapes grow best in those sub-areas.* These can be the basis for your branch-out buying strategy, as follows. If you know some of the major sub-AVAs and their grape affinities, you can do one of two things:

- Stick with your favorite varietals, but try new wineries from the AVAs known for success with that grape variety; or

- Try different grapes and styles than those you normally drink, choosing the ones that are well-matched to their growing area.

For example, the Pinot Noir lover would try new wineries' bottlings from areas such as Carneros (a sub-AVA of Napa and Sonoma), Russian River Valley (in Sonoma), and Santa Barbara (in the Central Coast growing area), which are all known for great Pinot. Someone who wanted to go beyond the Big Six and explore red Zinfandel might choose wines from Zin strongholds like the Dry Creek Valley (in Sonoma) and the Sierra Foothills (in Amador County). Either approach greatly increases your odds of getting a very good wine. The following maps will show you America's key wine-growing zones, and the tables will give you the best sub-AVAs for each grape and some wineries to try in each.

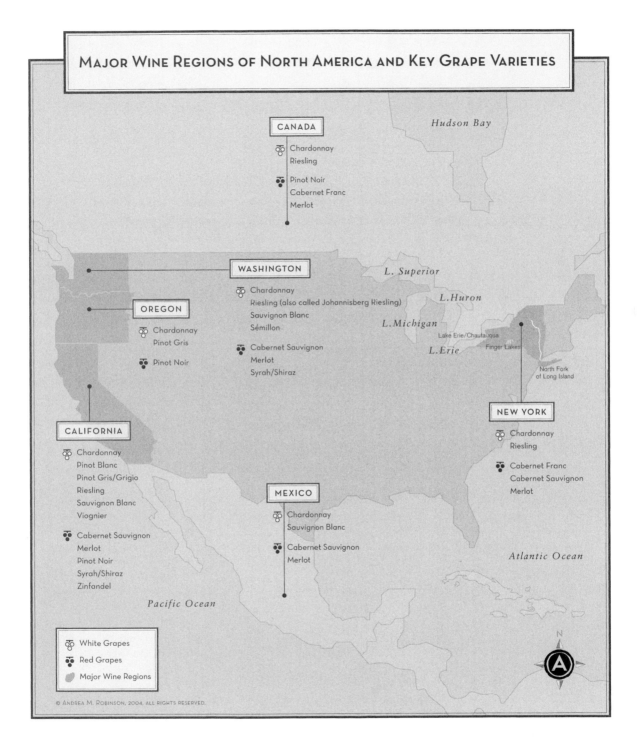

Major Wine Regions of North America and Key Grape Varieties

CANADA
White Grapes: Chardonnay, Riesling
Red Grapes: Pinot Noir, Cabernet Franc, Merlot

Hudson Bay

WASHINGTON
White Grapes: Chardonnay, Riesling (also called Johannisberg Riesling), Sauvignon Blanc, Sémillon
Red Grapes: Cabernet Sauvignon, Merlot, Syrah/Shiraz

L. Superior
L. Huron
L. Michigan
Lake Erie/Chautauqua
L. Erie
Finger Lakes
North Fork of Long Island

OREGON
White Grapes: Chardonnay, Pinot Gris
Red Grapes: Pinot Noir

NEW YORK
White Grapes: Chardonnay, Riesling
Red Grapes: Cabernet Franc, Cabernet Sauvignon, Merlot

CALIFORNIA
White Grapes: Chardonnay, Pinot Blanc, Pinot Gris/Grigio, Riesling, Sauvignon Blanc, Viognier
Red Grapes: Cabernet Sauvignon, Merlot, Pinot Noir, Syrah/Shiraz, Zinfandel

MEXICO
White Grapes: Chardonnay, Sauvignon Blanc
Red Grapes: Cabernet Sauvignon, Merlot

Atlantic Ocean

Pacific Ocean

Legend:
White Grapes
Red Grapes
Major Wine Regions

N

WHERE TO FIND BEST OF THE BIG SIX

WHITE		
GRAPE	REGION*	WINERIES
RIESLING Riesling doesn't get much acreage in the United States, partly because most of the growing areas have a moderate climate better suited to other grapes (Riesling grows best in cool climates), and partly because its popularity pales in comparison to the likes of Chardonnay.	*New York State:* Finger Lakes AVA grows world-class Riesling.	Hermann Wiemer, Dr. Konstantin Frank, Fox Run
	California: no particular AVA affinity, but grown in cool coastal climates	Kendall-Jackson, Bonny Doon, J. Lohr, Jekel, Trefethen, Smith-Madrone
	Washington State: Columbia Valley AVA	Chateau Ste. Michelle, Columbia Winery, Eroica
SAUVIGNON BLANC/FUMÉ BLANC	Sonoma	Simi, Murphy-Goode, Geyser Peak, Chateau Souverain, Iron Horse, Morgan, Kenwood, Kunde, Matanzas Creek, Ferrari-Carano, Rochioli (very rare but outstanding), Chalk Hill, Dry Creek
	Napa and the Stag's Leap District sub-AVA	Joseph Phelps, Sterling, Frog's Leap, Duckhorn, St. Supéry, Robert Mondavi, Grgich Hills, Silverado, Cakebread, Flora Springs, Soliloquy

* All in California except as noted

GRAPE	REGION*	WINERIES
SAUVIGNON BLANC/FUMÉ BLANC	Central Coast/Santa Barbara	Babcock, Byron, Meridian
	Washington State: Columbia Valley AVA	Hogue Cellars, Chateau Ste. Michelle, Chaleur Estate
CHARDONNAY California's best Chardonnay regions are the coolest subdistricts of Napa, Sonoma, and the Central Coast	Napa	Grgich Hills, Franciscan, Newton, Beringer, Robert Mondavi, Sterling, Chateau Montelena, Merryvale, Cakebread, Silverado, Staglin, Peter Michael
	Napa: Carneros AVA (part is in Sonoma)	Acacia, Robert Mondavi Carneros, Saintsbury, Joseph Phelps, Buena Vista, Beaulieu (BV), Carneros Creek, Truchard, Shafer
	Sonoma	Chateau St. Jean, Kunde, Simi, Ferrari-Carano, Matanzas Creek, Rodney Strong, Arrowood, Chalk Hill, Jordan, Iron Horse
	Sonoma: Russian River Valley AVA	Kistler Vineyard, Sonoma-Cutrer, Gallo (Sonoma and Laguna Ranch), Lynmar, Dutton Ranch
	Central Coast	Calera, Meridian, Wente, Edna Valley
	Central Coast: Monterey and Santa Lucia Highlands AVAs	Talbott, Morgan, Logan, Estancia, Mer Soleil (*Mair So-*LAY)
	Central Coast: Chalone AVA	Chalone Vineyard, Testarossa
	Central Coast: Santa Barbara and Santa Maria Valley AVAs	Au Bon Climat (*Oh bone clee-*MOTT), Cambria, Byron, Sanford

GRAPE	REGION*	WINERIES
PINOT NOIR Many of Pinot's best AVAs and wineries match those of Chardonnay —as in Burgundy, the two grapes flourish in similar growing conditions	Napa: Carneros AVA	Saintsbury, Kent Rasmussen, Etude, Buena Vista, Domaine Carneros, Carneros Creek, Robert Sinskey, Truchard
	Sonoma: Sonoma Coast AVA (an up-and-coming AVA)	Flowers

* All in California except as noted

GRAPE	REGION*	WINERIES
PINOT NOIR (*continued*)	Sonoma: Russian River Valley AVA	Kistler, Lynmar, Gary Farrell, 'J,' Merry Edwards, Dehlinger, Rochioli and Williams-Selyem (both very rare)
	Sonoma: Green Valley AVA	Iron Horse, Marimar Torres Estate
	Central Coast	Calera, Meridian
	Central Coast: Monterey AVA	Morgan, Estancia
	Central Coast: Chalone AVA	Chalone Vineyard
	Central Coast: Santa Barbara and Santa Maria Valley AVAs	Au Bon Climat, Cambria, Byron, Sanford
MERLOT/CABERNET SAUVIGNON	Napa	Duckhorn, Sterling, Cain, Robert Mondavi, Franciscan, Markham, Pahlmeyer, Newton, Shafer, Frog's Leap, Chateau Montelena, Beringer, BV, Mt. Veeder, St. Supéry, Joseph Phelps, Groth, Cakebread, Freemark Abbey, Forman, Heitz, Spottswoode, Etude, Dominus, Niebaum-Coppola, Opus One, Flora Springs, Far Niente
	Napa: Stag's Leap District	Shafer, Pine Ridge, Clos du Val, Stag's Leap Wine Cellars, Silverado, Chimney Rock
	Sonoma	Kunde, St. Francis, Benziger, Arrowood, Clos du Bois, Matanzas Creek, Simi, Laurel Glen, Kenwood, Arrowood, Chateau St. Jean
	Sonoma: Alexander Valley AVA	Alexander Valley Vineyards, Jordan, Geyser Peak, Stonestreet
	Washington State: Columbia Valley, Yakima, Red Mountain, and Walla Walla AVAs	Chateau Ste. Michelle, Columbia Crest, Andrew Will, Canoe Ridge, Leonetti, Woodward Canyon, L'Ecole No. 41, Delille Cellars, Columbia Winery

* All in California except as noted

BEYOND THE BIG SIX VARIETALS This is fun stuff, because what Americans lack in tradition, we make up for in our healthy taste for the new and different, and that includes grapes. Here are the best ones to try. I have listed them from light to full, rather than alphabetically, to help you remember their body style.

WHITE Like the other classic whites, these are French transplants.

Pinot Gris This is Oregon's white wine specialty, between Riesling and Sauvignon Blanc in body style. Although it is the same grape as Italian Pinot Grigio, Oregon Pinot Gris usually has a lot more vivid fruit character—to my taste a marked pear scent and flavor that is delicious, and no oak here, just pure fruit. Adelsheim, Ponzi, Sokol Blosser, King Estate, and WillaKenzie are good ones to try.

Sémillon A few wineries specialize in the Sémillon grape from Bordeaux. A rich, barrel-fermented style (as full as Chardonnay) is a specialty of California's Kalin Cellars and Washington's Columbia Winery blend. Most of the big Australian wineries bottle blends of these two grapes, often called Sem-Chard for short. They're tasty and inexpensive. A great value from Washington is Columbia Crest winery's Sémillon-Chardonnay.

Viognier Although plantings of this exotically scented grape from the Rhône in France are sparse, there are definitely several Viogniers worth trying. My favorites from California are Joseph Phelps, R. H. Phillips, Callaway, Westerly, Arrowood, Iron Horse, Stag's Leap, Cline Cellars, Andrew Murray, and Calera (a very full, barrel-fermented style). Believe it or not, Horton Vineyards in Virginia and Becker Vineyards of Texas also make good ones, available in their home states and a few big cities.

RED Now it gets really exciting.

Cabernet Franc I love the California versions of this grape from Bordeaux, where it is usually a blending partner to the dominant Merlot and Cabernet. In California, it really holds its own as a varietal wine, with slightly less weight and a lot more aromatic complexity than Cabernet Sauvignon. The best include Pride Mountain (tiny production, but find this wine!), Chateau St. Jean, Crocker & Starr, Ironstone, Smith-Wooton, Lang & Reed, La Jota, and Chappellet. Although it is too soon to make a definite conclusion, all of these examples are from Napa's mountain vineyards, which are planted at higher altitudes where the soil is poor, the wind strong, and the sunlight unfiltered by the fog that usually creeps up the Napa Valley from San Francisco—"above the fog line" as the locals say. Stay tuned. Outside the Golden State, Cabernet Franc is finding a niche in Virginia near Monticello, where Thomas Jefferson first tried (and failed) to make fine wine. Look for bottlings from Gabrielle Rausse and Williamsburg Winery.

Zinfandel They call us Zin-heads, we who are addicts of this beautiful wine, which ranges in style from medium-bodied, with bright and juicy raspberry flavors, to lush and full-bodied, with decadent fig, blueberry, and even chocolate flavors. Many of the best vineyards are old-vines, original pre-Prohibition plantings. The gnarled old vines, often "field blended" or interspersed with other grapes (formerly a common Old World practice, brought to California by immigrants from Italy), produce some unbelievably complex wines. The best regions and wineries for California Zinfandel are:

> Sonoma (especially the Dry Creek Valley AVA)—Ridge (which also makes a Paso Robles AVA bottling from outside Sonoma), Rosenblum, and Ravenswood (known lovingly among Zin-heads as the Three Rs), plus Rafanelli (easily their equal), Seghesio, Andrew Murray, and DeLoach.

> Sierra Foothills (especially the Amador AVA)—Renwood, Joel Gott, and Montevina

> Napa Valley Frog's Leap, Grgich Hills, Robert Mondavi, Mt. Veeder, Franus, and Chateau Montelena. Collectors covet Turley Zinfandels, but at upwards of 15 percent alcohol, I find them unbalanced and overpowering.

Petite Sirah There isn't much grown, but there are some delicious ones. This grape has no relationship to the Syrah grape, and is believed to be Durif, a lowbrow grape from the south of France. In any case, Stag's Leap Winery, Ridge, Bogle, and Concannon all make bottlings worth trying. Turley also makes a sought-after version (really intense, like its Zinfandels). Petite Sirah is an inky-dark wine, with lots of body, jammy fruit, and tannin.

All fifty states now produce commerical quantities of wine—so, just like the Europeans, we all have a "local wine" tradition to enjoy. Check yours out! For decades, most American farm wineries focused on native American grape varieties such as Catawba and Delaware (the species called *Vitis labrusca* that is better suited for making jelly) or French-American hybrids such as Seyval Blanc and Baco Noir, which range from mediocre (usually) to quite good. But nowadays more and more states are having success with the classic European grape varieties, whose species name is *Vitis vinifera*. In researching and shooting a "Fifty Wines, Fifty States" one-hour special edition of my Fine Living Network TV Show *Simply Wine*, I turned up an impressive list of new bright spots on the American wine map for classic *Vitis vinifera* wine grapes, from Cabernet to Viognier. They include: New York (Finger Lakes and North Fork of Long Island AVAs), Texas (Texas Hill country AVA), Idaho, Virginia, Massachusetts, Colorado, Arizona, New Jersey, Pennsylvania, and Rhode Island. As wineries continue to experiment, new AVAs in California and elsewhere will make their way onto bottle labels. Even in places like Napa and Sonoma, the exploration and discovery have just begun.

Chile

Although Chile's wine industry dates from the arrival of French vintners, grapes, and techniques in the 1650s, in my opinion progress on the quality front has been slow. The good news for buyers is the plentiful land and low labor costs help keep wine prices for the major brands quite attractive. Production is dominated by the Big Four wineries—Cocha y Toro, Santa Rita, San Pedro, and Santa Carolina, whose quality standard for the money is pretty good.

The future looks brighter than ever. Over the past two decades, top European and American vintners scoped out the potential, liked what they saw, and established vineyards and wineries:

Vintner	Chilean winery
Bruno Prats and Paul Pontailler of Bordeaux	Domaine Paul Bruno
Baroness Philippine de Rothschild of Bordeaux	Baron Philippe Chile Almaviva
Miguel Torres of Spain	Bodegas Torres

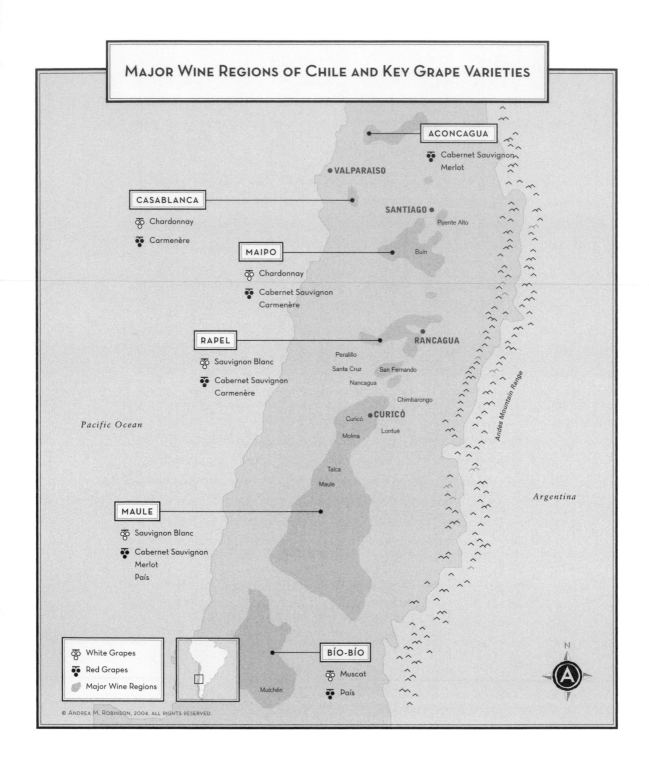

Major Wine Regions of Chile and Key Grape Varieties

ACONCAGUA
- Cabernet Sauvignon
- Merlot

• VALPARAISO

SANTIAGO •

Puente Alto

CASABLANCA
- Chardonnay
- Carmenère

MAIPO

Buin
- Chardonnay
- Cabernet Sauvignon
  Carmenère

RAPEL

RANCAGUA •

Peralillo
Santa Cruz   San Fernando
Nancagua
- Sauvignon Blanc
- Cabernet Sauvignon
  Carmenère

Chimbarongo

Curicó   • CURICÓ
Lontué
Molina

Pacific Ocean

Talca
Maule

Argentina

MAULE
- Sauvignon Blanc
- Cabernet Sauvignon
  Merlot
  País

Andes Mountain Range

BÍO-BÍO

Mulchén
- Muscat
- País

Legend:
- White Grapes
- Red Grapes
- Major Wine Regions

N

Vintner	Chilean winery
The Marnier-Lapostolle family (makers of Grand Marnier)	Casa Lapostolle
Jess Jackson of Kendall-Jackson	Viña Calina
Agustin Huneeus of Quintessa	Veramonte

The Central Valley (Valle Central) is Chile's major growing area, extending from slightly north of the capital city of Santiago to 250 kilometers south of the capital. The subdistricts most commonly seen on wine labels are Maipo (a river valley in the environs of Santiago), Rapel, Curicó, and Lontue. Casablanca and Aconcagua are two up-and-coming regions north of Santiago. Although there are now some very upscale, expensive wines made in Chile, I still think the optimal buying strategy is to focus on the value category. Here are some of the best:

Grape	Best Wineries
Sauvignon Blanc	Casa Lapostolle, Veramonte, Concha y Toro
Chardonnay	Casa Lapostolle, Veramonte, Baron Philippe
Merlot	Casa Lapostolle, Veramonte, Montes, Dallas Conte
Cabernet Sauvignon	Santa Rita, Casa Lapostolle, Cousino Macul, Concha y Toro, Los Vascos, Domaine Paul Bruno, Veramonte

CHECK OUT CHILE'S SIGNATURE RED

If you are looking for something different, but not too far afield from the Big Six, try the Carmenère (car-muh-nair-eh) grape, a Bordeaux import that was originally misidentified as Merlot in many Chilean Vineyards. Its smooth texture and plum fruit are framed by an exotically meaty-smoky scent. Yum!

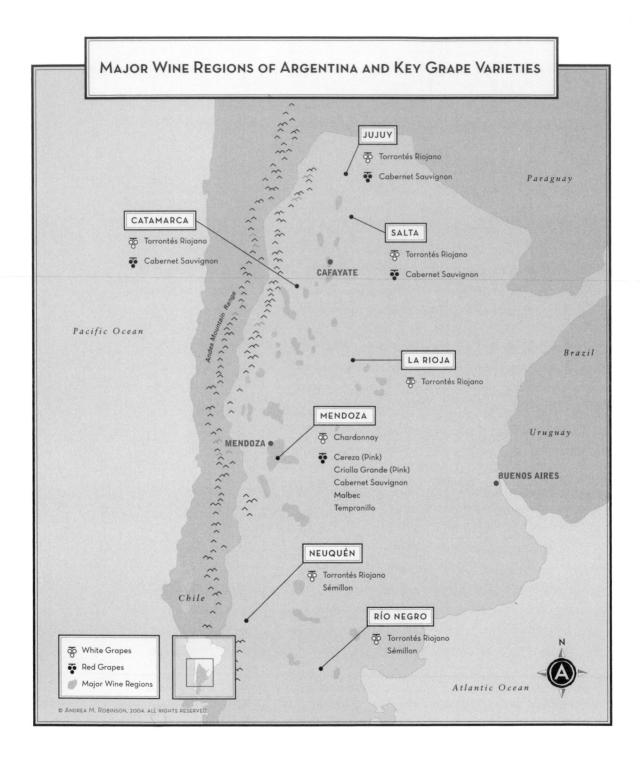

MAJOR WINE REGIONS OF ARGENTINA AND KEY GRAPE VARIETIES

JUJUY
- Torrontés Riojano
- Cabernet Sauvignon

Paraguay

CATAMARCA
- Torrontés Riojano
- Cabernet Sauvignon

SALTA
- Torrontés Riojano
- Cabernet Sauvignon

CAFAYATE

Pacific Ocean

Andes Mountain Range

Brazil

LA RIOJA
- Torrontés Riojano

MENDOZA
- Chardonnay
- Cereza (Pink)
  Criolla Grande (Pink)
  Cabernet Sauvignon
  Malbec
  Tempranillo

Uruguay

MENDOZA

BUENOS AIRES

NEUQUÉN
- Torrontés Riojano
  Sémillon

RÍO NEGRO
- Torrontés Riojano
  Sémillon

Chile

White Grapes
Red Grapes
Major Wine Regions

Atlantic Ocean

N

Argentina

The famously flavorful gaucho-tended Argentinean beef cattle share their acreage with vineyards—lots of them. Argentina ranks fifth after Italy, France, Spain, and the United States in world wine output, most of which is consumed on the home turf. But exports are growing rapidly, led by the signature red varietal Malbec, brought to Argentina from Bordeaux. Argentinean Cabernet Sauvignon is also very good, and a local specialty white grape called Torrontés, with a distinctive pineapple-cream flavor, is well worth trying as a "cheap but good" offering.

Mendoza is Argentina's (and the Western Hemisphere's) largest growing region, often listed on the label along with the varietal name. If not, one of these subregions may be: Agrelo, Tupungato, Lujan de Cuyo, or Maipu. Argentinean Malbec is definitely quite good (especially for the price) and getting better. My favorite wineries are Navarro Correas, Crios, Trapiche, Bodegas Salentein, Los Boldos, Altos la Hormigas, and Catena (who also make a sought-after Chardonnay). Santa Julia and Crios make delicious Torrontés.

Australia

Yabbies, leatherneck, rocket, and capsicums—dinner, I was told, when I arrived in Australia. And here I thought we spoke the same language. Actually, it turned out to be tasty and, on translation, familiar: freshwater prawns, fish, arugula, and bell peppers, respectively. (The kangaroo, on the other hand, was a new taste for me, but at least I knew it by name!)

They say behind every great Australian wine—and there are plenty of them—is a lot of beer. The land down under is a paradise of sunshine for grape vines, hence the lush, bold, exotically fruit-forward style of Australian wines—and the mean thirst that can develop after a long day of manning the fermenters during vintage (the brew of choice is Cooper's; Foster's is export stuff, mate). And yet, thanks to maritime breezes and higher altitudes in some areas, Australia enjoys impressive success with all of the Big Six grapes, including those with cool-climate affinity—Riesling, Chardonnay, and Pinot Noir. Add to that its very own blockbuster signature varietal, Shiraz (while it hails from France's Rhône Valley as Syrah, the Aussies' version put it on the consumer wine map), and some one-of-a-kind "stickies" (Australian for dessert wines), and you get one of the most smashing success stories in the wine world. Australia is hot.

Although grapes are grown and wine made in each of Australia's seven states (including the island of Tasmania), the majority comes from the state of South Australia, followed by New South Wales and Victoria. Western Australia also makes small amounts of excellent wine. The industry is dominated by a few large firms that own many wineries and brands, among them Southcorp Wines, Beringer Blass, Orlando-Jacob's Creek, and BRL Hardy. As in the United States, boutique wineries and expensive, luxury bottlings have also come on strong in the last decade. But the wines at the other end of the spectrum also get a lot of attention. It is deserved. I believe that at present, Australia is one of the wine world's quality and quantity leaders for everyday-priced wines—popular varietals and proprietary blends that are tasty, well-made, and affordable as an everyday dinner wine. Since Chile is still working to get there, and much of California, Italy, and France seem to have stopped trying, here's hoping it stays that way.

One of Australia's price advantages is plentiful land, and blending of grapes from far-flung vineyard sources is quite common. For example, the origin that you commonly see listed on value wines, South Eastern Australia, means the grapes could come from anywhere in the states of South Australia, New South Wales, or Victoria—a huge area. Consequently, South Eastern Australia doesn't connote a signature wine style or grape variety, but many of Australia's famous regions do. Here is a brief summary, by state, of the most famous Australian regions:

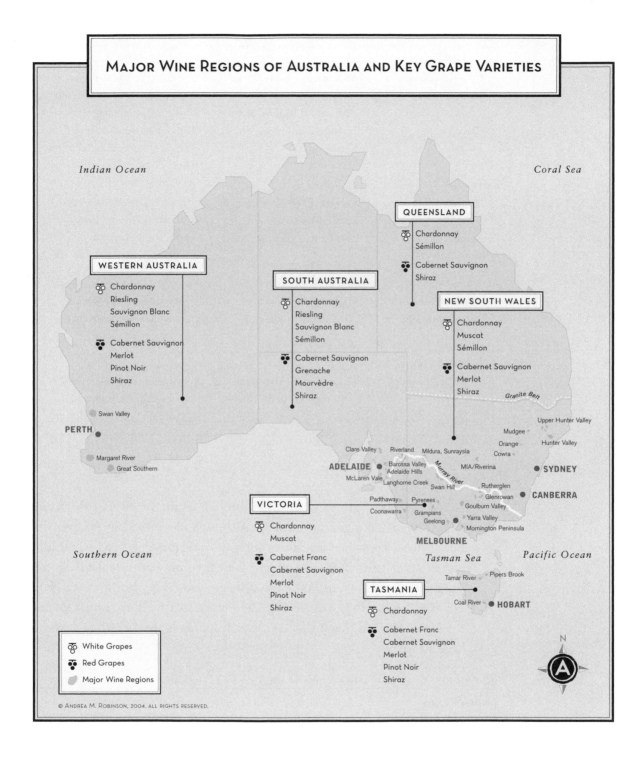

Major Wine Regions of Australia and Key Grape Varieties

Indian Ocean

Coral Sea

QUEENSLAND
Chardonnay
Sémillon

Cabernet Sauvignon
Shiraz

WESTERN AUSTRALIA
Chardonnay
Riesling
Sauvignon Blanc
Sémillon

Cabernet Sauvignon
Merlot
Pinot Noir
Shiraz

SOUTH AUSTRALIA
Chardonnay
Riesling
Sauvignon Blanc
Sémillon

Cabernet Sauvignon
Grenache
Mourvèdre
Shiraz

NEW SOUTH WALES
Chardonnay
Muscat
Sémillon

Cabernet Sauvignon
Merlot
Shiraz

Granite Belt

Swan Valley

PERTH

Margaret River
Great Southern

Clare Valley   Riverland   Mildura, Sunraysia

Upper Hunter Valley

Mudgee
Orange   Hunter Valley
Cowra

ADELAIDE   Barossa Valley
Adelaide Hills   MIA/Riverina   **SYDNEY**
McLaren Vale   Langhorne Creek
Swan Hill   **CANBERRA**
Murray River   Rutherglen
Glenrowan
Padthaway   Pyrenees   Goulburn Valley
Coonawarra   Grampians   Yarra Valley
Geelong   Mornington Peninsula

VICTORIA
Chardonnay
Muscat

Cabernet Franc
Cabernet Sauvignon
Merlot
Pinot Noir
Shiraz

MELBOURNE

Southern Ocean

Tasman Sea

Pacific Ocean

Tamar River   Pipers Brook

TASMANIA
Chardonnay

Coal River   **HOBART**

Cabernet Franc
Cabernet Sauvignon
Merlot
Pinot Noir
Shiraz

White Grapes
Red Grapes
Major Wine Regions

N

STATE AND WINE REGIONS	FAMOUS GRAPES AND STYLES	FAMOUS WINERIES
SOUTH AUSTRALIA		
Barossa Valley	Full-bodied, intense Shiraz	Penfolds, St. Hallett, Henschke
Adelaide Hills	Chardonnay, Pinot Noir	Lenswood, Petaluma, Penfolds
Coonawarra	Cabernet Sauvignon, Shiraz	Wynn's, Lindemans, Katnook
Clare Valley	Riesling, Chardonnay, Shiraz	Pike's, Grosset, Mt. Horrocks
McLaren Vale	Shiraz	Hardy's, d'Arenberg, Clarendon Hills, Chateau Reynella
VICTORIA		
Rutherglen	"Stickies" (dessert wines) called Liqueur Muscat & Tokay	Brown Brothers, Baileys, Chambers & Chambers
Yarra Valley	Pinot Noir	Yarra Yering, Coldstream Hills
Goulburn Valley	Shiraz	Jasper Hill, Château Tahbilk
NEW SOUTH WALES		
Lower Hunter Valley	Sémillon, Shiraz	Lindemans, Brokenwood
Upper Hunter Valley	Chardonnay	Lindemans, Rosemount, Tyrrells
WESTERN AUSTRALIA		
Margaret River	Shiraz, Chardonnay, Cabernet Sauvignon	Cape Mentelle, Leeuwin, Devil's Lair, Plantagenet, Vasse Felix

New Zealand

Sauvignon Blanc, grown in the Marlborough region on the South Island, is New Zealand's signature varietal. Although all of the Big Six are produced there, her other specialties are also cool-climate grapes—Chardonnay, Riesling, and Pinot Noir, which is fast becoming New Zealand's other signature wine (the Central Otago district is emerging as the Pinot HQ). Based on my tastings, I agree that the potential is truly exciting. Outside the Big Six, I think New Zealand Gewürztraminer is another white grape to keep an eye on.

WINE REGIONS	FAMOUS GRAPES AND STYLES	FAMOUS WINERIES
NORTH ISLAND		
Kumeu River	Chardonnay	Kumeu River Winery
Martinborough	Pinot Noir	Martinborough Winery, Ata Rangi Winery
Hawkes Bay	Cabernet Sauvignon	Te Mata Estate

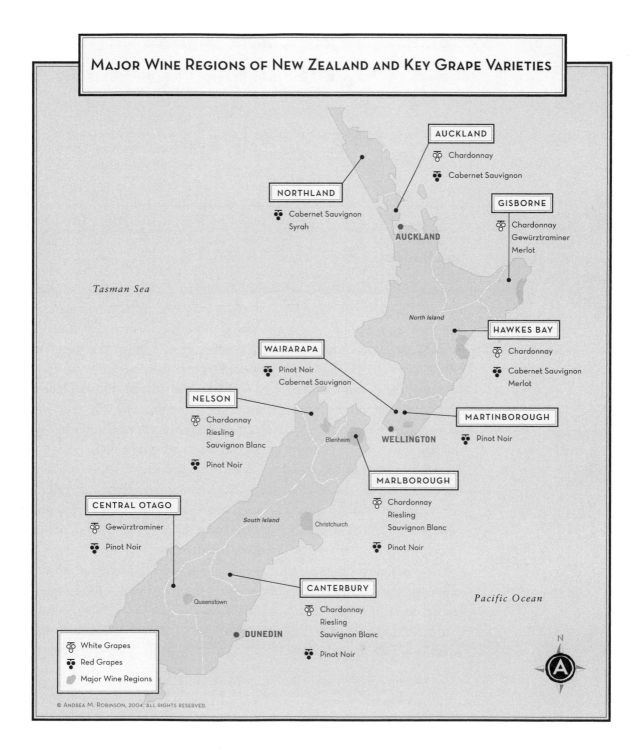

MAJOR WINE REGIONS OF NEW ZEALAND AND KEY GRAPE VARIETIES

NORTHLAND
Cabernet Sauvignon
Syrah

AUCKLAND
Chardonnay
Cabernet Sauvignon

AUCKLAND

GISBORNE
Chardonnay
Gewürztraminer
Merlot

Tasman Sea

North Island

HAWKES BAY
Chardonnay
Cabernet Sauvignon
Merlot

WAIRARAPA
Pinot Noir
Cabernet Sauvignon

NELSON
Chardonnay
Riesling
Sauvignon Blanc
Pinot Noir

MARTINBOROUGH
Pinot Noir

WELLINGTON

Blenheim

MARLBOROUGH
Chardonnay
Riesling
Sauvignon Blanc
Pinot Noir

CENTRAL OTAGO
Gewürztraminer
Pinot Noir

South Island

Christchurch

CANTERBURY
Chardonnay
Riesling
Sauvignon Blanc
Pinot Noir

Queenstown

Pacific Ocean

DUNEDIN

White Grapes
Red Grapes
Major Wine Regions

N

WINE REGIONS	FAMOUS GRAPES AND STYLES	FAMOUS WINERIES
SOUTH ISLAND		
Marlborough	Sauvignon Blanc, Chardonnay, Pinot Noir, Pinot Gris, Riesling	Cloudy Bay, Brancott, Huia, Babich, Seresin, Nobilo, Allan Scott, Villa Maria, Spy Valley
Central Otago	Pinot Noir, Pinot Gris, Chardonnay	Little is imported at present, but watch for Peregrine, Gibbston Farm, and Bannockburn

South Africa

A glass of Pinotage (*PEE-no-tahj*) with your roast warthog? Well . . . okay, sign me up. While working for a company called Restaurant Associates, I had the privilege of catering to the thirsts of a most distinctive and distinguished group of customers: most of Wall Street's CEOs (we did their corporate dining), the world's top musical talent (we fed Carnegie Hall, Lincoln Center, and the Kennedy Center, among others), and the global diplomatic community by way of the United Nations. The U.N. occasion was a celebration of South African culture, including its food and wine. By the way, warthog and Pinotage are a great food and wine match.

South Africa's top-quality wines are all Big Six varietals—notably Sauvignon Blanc, Chardonnay, and Cabernet Sauvignon, but its calling card is the red Pinotage, a cross between two French grapes: Pinot Noir and a Rhône red called Cinsaut (*San-SEW*). It is medium- to full-bodied, with a spicy, gamy *sauvage* character—definitely worth trying.

All of South Africa's quality growing regions are clustered in what is called the Coastal Region, one of the legally approved Wine of Origin districts, which are South Africa's appellations. The best Coastal Region subdistricts to look for are Stellenbosch, Paarl, and Constantia. The following wineries are among my favorites:

Thelema (*Tuh-LEE-muh*): known for Chardonnay and Cabernet Sauvignon

Glen Carlou: outstanding Chardonnay

Mulderbosch: one of the world's great Sauvignon Blancs

Kanonkop (*Cuh-NON-cop*): Pinotage

For value wines, look for Swartland and Indaba.

"WHO'S WHO" OF SOUTH AFRICAN WINE IMPORTERS Cape Classics and Cape Ventures are considered among the best importers of South African wines. They carry a lot of boutique wineries that are worth trying.

Buying Strategies for the Rest of the Old World

Although the French and Italian benchmark wines that we have explored are great, you should not limit your Old World wine buying to just these. For one, those wines are world classics, and are priced as such. Second, there is so much great wine that you would miss with this strategy, both in France and Italy, not to mention the rest of Europe, and we can't have that.

Besides, at one time or another most of us have discovered how much fun it can be to go off the beaten path and explore what only the locals and insiders know. That is what we will do here. I will give you a summary of the not-to-be-missed wines from the rest of the Old World wine countries that I think are worthy of your attention, specifically Spain, Portugal, Germany, and Austria. I will also give you, for these countries and for Italy and France, the importer names that will make buying these wines absolutely hassle-free.

Spain

I love Spain. I have been seduced by its people and pageantry; charmed by the cheeses, suckling pig, and tripe stew (they didn't tell me what it was before I tried it); and utterly humiliated in my flamenco attempts at Fazil's Dance Studio at Forty-eighth Street and Eighth Avenue in Manhattan (though I'm not giving up yet). But the wines won me over before all that. At first I tried them because I could afford them. Although, as in every wine-growing country, there is a burgeoning trend toward boutique wines (with prices to match), Spain's value for the money at every price point continues to impress me.

Quality is on a major roll. I first visited the Spanish wine country in

Although I have not included some European wine countries (e.g., Switzerland and Greece) in this summary, it is not because I don't think they make worthy wines. The commercial reality is that the quantities exported to the United States are so small, they are rarely seen in the typical wine shop.

1985 for college kicks during a summer abroad. I had no sense at the time of the significance of what I saw in the wineries, but I remembered it. When I returned in 1990, and again in 1993, the viticulture and winemaking changes that had taken place were dramatic. By all accounts, it is time for me to return, because the movement toward quality has reportedly continued on an exponential curve. You can certainly taste it in the wines. In my opinion, Spain is *the* wine source for the millennium—offering value, tradition, and innovation all rolled up into good-tasting vino with soul. For the wine lover who feels jaded by the homogeneity of many of the Big C's (Chardonnay and Cabernet), or clobbered by their all-too-common heaviness, it's great to have these wine styles that don't have "me, too" written all over them.

There are two classic Spanish wine styles, some one-of-a-kind specialties, and some cheap-but-good choices that any wine lover needs to know about. And it is really quite easy, because you can memorize a few of the top winery names, and for the rest go with my "who's who" roster of specialist Spanish wine importers.

SPAIN'S CLASICOS—RIOJA AND RIBERA DEL DUERO Spain's top-quality wine appellation, called *Denominacion de Origen (DO)*, compares to the AOC of France and, especially, the DOC(G) system of Italy, because the regulations emphasize barrel- and bottle-aging requirements.

Although there are more than sixty Spanish DOs, you can focus on just the two classics, Rioja (*Ree-OH-hah*) and Ribera del Duero (*Ree-BEAR-uh dell DWAIR-oh*). Both are known for their red wines, based on a grape called Tempranillo (*Tem-pruh-NEE-oh*) and blended with other grapes. In Rioja, these are Garnacha (*Gahr-NAH-chuh*, the Grenache of France), Mazuelo

(*Mah-SWEH-lo*), and Graciano (*Grah-see-AH-no*). In Ribera del Duero, one winery, Vega Sicilia (*VEH-guh Si-SEAL-yuh*), is permitted to blend Cabernet Sauvignon with Tinto Finol (the local variant of Tempranillo) because they have a long tradition of doing so. There are three quality levels, with the amount of body, flavor intensity, and barrel and bottle aging increasing as you go up the ranks:

> Crianza (*Cree-AHN-zuh*): soft, medium-bodied, a little spicy; good for everyday drinking (my house wine)

> Reserva (*Ruh-ZUHR-vuh*): fuller, more complex, more concentrated

> Gran Reserva (*Grahn Ruh-ZUHR-vuh*): intense; made only in the best years

The tradition of long aging in barrel and bottle means Gran Reservas are released already with a few years of development. This makes them good wines to try to see the effect of bottle aging on a red wine, as we did with the Amarone in Chapter 7. Rioja Gran Reserva, especially, will give you an excellent sense of the effect of age on color (it fades from a youthful purplish hue to rust and brick shades), aroma (it develops complex scents other than fruit, such as leather and spice), and texture (tannins become softer and more harmonious). They are often priced at a value compared to comparable-quality wines from better-known regions.

Although the grapes are the same and the regions not far apart, Ribera del Duero and the traditional Rioja style are different—Ribera the dark and powerful style to Rioja's less intense profile, ranging from rustic to elegant. I have noticed, though, from many new Rioja wineries as well as some of the old guard, a "new style" Rioja red that is closer in style to Ribera del Duero. Fortunately, you can try it, and have it, both ways. To me, the restraint of old-style Rioja is great with simple meats (chicken, leg of lamb, pork loin) that let the wine's subtlety show. But with bolder dishes, or a great Spanish Manchego cheese, the strapping "new style" is often better suited. Overall, I'd sum up the style of both as medium- to full-bodied, with similarities to Bordeaux due to the oak aging, but with a spiciness and rustic quality that is similar to Rhône wines due to the grapes used.

BUYING RIOJA AND RIBERA DEL DUERO There are several large Rioja wineries (called bodegas) that have been dominant forces in the market for years. My favorites are Marqués de Cáceres (*Mahr-KESS deh KAH-seh-ress*), Marqués de Arienzo (*Ah-ree-EN-zo*), Montecillo (*mohn-teh-SEE-yo*), and Cune (*KOO-neh*). These wineries' Crianza bottlings are some of the best everyday drinking wines from any source on the market right now. There is another group of smaller wineries producing only mid-priced and high-end wines that I consider some of the best Riojas made—Bodegas Muga, La Rioja Alta, Marqués de Murrieta (*Moo-ree-ETT-uh*), and Remelluri (*Reh-meh-YUH-ree*) are my picks among these. In Ribera del Duero, some of the major players are Vega Sicilia, whose "Unico" (*OOH-ni-co*) bottling is Spain's most expensive wine, Teofilo Reyes, and Pesquera (*Peh-SKEH-ruh*). Also look for Condado de Haza (*Cohn-DAH-do deh AH-suh*), a second estate launched a few years ago by the owner of Pesquera, and Abadia Retuerta (*Ah-buh-DEE-yuh Reh-TWAIR-tuh*), adjacent to the Ribera del Duero region and easily its equal in quality.

WHITE ALBARIÑO AND RED PRIORATO—SPAIN'S ONE-OF-A-KIND WINES A few years ago, the beautifully scented Albariño, from a little-known DO called Rías Baixas (*REE-yahss BIKE-sahss*) stole onto the wine scene, taking a lot of us in the trade by surprise. Spain was known for red wines, but this world-class white from the Galicia district really got our attention with its delicate fruit and mouthwatering acidity. It should be savored young, while the fruit character is fresh and vibrant. Look for Burgans (*Buhrr-GANZ*), Morgadío (*More-guh-DEE-oh*), Lagar de Cervera (*Luh-GARR deh Sair-VAIR-uh*), Lusco (*LOO-scoe*), and Martin Codax (*Martin COE-*

DON'T FORGET THE SHERRY

My Spanish friends may want to disown me right now for not giving Sherry (the real Spanish stuff, not the generic screw-cap California "sherry") its own section in this chapter, for indeed Sherry is one of the wine world's great and original masterpieces. But I have always found that it is best to teach and learn about wine in context, and when it comes to Sherry that means food. As such, we will consider Sherry in the next chapter, where we will discuss pairing wine and food.

dacks). We can thank some of the top Spanish importers mentioned below for introducing this one to the American market.

Ditto the intense, inky red wine called Priorato (*Pree-or-*RAH*-toe*) or sometimes Priorat. The region, a bit inland from Barcelona, had been in decline until a few talented winemakers saw the capability of its great old vineyards to make monumental red wines. Garnacha, Tempranillo, and Cabernet Sauvignon are the mainstay grapes, made into an intense, tannic, oak-aged style. You pay dearly for that intensity, but fans of Priorato are more than willing. I personally find the style overpowering for food and thus hard to work with in most wine situations. If you like this big style, Finca Dofí (*FING-cuh Doe-*FEE), Clos de l'Obac (*Cloe duh Loe-*BOCK), Clos Mogador (*Cloe Moe-guh-*DOOR), and L'Ermita (*Lair-*MEE*-tuh*) are some wines to be on the lookout for.

CHEAP BUT GOOD: SPANISH CAVA, PENEDES, AND NAVARRA WINES

Cava (*KAH-vuh*), Spain's sparkling wine made mainly in the Penedes (*PEH-nuh-dess*) region around Barcelona, is simply the best budget bubbly on the market. It is made by the Champagne method described in Chapter 6, yet good ones cost around ten dollars, and often less. In addition to the local grapes Parellada (*Pah-ray-*YAH*-duh*), Macabeo (*Mah-cuh-*BAY*-oh*), and Xarel-lo (*Shah-ray-*LOE), Chardonnay is widely used. The two biggest brands, Freixenet (*Freh-zhuh-*NETT) and Codorníu (*Coh-duhr-*NEW), are both good. Look also for Segura Viudas (*She-*GUH*-ruh Vee-*YOU*-duss*), Paul Cheneau (*Paul Shuh-*KNOW), and Mont Marcal (*Mohnt Mahr-*CAL).

Penedes In still (nonsparkling) wines from the Penedes, there is one name you should know: Torres. Like the Gallo family of California and the Antinoris of Italy, the Torres family are Spain's wine titans, with wine, liqueur, and brandy operations all over the country (and the world, with outposts in Chile and California). Their headquarters in the Penedes region is the source of some of the best everyday-priced white and red wines on the market. I always have fun pouring them, identity hidden, for guests. Being at my house, their wine expectations are usually pretty high, so I love seeing their delighted reactions to these ten dollar wines (some cost even less). All have proprietary names and use local grapes, sometimes in combination with the international varieties you know so well (Sauvignon Blanc, Cabernet, and so on). The whites are Viña Sol (aptly named, it is the perfect summer party time and anytime wine) and Gran Viña Sol; the reds

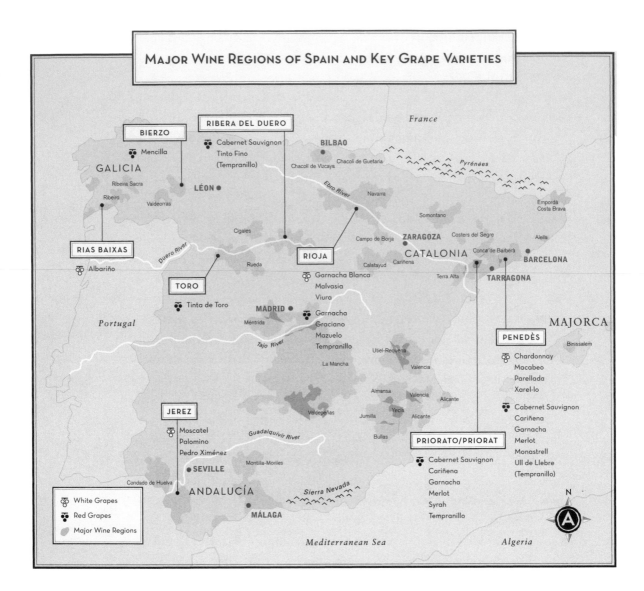

Major Wine Regions of Spain and Key Grape Varieties

GALICIA

BIERZO
Mencilla

Ribeira Sacra
Ribeiro
Valdeorras

RIAS BAIXAS
Albariño

RIBERA DEL DUERO
Cabernet Sauvignon
Tinto Fino
(Tempranillo)

LÉON

Cigales

Rueda

TORO
Tinta de Toro

France

BILBAO
Chacoli de Vizcaya
Chacoli de Guetaria

Ebro River

Navarra

Pyrénées

Somontano

Emporda
Costa Brava

Campo de Borja
ZARAGOZA
CATALONIA

Costers del Segre

Aleila

Conca de Barberá
BARCELONA

Calatayud
Cariñena

Terra Alta

TARRAGONA

Duero River

RIOJA
Garnacha Blanca
Malvasia
Viura

MADRID
Garnacha
Graciano
Mazuelo
Tempranillo

Méntrida

Tajo River

La Mancha

Utiel-Requena

Valencia

Portugal

MAJORCA

Binissalem

PENEDÈS
Chardonnay
Macabeo
Parellada
Xarel-lo

Cabernet Sauvignon
Cariñena
Garnacha
Merlot
Monastrell
Ull de Llebre
(Tempranillo)

Almansa

Valencia

Alicante

Valdepeñas

Jumilla

Yecla

Alicante

Bullas

JEREZ
Moscatel
Palomino
Pedro Ximénez

Guadalquivir River

SEVILLE

Montilla-Moriles

Condado de Huelva

ANDALUCÍA

Sierra Nevada

PRIORATO/PRIORAT
Cabernet Sauvignon
Cariñena
Garnacha
Merlot
Syrah
Tempranillo

MÁLAGA

Mediterranean Sea

Algeria

N

White Grapes
Red Grapes
Major Wine Regions

TOP RANKED

As in Italy with the DOCG rank, Spain added an even stricter level to its appellation system, the DOC—*Denominación de Origen Calificada*. So far, Rioja and Priorat are the only two.

are Sangre de Toro (*SAHN-greh deh* TORE-*oh*), Coronas, and Gran Coronas (a splurge wine).

Navarra For me, Spain's Navarra province was always Pamplona: San Fermin, the city's patron saint, and the week of passionate partying thrown every July in his honor that is best known to outsiders for the *encierro*—the running of the bulls (and crazy humans) every day at dawn. When it comes to wine, Navarra is Rosado (*Roh-SAH-doe*), tasty and refreshing rosé wines made from the Garnacha grape, and value-priced popular varietals — Chardonnay, Cabernet Sauvignon, and Merlot, or blends of these with local grapes. Look for Bodegas Nekeas wines under the brand Vega Sindoa (*VEH-guh Sin-DOE-uh*). Las Campanas and Chivite make good rosados to try.

"WHO'S WHO" — THESE SPANISH WINE IMPORTERS HAVE GOT THE JUICE Here are the best Spanish wine importers. Their names on a wine label represent a stamp of quality, and also originality. These importers source some of Spain's most interesting up-and-comers, unsung heroes, and the leaders in Spain's emergence as a great wine source for the millennium:

> Fine Estates from Spain, Jorge Ordoñez Selections Jorge, as everyone in the trade knows him, brings in great wines from all over Spain, the classic regions, as well as up-and-comers like Navarra, Toro, and the Levante district, near Alicante.
>
> Classical Wines Steve Metzler of Classical Wines represents top producers from the classic zones, as well as great values from little-known regions like Bierzo, Somontano, and Extremadura. They also bring in Hidalgo Sherries, which are among Spain's best.
>
> Europvin, Christopher Canaan Selections This company imports Vega Sicilia but also some great Riojas, Sherries from Lustau (*Loo-STAU*), a top producer, and a raft of wines from up-and-coming spanish DOs.

Portugal

The Portuguese wine story used to be about extremes, with Mateus and Vinho Verde (*VEEN-yo VAIRD*) at one end of the spectrum, and the famous fortified Port and Madeira wines at the other. The former were bought by the everyday consumer based on brand familiarity and novelty, the latter by a tiny group of aficionados. That is now changing rapidly, and with good reason. For one, the quality and availability of Portuguese still wines (regular whites and reds) is improving at warp speed, replacing the old budget standards with seriously good wine at excellent prices. Second, the emergence of restaurant wine-by-the-glass programs has given people access to the classic fortified wines in a single-serving size, making it easy and affordable to try them, and to sample the diversity of styles. As with Spanish Sherry, I will explore this latter group in the next chapter.

For the still wines, here is what you should know. Big Six varietal wines, which are popular in some Portuguese regions, are modeled on the French classics just like everywhere else, so buying them is a no-brainer. For the distinctive local wines, which are definitely worth exploring, here is a quick primer:

> **IPR** *Indicacao da Proveniencia Regulamentada* (literally "indication of regulated provenance") is the Portuguese appellation system. For rustic, spicy, medium- to full-bodied red wines, look for Douro (*DUHR-oh*), Dão (*Downg*), and Bairrada (*Bye-RAH-duh*).

> **VR**, or **Vinho Regional** (*VEEN-yo Reh-juh-NALL*) is a classification rank one step down from IPR that also makes some worthy wines. My favorites are the reds (again rustic, spicy, lots of character) from the Terras do Sado (*TEAR-uss do SAH-do*) and Ribatejo (*Ree-buh-TAY-jhoe*) VR districts.

> **Quinta** (*KEEN-tuh*) "Wine estate" in Portuguese, the equivalent of chateau or domain in French, tenuta or fattoria in Italian, bodega in Spanish.

> **Vinho Verde** A fun wine, some of which are a very nice quality now. Don't write it off, especially for the price. Although white, red, and rosé Vinho Verde is produced, white is the major export to this country.

"WHO'S WHO" OF PORTUGUESE WINE IMPORTERS Although Portugal as yet lacks a major specialty importer to champion her wines, there are a few names bringing some excellent wines in on a small scale:

Broadbent Selections Bartholomew Broadbent, an Englishman based in San Francisco, brings in great Ports and Madeiras and a few excellent still wines from high-quality estates in the Douro district (where Port is made).

Sogrape The producers and importers of Mateus, this company also owns and/or imports many high-quality still wines from all of Portugal's best-quality regions. You will see the Sogrape label on these wines.

Fran Kysela Another importer of great fortified wines, as well as top still wines.

Admiral Wine Merchants Both fortified and still wines.

Germany

When it comes to German wines, my message is very simple: You will love them. Here's why:

Riesling You already know how I feel about this grape. Germany is the headquarters for great Riesling, which is considered by some top wine experts to be the best white wine grape in the world. In Germany, it achieves a bewitching power and purity of fruit and an uncanny range of flavor, all in a sleek package. It is a lithe ballet dancer of a wine compared to the sumo wrestler bulk of Chardonnay. Which one would you rather invite to dinner?

Your budget The price range for truly great German wine starts at under twenty dollars per bottle. I can think of no other classic wine style or region capable of making this claim. What is more, there is real choice at that price level, not just a token wine or two that you have no hope of ever finding for sale. It is certainly possible to spend a lot more for great German wines, but the highest prices are for the rare dessert wine styles, which most people don't drink on a daily basis anyway.

Great meals, every day There is no better wine for a wide range of foods, especially the regular foods that people really eat (such as takeout, salads, and sandwiches) than German Riesling (we'll discuss this more in the next chapter). Although it's light in body, it never lacks for flavor that complements everything from a BLT to mac and cheese, and just about

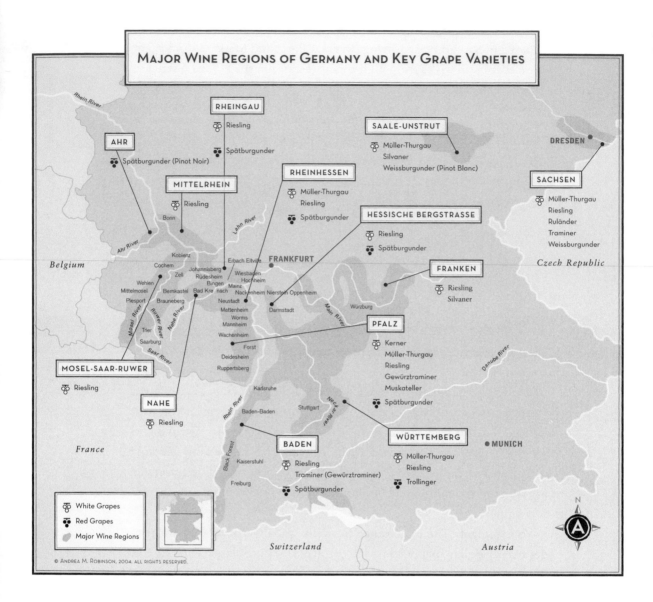

MAJOR WINE REGIONS OF GERMANY AND KEY GRAPE VARIETIES

RHEINGAU
Riesling
Spätburgunder

AHR
Spätburgunder (Pinot Noir)

MITTELRHEIN
Riesling

Bonn

RHEINHESSEN
Müller-Thurgau
Riesling
Spätburgunder

SAALE-UNSTRUT
Müller-Thurgau
Silvaner
Weissburgunder (Pinot Blanc)

DRESDEN

SACHSEN
Müller-Thurgau
Riesling
Ruländer
Traminer
Weissburgunder

HESSISCHE BERGSTRASSE
Riesling
Spätburgunder

FRANKEN
Riesling
Silvaner

Belgium

Czech Republic

Rhein River

Ahr River

Koblenz

Cochem

Zell

Wehlen

Mittelmosel

Piesport

Bernkastel

Braunberg

Trier

Saarburg

Mosel River

Ruwer River

Nahe River

Saar River

Johannisberg
Rüdesheim
Bingen
Bad Kreuznach

Erbach Eltville
Wiesbaden
Hochheim
Mainz
Nackenheim Nierstein Oppenheim

FRANKFURT

Lahn River

Neustadt
Mettenheim
Worms
Mannheim
Wachenheim
Forst
Deidesheim
Ruppertsberg

Darmstadt

Würzburg

Main River

PFALZ
Kerner
Müller-Thurgau
Riesling
Gewürztraminer
Muskateller
Spätburgunder

MOSEL-SAAR-RUWER
Riesling

NAHE
Riesling

Karlsruhe

Rhein River

Baden-Baden

Kaiserstuhl

Freiburg

Black Forest

Stuttgart

Neckar River

Danube River

WÜRTTEMBERG
Müller-Thurgau
Riesling
Trollinger

MUNICH

BADEN
Riesling
Traminer (Gewürztraminer)
Spätburgunder

France

Switzerland

Austria

White Grapes
Red Grapes
Major Wine Regions

N

anything else you might throw together or pick up. And in a restaurant setting, aside from its versatility with varied foods, German Riesling has an amazing ability to showcase a chef's talents, coaxing the final flourishes of flavor from great dishes. And because it's less popular than Chardonnay, it's usually less pricey.

WHEN IT COMES TO GERMAN RIESLING, YOU NEED TO START FRESH

In the context of all that, I find that people still need to be convinced about German Riesling, and it is very frustrating. But I know why. One look at the long flute-shaped bottle is all people need to make the Liebfraumilch association—and this is understandable, because at one point in the 1970s, Blue Nun was among the top-selling wines in the nation. Generally, wine tastes have evolved since then, leaving German Riesling on the back burner —by mistake, because *quality German Riesling bears no resemblance to Liebfraumilch.* Here is what you need to know about the real thing:

Sweetness German Rieslings generally do not taste sweeter than the other popular white wines drunk in this country—Chardonnay and white Zinfandel—except in the case of the late harvest and dessert styles. Because they remember Liebfraumilch, tasters prepare themselves for a sweetness in the wines, just as they take for granted that the popular whites are dry. Often, they are not—review Chapter 2's "dry" discussion if you need a frame of reference, or to remind yourself that you don't have to drink "dry" to get sophisticated taste.

Fruitiness German Rieslings do, however, typically have a very fruity taste, which can seem sweet. And what is wrong with that? It is exactly the quality that Americans adore in white Zinfandel and in mass-market Chardonnay. With Chardonnay, the sweetness is often more pronounced than in Riesling because of the addition of "sweet" oak (review the oak discussion in Chapter 2 if you need a refresher on this concept).

Balance German Rieslings have a major edge over the popular white wines, and this is it. Though they may be fruity or have a touch of sweetness, thanks to the Riesling grape itself and the cool growing region, German Rieslings have incredible balance and vibrancy due to their acidity. It balances the fruitiness and sweetness, making the wine refreshing, complex, and great for food. The wines are not oaky, either.

Labels They have changed, thank goodness. Yes, there are still busy labels with illegible gothic script and inscrutable multisyllabic names. I am not being critical of this tradition, but I do have a practical concern: Non-German speakers do not know how to confidently choose these wines. Happily, some of the greatest German winemakers realized this and have simplified their labels in two ways. First, many use cleaner lettering and simpler designs, so that it is easy to find the important things on the label, like the grape and winery name. Second, a lot of wineries are now leaving off the vineyard source and instead simply labeling their wine as "Estate Riesling." This can help a lot, because the vineyard labeling is usually where the very long, confusing words come in.

All of these changes make it easier than ever to buy German Riesling. Here is what to look for on the labels for day-to-day drinking:

Riesling If the label doesn't specifically list the Riesling grape, the wine is probably a blend of cheaper white grapes, and not really worth your time.

Kabinett or Spätlese (*Kab-uh-NETT, SPATE-lay-zuh*) These terms refer to how ripe the grapes were at harvest, and roughly equate to body of the wine, with Kabinett being the lighter of the two.

Halbtrocken Off-dry, and you may see it combined with either Kabinett or Spätlese.

Trocken Completely dry. Again, may be combined with Kabinett or Spätlese.

Vintage You have a wealth of riches from which to choose, because Germany, in spite of its marginal climate, hasn't seen a really bad vintage in years, and many recent years have been great.

Region name The best German regions for the Riesling grape are all named for the rivers that flow through them:

- Mosel-Saar-Ruwer (*MOE-zul Zahr ROO-ver*) The Saar and Ruwer rivers are both tributaries of the Mosel, which is the main river in this region. This region is called Mosel, for short.

- Nahe (*NAH-huh*) Named for the Nahe River.

  These regions are all named for the Rhine River:

- Rheingau (*RINE-gau*)

- Pfalz (*FAULTS*) Formerly called Rheinpfalz

- Rheinhessen (*RINE-hess-en*)

Vineyard names This is where it gets tricky. Usually the vineyard name follows a town name, as in: Piesporter (town name) Goldtropfchen (vineyard name). The town name of Piesport has "er" to signal "from" in much the same way that if you are *from* New York, you are a New York*er*. Sometimes you see this after the vintage, as in 2002er. This just means *from* 2002—no big deal. When the vineyard names get confusing, the "who's who" importer and producer lists below are a reliable fall-back.

And here are the label terms you will find on the dessert styles:

Auslese (*OUSE-lay-zuh*) *Aus* means out, *lese* means picked, referring to the fact that overripe clusters are isolated from the rest of the crop for this wine. This is the first ripeness level that might be considered dessert-style, although I still think many auslese wines are appropriate for savory dishes, and not at all too sweet.

Eiswein (*ICE-vine*) This is made from grapes that are harvested and pressed while frozen. The water stays behind in the press as ice pellets, making for a *very* sweet, flavorful, concentrated wine. Very little is made, because leaving fruit on the vine until a hard frost is risky—usually rain comes and rots the grapes before the weather gets cold enough to make eiswein. The result is expensive, as you would imagine, but also amazing. A good way to try it is to go in on a half bottle with some friends (a few ounces per person is more than satisfying).

Beerenauslese (*BEAR-ehn-OUSE-lay-zuh*) Commonly called BA, this is a rich, sweet dessert wine made from grapes affected by botrytis, which as you know concentrates their sugar. Quite expensive.

Trockenbeerenauslese (*TROCK-ehn-bear-ehn-OUSE-lay-zuh*) This is called TBA for convenience. It is a dense, unctuous, honeyed nectar made of grapes so shriveled by botrytis that they look like dried-out raisins (hence the *trocken*, or dry, in the name). It is extremely rare and expensive.

"WHO'S WHO" IN GERMAN WINE IMPORTERS German wines are where you really gain some buying efficiency by going with reputable importers—it's not what you know, it's who you know. Terry Theise Estate Selections, Cellars International—Rudi Wiest, and Classical Wines are the best companies, with absolutely uncompromising quality standards. Below is a short list of my favorite Riesling wineries, by major region.

Mosel-Saar-Ruwer Selbach-Oster (*SELL-bock OH-stir*), Dr. Loosen (*Low-zen*), Schaeffer, Fritz Haag (*Hahg*), JJ Prüm (*Proom*), Merkelbach (*MUHR-kuhl-BOCK*), von Schubert, Egon Müller (*AY-gone Muller*), Dr. Fischer, Maximin Grünhaus

Rheingau Robert Weil, Breuer (*BROY-er*), Staatsweingut Klostereberbach (*Stahts-wine-goot Closs-ter-AY-ber-bock*), Schloss Johannisberg, Josef Leitz, August Eser, Hans Lang

Rheinhessen Gunderloch, Strub, Wittman (*VITT-man*), Gysler (*GIZE-ler*)

Pfalz Darting, Müller-Catoir (*Muller-cah-TWAHR*), Lingenfelder, Burklin-Wolf (*BERK-lin Wolf*), von Buhl

Nahe Donnhoff, Hans Crusius (*Hanz CROO-zee-us*), Paul Anheuser, Schlossgut Diel (*SHLOSS-gut DEEL*)

THE REST OF GERMANY What about grapes other than Riesling? Some of them have very unique flavors and can be a lot of fun. Try them (Silvaner and Muskateller are my favorites) by choosing selections from one of our "who's who" importers or wineries.

Austria

Waltz into your wine shop and try one of these wines. You will have to go to a fine wine specialty store, because the quantities produced are small, so the average liquor store or supermarket doesn't carry them. They are, however, worth the extra effort to track down. The labeling and bottle shapes for whites are sometimes similar to those for German wines, with the grape variety shown, and often a ripeness level. But there are two big differences to keep in mind. First, the style: Except for a few specialty dessert types, Austrian wines are very dry and fuller-bodied than German wines. Second, Austria's growing regions are warmer than Germany's, so excellent red wines are also made.

When choosing Austrian wines, here is what to look for on the label:

	WHITE	RED
	None of the classic Austrian whites are oaky	The reds are sometimes oak aged, but the oakiness is always subtle
Grape variety	*Grüner Veltliner* (Groo-ner Velt-lin-er): Austria's specialty white grape , and the most widely planted; medium-bodied, spicy and earthy, with lots of acidity *Riesling:* As you know it, but a very dry style (more like Alsace than Germany) *Sauvignon Blanc:* Rare, but can be great; a crisp Loire Valley style, medium-bodied	*Zweigelt* (Zwye-gelt): Austria's most widely planted red grape; medium-bodied, juicy, not very tannic, a little spicy *Blaufrankisch* (Blauw-frank-ish): Medium-bodied also, with an earthier flavor that reminds me often of the highest quality French Beaujolais from one of the cru villages such as Morgon *St. Laurent:* Falls between the Zweigelt and Blaufrankisch in terms of body and flavor
Region	Wachau (Vock-au), Kremstal, and Kamptal: All make great (dry) Gruner Veltliner and Riesling Styria: For Sauvignon Blanc	Burgenland and Carnuntum (Car-nun-tum) are the two best regions for red wines
Ripeness level	If you see Kabinett, Spätlese, etc., remember the wines are dry, so as you move up the ripeness level, you get fuller body, not increased sweetness. Wachau has its own scale, from least to most ripe (and lightest to fullest body): Steinfeder (Stine-fay-der) Federspiel (Fay-der-speel) Smaragd (Smuh-rogged)	Not applicable
Winery (these are my favorites)	Nigl (Nee-gul), Heinrich (Hine-rick), Prager, Hirtzberger, Brundlmayer (Brun-dle-my-er), Hiedler (Heed-ler), Salomon, Tement (Tay-ment), Knoll (K-nole), Pichler (Pick-ler), Hirsch	Umathum (Oo-muh-toom), Tement (Tay-ment), Heinrich, Triebaumer (Tree-baum-er)

AUSTRIAN DESSERT WINES Austria makes great dessert wines, from late harvested or botrytis-affected (or both) grapes. The two best regions for these wines are Burgenland and Neusiedlersee (*Noy-SEED-ler-zay*). Often, the wines have proprietary names or unfamiliar grapes on the label, so the easiest way to buy them is by producer: Kracher (*KROCK-er*), Heidi Schrock, and Willi Opitz (*OH-pits*) are the best.

"WHO'S WHO" OF AUSTRIAN WINE IMPORTERS Once again, your backstage pass to great Austrian wines, without the hassle of studying all the label stuff, is the importer name. Here are the best ones:

> Terry Theise The German specialist also brings in great Austrian wines.

> Vin Divino A diverse portfolio of great producers.

Italy and France: Off the Beaten Track

If you're like me, you would take Italy and France via the backroads over the *autostrada* any day. Taking the more laid-back route to French and Italian wines can give you access to two great things: Italy and France's rich repertoire of other wines, which, though outside the classic zones, can range from fun to world class if well chosen; and, better wines and better deals than from the traditional regions. To illustrate, take two wines of the same type—Italian Chianti, for example. One is a name brand, the other from a little, no-name producer. With the name-brand wine, what does the name tell you? For one, it lets you know that money has been spent to build the brand. That money has to come from somewhere—either you, in the form of a higher price, or the wine, with resources funneled away from grape-growing and winemaking, and into marketing. That doesn't necessarily make the wines less good, but it may make them more expensive. Clearly, you are better off if you can pay less and get more from an unsung winery. It's just a question of finding them, and I have a simple answer.

Again, it's not what you know, but who you know. For French and Italian wines as with all others, a great importer is your quality ally, saving you all the trial-and-error needed to discover the gems in every wine region. Here are the players, and the wines and regions for which they are known.

"WHO'S WHO" AMONG FRANCE'S ELITE IMPORTERS A refreshing Provence rosé for your al fresco weekend gathering? A big, chewy Southern French red to go with your beef stew? A wonderful Loire Valley dessert wine to rock your world? Start with the importers here.

Kermit Lynch Kermit has been scouring the backroads of France for a long time. He represents elite, classic producers from great regions like the Rhône, Alsace, and Burgundy, and so much more.

Eric Solomon Some Burgundy, and nice rustic wines from the Rhône and the south of France.

Robert Kacher Selections Bobby Kacher is a marathon searcher, sourcing great producers from all over, but especially Burgundy, the Loire, the Rhône, and unsung appellations from southwest France.

In addition to these, there may be some talented regional importers in your local market. Any good retailer will know the names to look for (and will be carrying those wines), so ask.

"WHO'S WHO" FOR TUTTO ITALIA — BROUGHT TO YOU BY THE BEST IMPORTERS With twenty regions, it is obvious that there is much more to Italy than Tuscany, Piedmont, and Veneto. Here are the names that can help you explore it:

Marco DeGrazia Specializes in Piedmont and Tuscan wines, but represents great producers from all over; always finds the up-and-comers.

Neil Empson Represents some of the great Tuscan wineries, as well as top producers from the northern regions of Trentino, Veneto, and Friuli. Check out their Sardinian wines, too.

Leonardo Locascio Top wineries from all the classic regions, especially Tuscany, but also a specialist in southern Italian wines (southern Italy is where the deals are so check these wines out).

Vinifera Imports Mostly classic regions and styles in this portfolio, but a real "who's who" of winery names.

Vin Divino Quite a broad portfolio, but especially strong in northern Italy's quality regions such as Piedmont, Trentino, and Friuli.

CHAPTER NINE

Shop Talk

Buying Wine for All Occasions and
Selecting Wine for Food

Would you rather: do some serious shopping for wine, or go to the dentist? I haven't conducted an official poll, but I'm willing to bet the dentist ranks pretty high. After all, at the dentist's office, with a little mind over matter, you can fantasize that you're reclining in a chaise lounge surfside, and that grit in your mouth is just a bit of ambient sand.

In the wine shop, on the other hand, buyers often feel overwhelmed and skeptical, certain that they're going to be made to overspend or feel stupid. Worse, they fear getting suckered into buying some plonk that's passed off enthusiastically as a bargain. Restaurants don't always make wine buyers feel much better—with those markups above the retail price, patrons fear they won't get good value for their money. And then there's the attitude. Is that a bottle of wine you're buying, or a badge of status (and how will you be treated if you're not buying the top rank?).

We will deal with buying in this chapter. We're no longer talking about what specific buys will taste like or how to get what you want, because you are perfectly capable of assessing bottles and labels on your own now, and your tastes have become more firmly defined. Instead, we'll look at the practical side of retail buying from supermarkets to boutiques, including bin ends, case discounts, bargain hunting, and what to avoid. Then we'll examine buying in restaurants—finding reliable recommendations, getting good value and service, and having fun with wine and food.

From my years working with wine-buying consumers in both retail and restaurant settings, I find that people buy in one of three ways, depending on the situation:

1. The "Go-to List." This is your personal short list of a few classic styles that you know well and buy often. They're generally sure things, and priced accordingly, so you buy them for important occasions. My own short list includes French Champagne and a few favorite Pinot Noirs, Sauvignon Blancs, Rieslings, and red Bordeaux.

2. Theme buying. Whether it's the local specialty, a carafe of the house wine in a French bistro or a Tuscan trattoria, summer whites for a backyard barbecue, or a reasonably priced sparkler for a big New Year's blast, sometimes the context for the wine guides your choice.

3. Bargain hunting. I firmly believe that the rest of the time, people are simply looking for deals, both in stores and restaurants, though they're sometimes embarrassed to admit it for fear of looking cheap.

Don't be shy. Getting a good deal is where we're going to start.

How to Find Wine Values

Everyone wants value, regardless of their budget. Buyers of expensive wines expect tremendous quality and pleasure from them, and rightly so. But we've learned two important things about the price-to-quality relationship in wine that are worth restating. First, a wine's quality assessment and pleasure potential are personal, and a critic's highly rated wine might not be to your taste. And then you have to remember that the prices reflect everything from the winery's marketing objectives to critical acclaim, production cost, and supply and demand, just like any other consumer product—so they don't give you a value "number" either. It would not be possible to do so, because value is completely subjective.

That said, there's always joy in finding a good wine for a low price, and not least is the thrill factor. Everyone loves discoveries and deals

("Think how much money I saved — so I bought two!"). And many times, what's quirky and full of character—like a vintage jacket in the secondhand store or a great barbecue joint that only the locals know about—is as satisfying as the tried-and-true, prestigious, and expensive, if not more so.

I choose wine for several hundred Target stores, but that's not my job. My job is to make sure the wines sell, and that guests are pleased with what they bought and what they spent for it. Here is my strategy for finding deals, and it will work for you, too, in both stores and restaurants:

Buy the stuff most other people aren't buying. This is a notion we have covered before—branching out from plain vanilla into new territories of taste. Wine professionals sometimes call this ABC-land—Anything But Chardonnay (or Cabernet Sauvignon)—where the wines often give better value for the money because they have to, in order to compete with the better-known styles. Aside from the price advantage in this strategy, there's another major benefit of which few are aware. Any restaurant or wine shop with a reasonably thoughtful selection puts heart and soul into sourcing the very best stuff in this category of unique, ignored and therefore value-priced wine styles. (When we professional wine buyers get together, we commiserate over how some customers are scared off by the "cheap" prices of many of these lovely wines. If you're among that crowd, you're missing out, big time, on great deals.)

Following is my list of the categories where you're most likely to find great value for the money.

Whites

RIESLING Yes, here it is again. And you know where the excellent ones come from. The Old World classics are from Alsace, France (the driest and fullest), and Germany (fruity and more delicate). The best New World versions come from New Zealand, Australia, and the United States (somewhere in between Germany and Alsace, and more fruit-forward). If you want to avoid the super-sweet dessert Rieslings, steer clear of the really high-priced versions and half-bottle sizes. My favorites are:

Alsace Trimbach, Lucien Albrecht, Paul Blanck, Pierre Sparr, and Marcel Deiss

Germany Anything from the Strub, Selbach-Oster, and Robert Weil wineries

New World Allan Scott from New Zealand, Grosset and Pike's from Australia, and Chateau Ste. Michelle from Washington

SAUVIGNON BLANC Although I am a Riesling fanatic, I drink this more often at home because the great ones are easier to find and sometimes more affordable. We're talking Sancerre and Bordeaux from France, plus the varietal Sauvignon (and Fumé) Blancs from the United States, New Zealand, Chile, and Australia. My favorites:

Sancerre Jolivet, Crochet, and Château de Sancerre

Bordeaux from these chateaux Carbonnieux, Chantegrive, and La Louvière from Graves, and the basic Bordeaux white from Michel Lynch

Chile Casa Lapostolle, Veramonte, and Concha y Toro Casillero del Diablo

Reds

FUNKY AUSTRALIAN BLENDS It seems the Aussies are a little more democratic in their attitude about wine grapes. Rather than being slaves to fashion (in other words, Cabernet Sauvignon, Merlot, and Syrah/Shiraz), they take a "love all, blend all" approach, using lots of different grapes, often in interesting combinations. They make their share of single-grape varietal wines, too, but a lot of these nifty blends have the character of a boutique wine without the high cost. Look for Cabernet-Merlot, Shiraz-Cabernet, and Grenache/Syrah/Mourvèdre blends. They often have proprietary names.

My specific favorites are: Grenache/Shiraz, Hill of Content; Red Ochre Grenache/Shiraz, D'Arenberg Cellars ("Red Ochre" evokes the area's flame-colored cliffs, whose dust was used to tint Aboriginal body paint); Rosemount Cabernet-Merlot, and Penfolds Koonunga Hill Shiraz-Cabernet.

ZINFANDEL The red kind. If you are a fan of California Cabernet or Merlot, consider red Zinfandel, which offers at lower prices the full-throttle, juicy, California-red intensity you are looking for. Cline Cellars' plain California bottling and Joel Gott's Amador Zinfandel are two of the great values, but there are so many wonderful California Zins.

Here is my short list of the other great names: Rafanelli, Renwood, Ridge, Ravenswood, Rosenblum, Mt. Veeder, and Andrew Murray.

CHIANTI As we discussed in Chapter 7, Chianti has morphed into a seriously good wine at doable prices. Some winery names offering great Chianti values are: Badia a Coltibuono, Viticcio, Dievole, Brolio, Castello di Gabbiano, and Querciabella. Any of these are great food wines (my highest compliment), spicy and easy-drinking, yet with Chianti character.

BARBERA As you have learned, this is an Italian red grape, grown in the Piedmont district. It's soft and juicy and the inexpensive versions are the chameleons of the dinner table. They fit right in with nearly every food imaginable, so they're always a great bet in restaurants. There are a few expensive ones, which are a little less flexible, but great with cheese. My picks include: Barbera d'Alba, Moccagatta; Barbera d'Asti, Chiarlo; and Barbera d'Albas from Vietti, Pio Cesare, and Prunotto.

SPANISH RIOJA For my money, this is *the* red wine for value. Great boutique bottlings are sprouting up everywhere, yet you still have to look pretty hard to pay in excess of twenty-five bucks. Even mass-market bottlings offer good, reliable drinking year after year. Look for bottles with the term Crianza for day-to-day drinking with pretty much any food. Bottles labeled Reserva and Gran Reserva, which, as you know, are barrel- and bottle-aged longer, offer intensity that is well worth the trade-up in price. My top pick is the Rioja Crianza from Marqués de Cáceres. I also love Riojas from these bodegas: Loriñon, Remelluri, Sierra Cantabria, Contino, Montecillo, Finca Allende, and Marqués de Arienzo.

Theme Buying

There are many situations when buying considerations go beyond your own taste. A deal-closing steak dinner with a client, pot roast with the whole family, wine and cheese with a date you want to impress—all might call for a full-bodied red, but perhaps not the same one. A blue chip Cabernet Sauvignon could aptly symbolize your commitment to your client. The Sunday crowd may be better off with an everyday-priced crowd-pleaser. And something a little unusual makes for great date conversation (no winespeak, of course) and shows your creativity.

Every week I get letters, calls, and e-mails from around the country, from readers of my magazine column, guests I have served, trade colleagues, and so on, seeking advice for common wine-buying dilemmas. Although you know a lot about choosing wine, some no-brainer answers can be handy when you don't have time to think about it.

When You Want to Impress

The first strategy applies when you don't know the preferences of your dining partner, or the recipient if it's a gift; the second if you know you're dealing with a wine lover.

GO WITH THE ALL-STAR TEAM They may not be the hippest and newest kids on the block, but on my wine radar screen, these winery names are a permanent fixture; they offer excellent wine, year in and year out, at fair prices. They anchor (or should) most wine lists and wine shop shelves, and probably will for years to come. Here are some of my favorite all-star winery names:

> California Cakebread, Simi, Robert Mondavi, Beringer, Frog's Leap, Jordan, Iron Horse, Chateau St. Jean, Franciscan, Ridge, Ravenswood, Joseph Phelps, Sonoma-Cutrer, Trefethen, Chalone, Stag's Leap

> Washington State Chateau Ste. Michelle, Columbia Winery

> Australia Penfolds, Lindemans, Rosemount

> France

>> Champagne—Veuve Clicquot, Taittinger, Perrier-Jouët, Moët et Chandon, Bollinger, Krug

>> Rhône—Chapoutier, Jaboulet, Guigal

Bordeaux—Château Lynch-Bages, Château Talbot, Château Pichon Longueville-Baron, Château Leoville-Barton

Burgundy—Louis Jadot, Joseph Drouhin, Bouchard Père et Fils, Louis Latour, Faiveley, Olivier Leflaive

Alsace—Trimbach, Hugel, Zind-Humbrecht, Weinbach

Italy

Tuscany—Antinori, Banfi, Badia a Coltibuono, Castello di Gabbiano, Frescobaldi

Piedmont—Pio Cesare, Ceretto, Marchesi di Barolo, Produttori del Barbaresco, Prunotto

BOUTIQUES WITH ROOTS If you know your dining partner or gift recipient is into wine, a boutique bottling might impress them. It seems like a new crop of boutique wineries emerges every day, but when it comes to impressing someone, I'd stay with boutique wineries that have a track record, such as these:

California Kistler Vineyard, Au Bon Climat, Qupé, Shafer, Rochioli, Far Niente, Chateau Montelena, Etude, Williams-Selyem

Washington State Woodward Canyon, L'Ecole No. 41

New Zealand Cloudy Bay, Martinborough

Australia Leeuwin Estate (*LEE*-win), Cape Mentelle, Henschke, Clarendon Hills

France The Alsace, Rhône, Loire, Burgundy, and Bordeaux estates at the "impress" level are essentially all boutiques with track records. (Refer to Chapter 6 for those recommendations.)

Italy

Tuscany—Fonterutoli, Castellare di Castellina, Selvapiana, Monsanto, Castello di Ama

Piedmont—Gaja, Giacosa, Giacomo Conterno, Marchesi di Gresy, Scavino

Pleasing a Crowd

The two issues here are varying preferences when you have a large group, and budget. Obviously, the "deal" categories above are the place to start, but here are some specific suggestions for the big gatherings people ask me about again and again:

Cocktail parties I have found that the best "cocktail" wines are fruit-forward styles, which don't need to be served with a meal to show their best. For whites, I prefer California Sauvignon Blanc or Australian Chardonnay; for reds, California Zinfandel or Australian Shiraz.

Thanksgiving I get dozens of frantic calls every November, because the traditional Thanksgiving spread is a huge array of flavors with which to pair wine. I tell everyone, "Don't sweat it." Just get a good-tasting wine that goes well with lots of foods, and be done with it. I have found that reds go better overall with Thanksgiving food, but you need something for the white wine drinkers—Riesling, Gewürztraminer, Pinot Grigio, and Sauvignon Blanc are the best bets. Great reds for Thanksgiving are Spanish Rioja Crianza or Reserva, California Zinfandel, Italian Barbera and Chianti, and Australian Shiraz.

Weddings For whites and reds, go with the cocktail party strategy above. For sparkling wine Spanish Cava offers the best quality for the money. I also like the Domaine Ste. Michelle sparklers from Washington State.

Barbecues, picnics, and other outdoor stuff Where I grew up, rodeos and truck pulls were the main outdoor activities—not a lot of wine action there. Then in high school, I had a boyfriend whose family owned a local winery. It was southern Indiana, so the wines were made from strawberries and hybrid grapes, but on summer nights, as a bluegrass band played near the winery, people danced, wine flowed, and I discovered the magic of vino al fresco. There is nothing like it—being outside heightens the wine experience. For outdoor activities, I lean toward lighter styles: Champagne is my splurge choice, then Riesling, Pinot Grigio, and Sauvignon Blanc for whites; Pinot Noir, Beaujolais, and Rioja Crianza for reds. You can even chill them a bit for extra refreshment.

All of these tips apply whether you are choosing from a retail shelf or the wine list at a restaurant or catering venue. Now we'll turn to the things every buyer should know about retail stores and restaurants.

The Merchant of Vinos—Retail Wine Buying

Supermarkets, pharmacies, price clubs, catalogs, state stores, megastores, cellar doors, dot.coms, and boutiques . . . where you shop for wine depends a lot on the state where you live. That is because selling wine requires a license from the state in question, and most people do not realize how much the licensing laws vary from one state to the next.

In most states, the regulations affect the prices you pay for wine, what wines are available, and how you get your hands on them (ideally, they are delivered to your door or poured at your table, but this isn't always legal). Here is a quick summary of the retail scene to help you make the most of your buying power wherever you live.

Wine availability The single biggest frustration for every wine buyer and winery is bureaucracy. To ensure the collection of excise taxes, in nearly all states, every single wine must be registered and approved in some way before it can be sold. If a wine you're seeking isn't available in your area, this is probably the reason. For many small boutique wineries, it just isn't worth the bother to get approved for the few cases of wine they would sell in a particular state. One extreme example is Pennsylvania, a "control state" where wine is sold exclusively by a state-run monopoly that, without competition, has had little incentive over the years to source a lot of boutique wines (this is changing now, as it is responding to a growing demand for them). By contrast, California, New York, and Chicago, where both demand and competition are high, are good markets for wine availability.

Wine prices Wine prices can vary from one state to the next due to different tax rates. And in general, prices are lower in competitive markets, where stores can use discounts, sale prices, and so on to vie for your business.

Case discounts Where they are legal, case discounts of 10 to 15 percent are a great way to get the best possible prices for your favorite wines. On the more expensive wines, many people I know coordinate their buying with friends and family so they can buy full cases and get these discounts. Also ask the store about discounts on a mixed case, when you don't need or want multiple bottles of the same wine but still plan to fill a case with your selection.

Delivery In many states, it is not legal for stores to deliver wine to the purchaser.

Wine-by-mail Many catalogs and websites sell wine by mail. Some are affiliated with retail stores or wineries, while others are strictly virtual stores. The conveniences include shopping on your own time and terms, from home or office, helpful buying recommendations and information, and usually home delivery. But the laws governing such shipping are complex, and vary from state to state (in some states it is completely prohibited). When you add in shipping costs, there may not be a price advantage to shopping online, but some people swear by the convenience and buying advice it offers. It's also an easy way to send wine gifts.

Where should I shop? That depends on what you're buying. If you know what you want, then price is your main consideration, and you'll get your best deals at venues that concentrate on volume sales—discount stores, price clubs, and so on. If you want buying advice, or are buying rare wines, you're better off in a wine shop or merchant specializing in fine wines. These stores have trained buyers who taste and know their inventory well; they can help you with your decision. The better stores also have temperature-controlled storage for their rare wines, which is critical to ensure you get a product in good condition. There are also web-based fine and rare wine specialists, but that is a fairly new market. I suggest you purchase fine and rare wines only through sources with a good track record of customer service. In that way, if you have problems with a shipment, you will have some recourse.

Can I take that bottle on the wine list home with me? In most states, restaurants' wine licenses allow for sale and consumption "on-premise" only, meaning they cannot sell you a bottle to take home. There are some exceptions, though, such as California.

Is that a deal or a disaster? Floor stacks, "end caps," private labels, and bin ends can be a boon for the buyer, or a bust, depending on where you are shopping. Here is how to tell the difference:

IF YOU SEE:	FINE WINE SHOPS WITH TRAINED WINE BUYERS	VOLUME-BASED LIQUOR MARTS OR SUPERMARKETS
"Floor Stacks" of large-volume categories and brands (e.g., branded varietal wines)	Usually not the best prices	Best bet; great for stocking up on everyday wines, and buying for parties

IF YOU SEE:	FINE WINE SHOPS WITH TRAINED WINE BUYERS	VOLUME-BASED LIQUOR MARTS OR SUPERMARKETS
"End Caps"—wine displays featured at the ends of aisles	A good bet; you may not have heard of the wine, but these are usually "finds" that the buyer bought in volume to pass the savings along to you	Be careful, unless it's a brand you've heard of; if not, careful selection may not be given utmost importance
Bin ends—clearing out the last few bottles of something at a discount	A good bet; the store is clearing out inventory stragglers, but they're still good quality	Be careful; the wines may be past their prime or oxidized
Private labels—a wine blended and bottled exclusively for the store	A good bet; the store stakes its reputation on your satisfaction with its private labels	Be careful: The prices are competitive, but the quality may not be the store's top priority
"Shelf-talkers"—written signs, reviews, and ratings	Good shops offer their own recommendations in lieu of, or along with, critics' scores	Be careful; the posted score may be for a different vintage than the one being sold

Burgundy Buyers, Beware

With the exception of volume categories such as Beaujolais, Mâcon, and Pouilly-Fuissé, buyers of French white and red Burgundy should shop only at fine wine merchants, preferably those that specialize in Burgundy, for two reasons. First, storage: Burgundy is simply too fragile to endure the storage conditions in most stores. Even many fine wine stores do not have temperature-controlled storage for their wines. Before you buy, ask if they do. Second, selection is a major factor, because quality varies a lot from one winery to the next, and from one vintage to the next. Specialist stores have the needed buying expertise to ensure the quality of their offerings.

Restaurant Wine Buying

For me, it just isn't a restaurant experience worth having if there isn't an interesting wine list involved. (The exceptions are coastal or south of the border-esque experiences—I'll happily do bivalves and beer or margaritas and Mexican.) But I often get the impression that people think bad restaurant wine experiences happen to them alone, maybe when they're eating in a (shoulda-known-better) snobby French restaurant and feeling self-conscious. Well, bad wine-buying experiences can happen to anyone, including me.

When I was leaving Windows on the World's 50,000-bottle cellar for a giant hotel company with 600,000 *cases* per year of wine bought and sold, my wine colleagues gathered for a little celebration. I had saved up and set aside a little wine budget of $1,500 to commemorate the occasion. I say *little* budget because in this restaurant you could, if you wanted to, spend that on just one bottle. Since that wouldn't go very far among six of us, I planned to spend a few hundred dollars per bottle on average, and enjoy the most luxurious night of my entire wine life.

It was not to be. I kid you not: The wine waiter broke absolutely every rule of decent wine service. Yes, I am a Master Sommelier, but that hardly makes me a tough customer. Far from it; I know firsthand the blood, sweat, and tears behind every nightly performance. But there are certain service basics that everyone has the right to expect when paying restaurant prices for wine. We'll discuss more specifics of professional service in Chapter 10, but here are the basics you have the right to expect, along with strategies to help you get the best service possible.

What Is Good Restaurant Wine Service?

BASIC WINE SERVICE RULE #1: SPEED "What does it take to get a drink around here" is a phrase you usually associate with airport lounges, not good restaurants with a clientele to cultivate. I teach waiters to get the first drink, no matter what it is, on the table immediately. It's a fact that humans, from birth, are happier (or at least a lot less cranky) when they have something to drink. And wine service already takes more time than a bottle of beer or a soda, making an extra sense of urgency that much more important.

What you should do:

- Ask for the wine list (and wine-by-the-glass list in case they're separate) as soon as, or even before, you're seated (maybe the host can pick it up as you're led to your table).

- Assess your table's needs (either to yourself or in discussion with your party)—budget, likes and dislikes, one wine or several—so you'll be able to focus your search of the list and your questions for the waiter.

- Ask to keep the list with you during the meal so that it's handy when you're ready to choose something new.

What the restaurant should do:

- Make sure that every table gets a copy of the wine list upon seating (be sure you have enough lists; with laser printers, this is easy). If a guest has to ask for the wine list, chances are they won't.
- Take the first wine order and serve it right away. People hate to wait, especially at the beginning of their meal.
- Leave the list with the guest if they'd like it, or at least be ready to return with a copy before the last wine is finished. Good service means always anticipating the guest's next need.
- Serve the wine before the accompanying food dish. While guests wait for the wine they ordered to drink with this appetizer or that entrèe, sizzles turn to fizzles, sauces congeal, and garnishes wilt—not what the chef or the guest had in mind. And when waiters have to play catch-up with wine service, mistakes (like opening the wrong wine) happen.

BASIC WINE SERVICE RULE #2: WINE SERVED IN GOOD CONDITION
This is usually harder for the customer than the server. The cork is presented, the ritual taste is poured, and *you're on*—performance anxiety at its worst. If you don't like it, is that the wine's fault or yours? It depends.

What you should do: If the wine you order is simply not to your taste, you'll have to chalk it up to experience, because it's not appropriate to send it back. (The exception is if you put your choice in the hands of the sommelier; more on this in Chapter 10.) It's different if the wine is actually flawed (again, we'll discuss this more in Chapter 10). In any case, the first taste of any wine is a shock to your tastebuds, so give the wine and your sensors a moment to warm up to each other before you make a final call.

What the restaurant should do: If the wine *is* flawed, the waiter should replace it immediately with another bottle of the same wine or an alternate, your choice.

Beyond the Basics—Getting Really Good Wine Service

And *great* wine service? It starts with fundamentals, like the wine list. Size isn't everything, and to many guests, a big list is a hindrance. What serves the customer well is a list that's legible, simply organized, and thoughtfully selected at every price point. Great restaurants put as much passion and enthusiasm into their bargain offerings as they do the boutiques, because they want guests of every budget to be happy. It also makes good business sense to sell a twenty-dollar bottle of wine rather than two iced teas, because both the bottom line and the customer will be better satisfied.

I also believe great wine service means creativity and flexibility. If you and your cohorts can't decide between white and red, the waiter suggests a half bottle of each. If you're undecided among two wines by the glass, they'll offer a small taste to help you pick. Many restaurants these days also offer half glasses—half the amount, half the price—so that you can try several different wines. And when there is a problem with a wine, great wine service is a restaurant that really cares, and knows what to do: get something else on the table that's drinkable and acceptable *fast*, while there's still time to enjoy it with your food. The bottom line is that great wine service is a restaurant with a sincere desire to make you really happy with your wine experience—whatever that takes. (This doesn't apply to customers who are rude or who take advantage of the restaurant's sincerity.)

A lot of getting good wine service is about going to restaurants that make wine service a priority. As I pointed out, that doesn't mean just the fancy restaurants with huge cellars, rare bottles, and big markups. There are restaurants of all types and price points across the country that see wine as an important part of the overall dining experience, rather than just a necessary amenity along with bathrooms and matchbooks. Magazines like *Wine & Spirits* and *Wine Spectator* regularly profile them, and wine Web sites often keep up-to-the-minute listings with reviews from critics and patrons. But do be wary of wine-*list* awards, which recognize restaurants for their wine-list content but do not rate wine service. I have had some of my worst wine service experiences at restaurants with "award-winning" lists.

Having Fun with Wine in Restaurants

WINE BY THE GLASS To me, one major test of a great restaurant is their wine-by-the-glass selection. If it offers a creative array of choices and prices, you're on to something. I remember my early days at Windows on the World, when wine by the glass at our competition meant house "chablis" for white and house "burgundy" for red. However, we were pioneers, offering premium varietal wines, and even dessert wines, by the glass.

Nowadays, premium wines by the glass are the industry standard, with many restaurants offering super-premium wine selections that most of us never thought we'd see in a single-serving size. What a great thing for wine lovers! As you continue to taste and learn about wine, you can use this to your advantage. Ordering a few different wines by the glass at the same time is a great way to taste and compare them. And remember the half-glass idea—even if the restaurant doesn't specifically offer it, ask. You and your dining partner can each choose a different glass, but let them pour half for each of you, so you can both taste each wine and share impressions. At home and whenever I travel, I am always in search of restaurants with great wine-by-the-glass programs where I can try new things.

DESSERT WINE If you have not yet experimented with dessert wines, you're missing out on one of the greatest categories in the world of wine. Restaurants are great places to begin your exploration, because many offer at least a Port or two by the glass, and often several other dessert wine styles. This lets you try different types to see what you want to buy for home. Here are the main dessert wine categories and a few brands you're likely to see when dining out:

STYLE	FAMOUS EXAMPLES	WHAT TO DO WITH THEM	HOW SWEET IS IT?
• Botrytis (noble rot) and late harvest wines *Buyer's tip:* look for half bottles *Handy to know:* These age very well, so do not be concerned if the vintage offered is older	Sauternes (Bordeaux, France)/Château Rieussec, Château Suduiraut	Serve with Roquefort cheese or foie gras	Honeyed, apricot flavor Very sweet
	German and Austrian: Auslese, Beerenauslese, Trockenbeerenauslese Ausbruch/Strub, Lingenfelder, Kracher, Heidi Schrock	Serve with fruit or crème brûlée or as dessert (fat free!)	Mango-peach flavor Very sweet, but great acidity, too

STYLE	FAMOUS EXAMPLES	WHAT TO DO WITH THEM	HOW SWEET IS IT?
• Botrytis and late harvest wines (*continued*)	American Late Harvest wines/Dolce by Far Niente, Chalk Hill Late Harvest	All of the above; great with fruit tarts, too	Orange marmalade, peach flavor Range from quite sweet to very sweet
	Vouvray Moellux (Loire Valley, France), Bourillon d'Orleans, Huet	All of the above	Honeyed, baked apple flavor Very sweet
	Tokaji from Hungary/ Château Pajzos, Disnoko, Royal Tokaji Wine Company	Puttonyos (*Puh-TONE-yos*) on the label refers to the level of noble rot; the higher the number, the sweeter the wine	Honeyed, baked apple flavor 4–6 Puttonyos—ranges from quite sweet to very sweet
• Fortified Wines *Buyer's tip:* Wines with a regular cork will keep about one week (see next chapter for preservation tips); wines with a stopper cork (embedded in the cap) will keep several weeks *Tip two:* Generic "port" and "sherry" aren't the same; avoid them	Vintage Port: This is a world-famous style and highly collectible/Graham's, Taylor-Fladgate	Age them (15 years plus); decant before serving alone or with Stilton cheese or chocolate	Fig, berry licorice, chocolate Very sweet
	Tawny Port: Great value for the money; look for 10- and 20-year-old (average age) styles/ Fonseca, Dow's	Serve alone or with caramel or nut desserts (tarts, cookies, etc.)	Toffee-caramel flavor Very sweet and smooth as silk
	Pedro Ximénez (*Hee-MEN-ezz*) Sherry from Spain (amazing value)/Argueso, Lustau	Serve alone or with vanilla ice cream (some in the glass, some poured on top!)	Dried figs & raisin flavor Very sweet
	Madeira from Portugal Styles to try: *Specialty:* Rainwater *Varietal:* Sercial, Verdelho, Bual, and Malmsey *Vintage:* very rare *Blended:* 10-year-old/ Blandy's, Broadbent, Leacock's	Serve with caramel, dark chocolate, or nut desserts; great with pineapple upside-down cake and pumpkin pie	Burnt sugar, candied orange peel Main grapes/styles *Sercial:* Off-dry *Bual:* Quite sweet *Malmsey:* Very sweet

Chefs have always known this, and regularly use it to their advantage. It is no accident that nearly every famous sauce in classic cooking uses at least a dash of an acidic ingredient—wine, vinegar, tomatoes, mustard, and lemon juice are the main ones—to enhance the flavor. Many of the hot ethnic cuisines rely on acidity as a flavor-booster, too—lime in Mexican and Thai food, pickled ginger with sushi and so on.

Maybe you weren't consciously thinking about it, but I am sure you have used this principle, too. Whether it was a squeeze of lemon on your fish and chips, pickles on your hamburger, or Worcestershire sauce on your steak, you've undoubtedly enjoyed the flavor wake-up call that acidity can bring to anything you are eating. As if that weren't enough, acidity has another great virtue: It brings balance into the picture, playing against and harmonizing with other tastes, textures, and flavors so they don't dominate or overpower. For example, the lemon squeeze keeps fish from seeming "fishy," and the steak sauce balances the meatiness and fattiness of a steak.

Thanks to its acidity, wine is *the* beverage for food. Is it any wonder that Europe's best eating cultures, France and Italy and Spain, enjoy a glass of wine with virtually every meal, not just special occasions? Acidity is the reason that, regardless of which dish is cast in the starring role at dinner, wine definitely takes "Best Supporting Actor" honors.

AND THE WINNERS ARE . . .

For best supporting actor in a:

Potluck supper: Beaujolais
Saturday night stir-fry: Pinot Grigio
Weekend clambake: Chardonnay
Backyard barbecue: red Zinfandel
Leftovers "Fridge Fest": Chianti

Taste Dynamics

How Wine and Food Change Each Other

As far as I'm concerned, if the food is on the table, and the wine's cork is out, it's a match. But on a day-to-day basis, your wine and food need not be locked in a passionate embrace—a handshake will do. Still, the dynamics of wine and food are fascinating. In the pairings below, I show how wine and food tastes can be completely transformed when the two are sampled together. (Yes, there is such a thing as wine and food nirvana, and so that you can experience it for yourself, later I will tell you about some matches made in heaven.)

I do this tasting with the waiters I teach, and it is a real eye-opener:

Fresh Goat Cheese with Sancerre

Use a fresh goat cheese such as chèvre, Montrachet, or Crottin Chavignol. You have had Sancerre before, but taste the wine first to refresh your taste memory—vibrant, mouthwatering acidity. Now taste the goat cheese and notice its tangy, acidic character. At this point, my students always brace themselves for a teeth-jarring taste experience—very acidic wine, very acidic food—ouch! But it is not so. Tasting the two together shows how acidity in both the wine and the food actually tone each other down. It shows that acidic wines go well with acidic foods (you *can* drink wine with salad).

Parmigiano Cheese with Cabernet Sauvignon

In the love affair between red wines and steak, or red wines and cheese, tannin is the tie that binds. Tannin, which gives the wine its structure, combats the heavy taste of the fat and protein in the cheese (or steak). At the same time, the fat and protein coat your mouth, mellowing the astringency of the tannin. Choose a good-quality Italian Parmigiano Reggiano and a tannic Cabernet Sauvignon (or you could use a tannic Rhône red such as Crozes-Hermitage, or another tannic red that your store suggests). The wine tasted by itself leaves your mouth dried out, which makes it hard to taste the fruit. But now eat some cheese, and then taste the wine. You will find that the cheese softens the wine's hard edges, and lets the fruit flavor come forward.

Shop Talk

287

Dessert Wine and Blue Cheese

This is an "opposites attract" comparison. Choose a Sauternes, or a Port wine from Portugal (either late bottled vintage Port, or a true vintage Port if you want to splurge). The best blue cheeses to use are either Roquefort from France, English Stilton, or a German blue called Cambazzola. (Supermarket blue cheese is not a good idea; it's too crumbly and salty.) People often think this combination sounds crazy, but it is fabulous. The saltiness of the cheese really makes the flavor of the dessert wine explode. It has to be experienced to be believed.

Off-Dry Wine—Moscato or Riesling—with Chips and Salsa

Another "opposites attract" combo, but of a different nature. What you will discover is that a little bit of sweetness really helps to cool the heat of spicy foods—one of the reasons a margarita tastes so good with Mexican food. Try Moscato d'Asti or a German Riesling Spätlese with some corn chips (not too salty) and salsa (medium or hot). To really see the difference that the sweetness makes, open a full-bodied California Chardonnay and taste *it* with the chips and salsa. You may start to sweat, because the alcohol in the wine really emphasizes the spicy heat. Not refreshing at all. Taking this lesson to its logical conclusion, go with off-dry wines when you're eating spicy ethnic foods (Mexican, Thai, Indian, and so on).

Matches Made in Heaven

Classic combinations are "classic" for a reason. They work beautifully. Here are some of the famous ones, and a few tips to use when trying them.

Wine and Cheese

"Cheese," to the average American, often means bright yellow cellophane-wrapped singles or the multipurpose, bland "Cheddar" that has little to do with the flavorful English original. When we graduate to grown-up cheese, we figure it has to be somewhat stinky to be real, so we go with triangles of Brie from the supermarket dairy case.

The wine lover needs to look at cheese a little differently. For most wines, the moldy rind of Brie (one of its great virtues) overpowers the flavor and leaves a metallic taste in your mouth. Although there are exceptions, generally the best cheeses for wine are the subtler ones. My favorite cheese by far for all wine is Spanish Manchego, an aged sheep's milk cheese from the La Mancha district. Italian Parmigiano Reggiano (the real stuff), which is an aged cow's milk cheese, runs a close second. These two just seem to go with every wine, but especially the full-bodied reds that are the best candidates for cheese in general.

You should also try Muenster (the real French kind) with Alsatian Gewürztraminer, and Brunello di Montalcino with Pecorino Toscano.

Foie Gras and Sauternes

It sounds trite, but it's true: You haven't lived until you have tried this combination. (This does not apply if you are put off by the idea of liver, because foie gras is just that —specifically, fattened goose or duck liver, a delicacy worshiped by the French.) This match is a glorious illustration of both contrast and complement. The contrast is flavor—sweet wine and savory foie gras. The complement is texture—luscious, almost syrupy wine and meltingly rich, silken foie gras. It is also an utterly decadent match, featuring two of the most expensive stars in the gastronomic universe.

Champagne and Caviar

Speaking of decadence, here is another classic combination that I think is well worth saving up for. Some wine and food commentators argue that it is not a great combination, because the caviar, which some say can seem fishy, can overpower the delicacy of Champagne. But I have never been disappointed. The key is to get good caviar—specifically, farmed American sturgeon roe from companies such as Sterling Farms or Tsar Nicoulai. (Due to overfishing, Caspian sturgeon have become so seriously endangered that I cannot recommend imported caviar). I have also found that the best Champagnes for caviar are the light and medium house styles (see Appendix B for a list), and especially the category called Blanc de Blancs. Its vibrant acidity is a great counterpoint to the fishy-salty-oily caviar.

Try other roe (fish eggs), too, such as salmon roe or flying fish roe (*tobiko* in Japanese markets).

French Chablis and Oysters

The same idea, acidity as a refresher to fishiness (or in this case, brininess), applies here. With bivalves, who needs a squeeze of lemon when you can have Chablis? In fact, I like all forms of bivalves and raw seafood (including sushi and sashimi) with Chablis (and also Champagne).

Big Red Wines and Steak

So classic it is practically a cliché, but worthy of its status because the dynamics are textbook: A boldly flavored, tannic red wine meets its match with a smoky, meaty, succulent steak. The fat and protein of the meat tame the tannins in the wine, unleashing the bold flavor and fruit. No wonder this one has survived nouvelle cuisine, macrobiotics, and everything else. It's just too perfect.

Spanish Sherry and Tapas

I have mentioned dessert-style Spanish Sherry, but you really must try the dry styles of Spanish Sherry with food. They are truly classic, original wines and you will add a lot of Spanish excitement and flair—let's call it *allegría* —to your life if you try some of these combinations. The basic Sherry styles for savory food are:

Fino This has a pale straw color, a nutty scent of almonds, and a crisp, fresh taste. When it comes to food, fino Sherry goes best with appetizers and salty nibbles, such as:

- toasted almonds (the classic pairing)
- aged ham such as prosciutto or serrano ham
- olives (the other classic pairing)
- fried foods (calamari, fish'n'chips, vegetable tempura, and so on)
- charcuterie (cured sausages and meats)

Oloroso This has a nut brown color, with a scent and taste of toasted pecans or walnuts. Oloroso Sherry is fabulous with:

- soups (from consommé to mushroom soup to lobster bisque)
- pâtés
- cheeses (mild, firm varieties)
- sautéed mushrooms

CHAPTER TEN

Corkscrews, Decanters, and All Those Glasses

Choosing and Using Wine Gear

They say the devil is in the details. But if I've done my job right, you have now conquered your demons, or most of them, when it comes to the anxieties of choosing wine. We've explored wine styles, pronunciation, rules of thumb for buying wine, and food and wine dynamics. We're left with just a few housekeeping details—wine-related gear, how-tos for serving and storing, cellaring if you want to, and, of course, getting the bottles open in a manner that befits a person of your wine prowess.

Opening Wine

My dream is coming true. In the first edition of this book, I fantasized about a world in which the affordable-but-tasty wines that appeal to most wine lovers came packaged in a bag-in-a-box. Further, I dreamt of a day when wine consumers would ditch their snobbery about the package and start embracing the bag-in-a-box virtues—easy-to-open (what a concept) with an easy-to-serve spigot and none of the disappointment and expense of spoiled, wasted wine, no spoilage from a flawed cork (more on these below), and none of the oxidation that occurs with bottled wine leftovers, because the bag inside deflates as the wine is consumed, so that no air gets in. Well, it has started to happen, with a growing number of wineries creating tasty, affordable bag-in-a-box wines that are perfect for everyday dinner enjoyment. Check 'em out. No corkscrew needed!

Bottles and corks do have virtues. They're beautiful and traditional. The standard size, 750 milliliters, is a practical quantity for sharing between dining partners, for placing on the dining table, and for trading up to a finer wine, where you may want to drink less but better, and the manageable size keeps the cost in check. Finally, they are a pretty good (though not perfect) container for aging wines when that is appropriate, as I'll explain below.

HOW DO EUROPEANS DO IT?

Per capita wine consumption in Italy and France is around ten times that of the United States. What is their solution to the cork conundrum? It's a combination of attitude and options. Europeans grow up drinking wine every day, so they get more practice with the corkscrew, and are a lot less uptight about both product and package. They also have more options. For example, in French bistros and Italian trattorias there is no stigma around carafe wine, and it is indeed good stuff. And screw-caps? In Europe, the single-serving screw-cap bottles sold on trains and ferry boats actually contain real wine that is perfectly pleasant (e.g., a French Côtes du Rhône or Beaujolais). And the markets sell wine in bulk, priced per liter, to patrons who bring in large plastic jugs they refer to as cubitainers and request the Euro equivalent of "fill'er up." The point is that in Europe they have options to skirt the hassles without having to skip the wine, and thus letting them get down to what is really important—the meal experience and the company.

They're also not that hard to open with some practice. And since you are probably reading this in the United States, where most of the quality wines, even at everyday prices, are sold in bottles, you will get plenty of uncorking practice. Here is how to do it, step by step.

Openers

I am frequently asked, "What's the best wine opener?" For most wine lovers I recommend the first two of the following choices.

WAITER'S FRIEND   For portability, I like and always carry a "waiter's friend," so-called for its compact design with both the augur, or screw, and blade (for cutting the capsule cover on the bottle top) folded into the handle like a pocketknife. It may take a little practice to get comfortable using it, but make it fun by tasting lots of different bottles along the way.

The technique—using a Waiter's Friend corkscrew

- Open the blade, and cut off the top of the capsule (also called a foil because it is sometimes made from a foil-like metal; plastic is also commonly used). This is the covering that stretches like a skin over the top of the bottle. The best place to cut is below the bottle neck's bottom "lip," the ridge of glass that sticks out slightly near the bottle opening. Cutting below this lip prevents the wine from coming in contact with the capsule when you pour, which might wash into the glass small capsule pieces or any mold that is clinging to the capsule.

- Wipe the bottle opening with a cloth or paper towel. It's perfectly normal to see a bit of mold or condensation there, so just clean it off.

- Close the blade, extend the augur screw, and push the tip a little way into the cork to get it started. From there, twist the handle to screw it in—all the way, so that the curved part of the augur is nearly buried in the cork (this will feel funny to lefties, because most corkscrews are engineered to twist in clockwise). If you only go halfway you may get only half a cork. This also helps you get the lever on the end of the corkscrew close to the bottle opening, for the next step.

- Extend the hinged metal lever at the end of the corkscrew, and anchor it against the bottle top. It is notched to help it stay in place, but hold it there by grasping around the bottle top with your nondominant hand, as you would grip a baseball bat.

- With your other hand, pull up on the handle. The lever pushes against the bottle lip, so it's easy to lift most corks without brute force. For extra-stubborn corks, take your time and be patient. Sometimes you can loosen the seal by wiggling or rocking the corkscrew.

A few special notes:

- Opening flange bottles: These are the bottles that many mass-market wineries use, with a flange, or lip, that flairs out at the top of the bottle. They usually have no capsule, but instead a paper or wax seal. Don't remove the seal before opening the bottle. Just insert the augur right through the seal. Waiter's Friend corkscrews work best with this bottle type.

- Opening synthetic corks: You may have seen these closures made of a smooth, plasticlike material. Open them as you would a normal cork—the augur goes right in.

SCREW-PULL AND LEVER-PULL   For home use, these corkscrews are among the fastest and most popular (I rarely use them because I am so accustomed to the Waiter's Friend, though I find the Lever-pull speedy for opening many bottles at once, say for a party or tasting). They have an extra-long, thin augur, usually covered with a nonstick coating. With the Screw-pull, twisting the handle inserts the augur. Continued twisting causes the cork to slide up the augur, so you need never pull on the cork to raise it. With the Lever-pull, instead of twisting, the user gives one quick stroke with the lever to penetrate and remove the cork. Both models work well on all but the most fragile corks, but they do not penetrate some of the flange-top seals, nor synthetic corks, easily. Note: There are lots of cheap knock-off versions of the Screw-pull and I say proceed with caution. Even the $39.95 versions I have tried broke after just a few cork extractions.

THE AH-SO   This model is also portable, and it is one of the best for very fragile, old, or soft corks that might be easily broken if penetrated by an augur. It is key-shaped, with a metal loop handle attached to two flexible, bladelike prongs inside a sheath. You remove the sheath, and slide the prongs into the bottle opening between the cork and the glass, gently working the prongs down the cork's edges. It is similar to running a knife blade around the edge of a muffin to loosen it from the tin. Once the prongs are all the way down the sides of the cork, you twist and slowly lift the loop handle to slide the cork out.

THE "WING"-TYPE CORKSCREW   My least favorite opener is the one everyone gets as a wedding gift, with two metal levers that open up as you twist the augur into the cork. You then push the levers back down to (if you're lucky) lift the cork. I think this model is bulky, awkward, and probably responsible for most of the world's broken and pushed-in corks, because its augur is thick and dull, and often chews up the cork as it goes in, making it a lot harder to get out in one piece. You can usually make it work, but it's not ideal.

A Restaurant Wine Service Primer

(For professionals and everyone else who has ever wondered about the rituals of restaurant wine service.)

When opening wine for restaurant guests, I complete a few additional steps for proper, professional wine service, before and after the cork is pulled. Here are the techniques I teach all wine waiters, from opening and showing the cork to decanting and pouring, and why each is done. You'll also learn about being on the receiving end of wine service in a restaurant, as well as something about the serving of fine wines at home.

> **Waiter's tip:** *No matter how experienced you are, always have a service napkin when you are serving wine to customers. Accidents and drips can happen to anyone.*

BEFORE THE WINE IS OPENED

Confirm you have the right wine before you are at the table. Otherwise, you lose precious time correcting your mistake. Generally, guests are in a hurry to get their wine, and busy waiters are always in a hurry.

Present the bottle. Show the bottle to the guest who ordered it, point to the label, and say the name of the wine and the vintage (if your guest uses reading glasses, they won't be able to see what wine you've brought if you just point). This is your last chance to make sure you don't mistakenly open the wrong wine.

AFTER THE WINE IS OPENED

Present the cork. This means remove the cork from the augur and place it on the table to the right of the guest's wineglass; formal restaurants present the cork on a small doily-lined plate. Receiving the cork means major performance anxiety for a lot of people, because many think they are supposed to do something with it, such as smell it. Feel free to do so, but the scent of the cork will tell you very little about the quality and condition of the wine. Only smelling and tasting the *wine* will tell you that. Some people touch the cork's end to see if it's wet, indicating the bottle was properly stored on its side. This is relevant for wines in medium- to long-term storage in a cellar, because keeping the cork moist helps to maintain a tight seal, thereby guarding against premature oxidation. But for restaurants selling current wine stocks that rotate often—and this is the majority—this is a nonissue.

WHY THE CORK RITUAL?

I must acknowledge that traditional European sommeliers smell the cork themselves before presenting it to the guest. When I have asked why, they say the main reasons are habit and tradition. They don't trust the cork to tell them whether or not the wine is okay, either.

Presenting the cork originally came about during the world wars, as a precaution against wine fraud by counterfeiters, who would take emptied bottles from famous wine estates, fill them with cheap wine, then recork and sell them for high prices as the genuine article. Presenting the cork allowed the diner to see the mark of the winery thereon, verifying that the wine inside was authentic. At one very formal restaurant where I worked as the mâitre d' and sommelier, we decided to dispense with the cork ritual. Our service still got top reviews, and not one customer ever mentioned missing it. I think they were happy to be off the hook.

Waiter's tip: *Don't make a big deal about presenting the cork. Just place it down casually, then wipe the bottle top with your service napkin. This creates a pause for you to see if your guest cares to do anything with the cork. If not, proceed with service.*

Pour a sample taste for the person who ordered the wine. This is a crucial step, needed to verify that the wine is sound. If you are buying wine in a restaurant, do not pass on the sample taste. Many wine professionals point out that it is difficult to tell from one quick sip if a wine is flawed. You should pause to smell the wine and taste it, as we have done so many times in the tastings in this book.

But also remember this is about the condition of the wine, not whether you like it. Fortunately, you have all the knowledge and tasting experience you need to make satisfying wine choices. The exception would be if the waiter recommended a wine that you weren't previously considering. In that case, it's okay to send the bottle back in favor of a different choice.

Most of the time, the bottle will be fine, but like any natural product, wine can spoil. If the bottle is not sound, a fresh bottle should be brought. Below, I will tell you how to spot spoiled wine although it is not always obvious at first, especially if the flaw is subtle—for example, very slight oxidation or corkiness (see below). I have said to customers who seemed uncertain after the first taste, "Let's give it a moment of air, and then I will check back with you to see if you're happy with the bottle." And I have myself asked a waiter to come back in five minutes because I wasn't sure about a wine at first whiff. A restaurant that is serious about wine has no problem with this.

Pour for those who wish to drink wine. It sounds straightforward, but here are a few things to keep in mind:

- Pouring order. Traditional serving order is ladies first, then gentlemen, with the person who ordered the wine last (regardless of gender), clockwise around the table.

- Pouring correctly. This takes practice. Do not touch the bottle to the glass rim (the guest drinks from there). Hold the bottle about one and a half inches above the rim to pour, and stop the flow before you pull away by tilting the bottle tip up, and twisting your wrist slightly. Wipe the bottle with the service towel every time you pull it away to catch any drips.

- Pouring evenly. Share the bottle evenly among those who are drinking. It is not appropriate to "run out" so that a second bottle is needed to serve the rest of the table. That is the guest's choice, which means you must stretch what they have ordered to fit the group size. Chances are, someone will pass on wine or order something different, and you will have more to go around than you thought. If so, it is perfectly fine to top up glasses to the proper level (see next) after everyone on the table has been offered wine.

- Pouring the right amount. When serving a bottle of wine, which is a little more than twenty-five ounces, three or four ounces is about right for the first pour, unless more than four people are sharing the bottle. In that case, a little less will ensure you have enough to top up the glasses of those who need it. Some guests may want to drink less wine than others, or may drink more slowly.

- Place the bottle appropriately. (Depending on the wine and the restaurant, this may mean on the dining table, at a nearby side stand, in the ice bucket, etc.) The capsule and empty bottles do not belong on the table or in the ice bucket. Remove them from the dining room.

Remove the cork and say, "Enjoy." Let the guest keep the cork if he or she wants to.

Opening Sparkling Wine and Champagne

While in the bridal party at a friend's very formal wedding, I watched a waiter remove the wire cover from the top of a Champagne bottle and then place the bottle on our table, right beneath a crystal chandelier. Having once seen a bartender take out the entire single-malt Scotch section of his back bar by doing the same thing, I dived for cover—taffeta gown, silk gloves, and all.

When opening Champagne or sparkling wine, you have to be careful. The carbon dioxide pressure in the bottle averages about six atmospheres, or ninety psi—enough to cause the cork to eject at high speeds, causing extreme injury. Whether you are a wine lover or a service professional or both, please read and follow these steps carefully.

1. Never use a corkscrew.

2. Ensure the wine is well-chilled, as this helps to mute the pressure.

3. Always open a sparkling wine bottle *pointing away from all people.* You can either hold the bottle with both hands, or rest it in an ice bucket, or the kitchen sink if you are at home. If needed, wipe the condensation from the bottle so that you get a firmer grip. Also watch out for wet labels that can slide and cause you to lose your grip.

4. Remove the foil that covers the wire cage around the cork. Many bottles have pull-tabs to help with this. Otherwise, cut the foil with the blade of your corkscrew.

5. Have a towel handy. In restaurant settings, use a service napkin.

6. Place your thumb or the palm of one hand firmly over the cork before you begin loosening or removing the wire cage.

7. While maintaining downward pressure on the cork with your thumb or palm, loosen the wire cage with your other hand by untwisting the loop that is attached. Once the wire is loose, *never release your firm grip on the cork*. It is not necessary to completely remove the cage, and in fact I don't, because it helps me to keep a tight grip on the cork.

8. Holding the cork tightly, *gently begin turning the bottle* in one direction, and the cork in the opposite (or just hold it steady). The pressure in the bottle will begin to push the cork out. Control the pressure with your grip, slowly easing the cork out.

9. Don't pop the cork. I know people like the festive sound, but a popping cork could get away from you and hurt someone. You also lose a lot of the carbon dioxide when the cork pops (those are the bubbles for which you paid extra), and sometimes the wine spews forth as well. If you want sound effects, clink glasses for a toast.

Waiter's tip: *When serving Champagne and sparkling wine, present the cork and pour a taste for approval just as you would any other wine. Sparklers can spoil, too.*

Decanting Wine

The Purpose

It's that cool thing that you have seen in restaurants—the waiter or wine steward lights a candle, then pours the wine from its bottle into a carafe before serving. Decanting is very beautiful and romantic, but also practical. There are two reasons for wines to be decanted (actually three if you count showmanship, which is an important part of restaurant dining).

Aeration This is mainly for full-bodied red wines whose aroma, flavor, and complexity can improve with aeration. I am sure that in some of our tastings you have noticed how wines evolved between your first taste, and later when perhaps you drank a glass with dinner, or went back to taste the wine after the bottle had been open for a while. Decanting speeds up that process.

Removal of sediment This process is also for full-bodied reds, which, as they age, naturally develop a deposit that settles to the bottom of the bottle. Decanting separates the clear wine for drinking from the sediment, which isn't so pleasant.

Which Wines Should Be Decanted?

Rule of thumb: *Older red wines* (typically ten years and older, but visually inspect bottles with 3 or more years of age to be sure) may have sediment, and

LET IT BREATHE

"Shall I open that and let it breathe?" It's the classic line of the attentive waiter seeking to enhance your enjoyment and your wine by aerating it. But whether you are at home or in a restaurant, simply pulling the cork does no good, because the sliver of a bottle opening lets in very little air. Instead, I ask guests, "May I pour your wine into the glasses for you so it can aerate?" Aeration is exactly what red wineglasses are designed for, with their wide balloon shape providing maximum surface area for oxygen to reach the wine.

are thus candidates for decanting. All *vintage Port* has sediment, and should be decanted—the older the wine, the thicker the sediment. *Young, very full-bodied red wines* can benefit from decanting for aeration.

The Tools for Decanting

The tools are:

- *A candle* to illuminate the neck of the bottle as you pour. This allows you to see the clear wine as it flows from the bottle into the decanter, and to stop when the dark trail of sediment reaches the neck of the bottle, before it flows into the decanter. You can use a taper or votive, but avoid scented candles. Some have staying power that can compete with the scents of the wine and food.
- *A carafe* or decanter to contain the decanted wine.

DO I NEED A DECANTER?   You can decant into any glass or crystal vessel of sufficient size to hold the wine. In a pinch, I have used water pitchers, ice buckets, and even my mom's Pyrex pancake mixing bowl, which worked great because of the built-in pouring spout. Glass and crystal are neutral, and thus won't alter the wine's taste. If you do buy a decanter, consider the size and shape. A good decanter should hold the contents of a bottle of wine with plenty of room to spare and should ideally have a wide circumference so that the wine inside has a broad surface area exposed to air (same concept as the balloon shape for red-wine glasses). The ones I use, from the Riedel company, are shaped rather like a large chemist's beaker. Etching, facets, or other decorative features are a matter of personal taste. I prefer the plain ones because they show off the color and shimmer of the wine.

SETTLING WINES AT HOME

If you store wines on their sides in a cellar or wine rack, make sure the label is facing up. That way, you will know that the sediment is opposite the label when you get ready to decant. If you remove the bottle from its rack carefully, you can decant by grasping the bottle with the label facing up (underneath your hand), to avoid mixing in the sediment.

How to Decant

First, let the wine settle. If you just got the bottle home from the store, or the wine is otherwise shaken up, the sediment will be mixed in. Give the bottle a day or two to settle. You can stand the wine up to settle (sediment goes to the bottom).

Waiter's tip: *Present the bottle as you normally would before opening. Formal restaurants use a decanting cradle or basket for this, to keep the wine on its side. Otherwise, just hold the bottle carefully, avoid shaking, and stand it up gently.*

1. Set up: On a counter or other firm surface, put the decanter to the left of the candle, and the bottle to the right of the candle (lefties can reverse this). The top of the candle needs to be six to twelve inches from the counter surface so that you can easily backlight the bottle neck. When using a votive or tea light, I invert a wineglass and place the candle on it like a pedestal. Light the candle. Wooden cigar matches are best, as they minimize sulphur smells that will compete with your wine experience.

2. Remove the entire capsule so you can easily see the sediment in the neck of the bottle when decanting. Cut a vertical slit on the side of the capsule with your corkscrew blade and it will come off easily.

3. Wipe the bottle top with a paper towel or service napkin before opening the wine.

4. Open the wine as you normally would.

5. Grasp the bottle with the *label facing up* under your hand. Grasp the decanter by the neck (or wherever it is comfortable for you).

6. Pour the wine slowly into the decanter in one smooth, gentle motion (avoid starting and stopping, which mixes up the sediment). As you do this, hold the neck of the bottle a few inches over the candle to backlight it so that you can see the sediment through it. Stop when you see sediment in the neck of the bottle. You will initially see a dusty wisp of sediment. Keep decanting through this, and stop when you see the grainy sediment. Some people like to strain the leftovers through a coffee filter, and this is fine.

(However, it is not "standard" restaurant wine service, so in that setting, do it only if a guest requests.)

Waiter's tip: *From here, simply pour the host's taste for approval and then pour the wine as you would in normal bottle service, wiping the decanter mouth after each pour as you would a wine bottle. I usually keep the bottle and the decanter together during service, because although you are not serving from the bottle, people still like to enjoy the label. For the same reason, I do not leave a napkin with the bottle or decanter. It just gets in the way.*

Wine Problems

When it comes to opening and serving wine, stuff happens. Here are the main problems, and what to do about them.

Broken corks. Everyone breaks corks from time to time, so don't sweat it. Prevent it if you can by using a good corkscrew (avoid the wing kind), and ensuring that you screw the augur into the full length of the cork. When a piece of cork does remain, I simply use my corkscrew again, gently, to get the rest out. My trick is to point the augur in at an angle, rather than straight down, to avoid pushing the fragment into the bottle. Then I press the cork against the neck of the bottle as I lift it, to keep it from slipping down. The Ah-So also works well, used as I described above, but wield it with a light touch so you don't push the cork in.

Pushed-in corks. You have two choices. Either you can chalk it up to experience and of course you can still serve the wine if you are at home (this won't fly in a restaurant setting). Alternatively, buy a Cork Retriever. They are inexpensive and easy to use. It consists of three long wires on a handle, with a slide that opens and closes the wires like a claw. You insert the wires, and lower the slide until they grasp the cork and flip it to vertical position. Lift, and out comes the cork. These are a must for restaurants.

Waiter's tip: *If you push a cork in or break it in front of a customer, remember that they won't sweat it if you don't. Apologize graciously and tell them you'll have the problem solved quickly, then do it. I have said things like, "I'm sorry. This cork is a bit difficult. I'm just going to step away and solve this, and I will be right back with your wine." Then go perform the necessary surgery as described above. It's best to do this away from the table. When you return, smile and thank them for waiting. The key here is speed. If you are gracious and efficient, people will be patient with the problem.*

Bad Wine

The term *bad* refers not to wine that isn't to your taste but to wine that is flawed or spoiled. Here are the two main forms of wine spoilage:

Oxidized wine. A wine that is prematurely oxidized loses its fresh fruit character, and begins to smell and taste flat and dull, or reminiscent of dried fruit (usually dried apples in the case of white wine, and prunes for reds). But even before you taste an oxidized wine, you will probably notice that the wine's color is browner than is typical for the wine style, or that it lacks its usual brilliant shimmer. A faulty cork seal or warm storage conditions are usually the causes of oxidation. To see what oxidation is like, leave a few ounces of your everyday house white and red on the kitchen counter. Check the color, scent, and taste every couple of days, and you will see progressive oxidation.

"Corked" wine or corky wine. This does not mean little bits of cork are floating in the glass, which is not a flaw—you can simply fish them out with a spoon. A wine with a musty smell of wet newspaper or wet cardboard that overpowers the fruit character is "corked," or is described as smelling "corky." The cause is a cork tainted by trace amounts of a chemical that, though not dangerous, can leech into the wine and cause this smell. In my experience, about 6 percent of wines are corked to some degree. The corky smell can range from very faint and hardly noticeable to very strong—and awful. Reputable wine shops will usually replace a corked bottle at no charge if you return to the store with the wine in question (don't pour it out if you plan to do this).

Many wineries have sought to combat the problem of corkiness by using the synthetic corks mentioned above, but their merits are the subject of some intense debate in the wine world. A few wineries think synthetics give an undesirable smell to the wine, and others say they don't provide the right conditions for a wine meant to age and develop in the bottle. I think synthetic corks are fine for everyday wines meant for consumption within a few years of the vintage.

Waiter's tip: *Never serve a bottle of wine that hasn't been checked for spoilage (tasted by the customer or sommelier, if you have one), and always bring a* *fresh glass for this purpose, even if you are serving a second bottle of the same wine. The reason is simple: If the second bottle is flawed, topping up glasses with the bad bottle ruins what has already been poured. Sometimes guests will say "Just serve it," but don't. In those situations, smile and say, "Certainly, I'll just confirm that it's in good condition for you." Then quickly take a clean glass, pour a splash, and smell it. If all's clear, you can serve it right up, and if not, you can catch the problem and bring a different bottle.*

WHAT IS CORK?

Cork is the bark of a species of cork oak trees grown mostly in Spain and Portugal (the main source of the world's wine corks). The bark is stripped from the tree, and the corks are stamped out like cookies with a cookie cutter, then processed (cleaning, imprinting, etc.). The bark then grows back, and after about nine years, the tree is ready to yield a new harvest of corks.

Serving Wine

I am often asked about wineglasses. The main concerns are whether it's necessary to have different wineglass shapes for different kinds of wine, and whether the glasses have to be expensive to be good.

WINEGLASSES—WHAT SIZE? WHAT SHAPE? Most of us lack the storage space and patience to hassle with a bunch of different wineglasses, and you don't need to. The classic wineglasses are a balloon shape for red wines and a tulip shape for whites, but one good, all-purpose glass, whether tulip- or balloon-shaped, is perfectly great for drinking just about any wine.

The main feature you want is ample size, around twelve to fourteen ounces. This isn't to accommodate more wine, though—only fill halfway or even less. Both classic shapes are designed to be filled to the widest part of the bowl, to equal about a five- or six-ounce glassful. The wide bowl of the balloon-shaped glass for reds is designed to provide a broader surface area to aerate the red wines once poured. The extra capacity also gives you enough room for swirling the wine, as well as leaving head space in the glass so the scents can collect there and enhance the experience.

A good wineglass should also have a clear bowl (the facets and etching of the classic wedding crystal complete with the color and shimmer of the wine) and most important, a thin rim. Here's why: A thin rim allows you to "pour" each sip so it slides effortlessly onto your palate. The wine's scents vaporize as you breathe through your nose, triggering the olfactory response that launches its flavor. With a rolled jelly jar–type rim, you draw each sip over the rim by sucking, which pushes each breath into your windpipe—but there are no smell receptors therre! So you miss much of the wine's secnt, and thus its complexity and flavor.

What about all the other wineglass shapes and sizes? Some wineglass makers produce different shapes specifically tailored to a multitude of different wine types beyond white and red—there are glasses for Bordeaux, Burgundy, Chianti, Sauternes, and the list goes on. For the wine drinker who enjoys a variety of tastes, it certainly seems like a way to entice them to buy a variety of crystal glasses, but do these glasses really improve the taste of the specified wine type? When comparatively tasting the same wine from two different glasses, I have found that the specially made glasses do showcase the scent of the indicated wine type—sometimes quite a lot. But investing in all these glasses takes resources—money and storage space, because the glasses themselves are often quite large and expensive—twenty-five to sixty-five dollars *per stem*. A good compromise is to target your selection. In my house, we use Riedel's Burgundy/Pinot Noir and Bordeaux/Cabernet stems from the Vinum line for all of our reds.

WINEGLASSES—HOW MUCH SHOULD YOU SPEND? No doubt about it, expensive crystal stems can be beautiful. But no amount of beauty is worth it if a broken glass would ruin your day or end a friendship. You can get good glasses with a fairly thin rim and ample size from places such as Pot-

THE CHAMPAGNE EXCEPTION

I do recommend one specialty wineglass shape. A flute or tulip is necessary for Champagne, because the elongated shape and narrower opening help to preserve the bubbles longer. The small capacity also means the contents won't warm up quickly.

tery Barn or Crate & Barrel for less than ten dollars each. My all-purpose glass at home is glass (not crystal) from Riedel's budget line, called Ouverture, in the Bordeaux shape, although I use it for everything. I also have a couple of larger finer crystal stems (red Bordeaux and Burgundy shapes) from Riedel's Vinum line that cost about twenty-five dollars each. I wash all of these in the dishwasher, being careful to arrange them with space in between. Many fine wine retail shops sell these glasses, or you can order them from Wine Enthusiast or International Wine Accessories catalogs.

Wine Leftovers

Dealing with wine leftovers is easy, since your primary concern is to keep oxygen away from the wine.

Still Wines

For home and in restaurants, I use a hand-pump vacuum sealer. They are sold in the accessories catalogs mentioned above, in wine shops, and in kitchenware sections of department stores and specialty stores such as Bed, Bath and Beyond. You simply seal the bottle with a rubber stopper that has a one-way valve (you can buy extra stoppers). The plastic vacuum pump is then placed on top of the stopper; you pump the handle repeatedly until the resistance tightens, indicating much of the air has been pumped out of the bottle.

Refrigerate stoppered and pumped bottles, whether white, pink, or red. Refrigeration of anything slows the spoilage, and your red wine, once removed from the fridge and poured in the glass, will quickly come to serving temperature. If you do not have a vacuum sealer, or if you run out of stoppers (which can happen when you do a comparative tasting of several wines), recork the bottles and refrigerate, and they will last at least a day or two. (You can check my *Wine Buying Guide for Everyone*'s Kitchen Survivor™ grades for an indication of the freshness-longevity of leftovers of specific wines.)

Note: A few wine experts don't think rubber stoppers work, but I have used them for years, particularly in my restaurants, where I have found they extended the life of bottles opened for by-the-glass service at least two days longer than just sealing with the original cork.

Another excellent option is preservation of partial bottles with inert gas. I recommend it especially when you are tasting more expensive wines. There are several brands available for purchase from wine accessories catalogs and wine shops—Wine Life and Private Preserve are two that I have used. These preservers come in a can that feels light, as if it's empty. Inside is an inert gas mixture that is heavier than air. The can's spray nozzle has a long strawlike extension that is inserted into the bottle. A one-second spray fills the empty bottle space with the inert gas, displacing the air inside, which is the key because no air in contact with the wine means no oxidation. Then you quickly replace the cork (make sure the fit is tight). My experience using gas systems in restaurants for very upscale wines by the glass is that they keep well for a week or more. You should also keep in mind that older wines are fragile and deteriorate far more rapidly. With very old wines, you may notice some deterioration even as you drink them, with the scent of a wine that seemed fine when first poured becoming oxidized after some time in the glass.

Sparkling Wines

Your best bet is to purchase "clam shell" Champagne stoppers, with two hinged metal clamps attached to a stopper top with a rubber or plastic gasket for a tight seal. You place the stopper on top, press down, and then close the clamps like a clam's shell, and they anchor to the bottle lip. If you opened your sparkler carefully and didn't "pop" the cork, losing precious carbonation, a stoppered partial bottle will keep its effervescence for at least another day or so. (In my experience, many bubblies keep their fizz and freshness in the fridge far longer—and yet, ironically, fear of flatness keeps so many people from enjoying bubbly regularly.)

Of course, preventing wine leftovers is usually as easy as a phone call. I have found that friends are always happy to do sharing duty over dinner or when I want to do a tasting.

Storing Wine

It is said in the trade that the average aging time for a bottle of wine in this country is seventeen minutes—the amount of time it takes to get the bottle home from the store and pull the cork. The fact is that for most people, storing wine isn't a major issue, because we buy for current consumption. But when you do buy multiple bottles at a time for convenience and quantity discounts, or get extras as gifts, you need to know the best way to store them.

Decorative racks over the fridge in the kitchen may look nice, but they are not a good place for wine. Actually, at five foot one and three-quarters, I find that over the fridge isn't a good place for anything—and I especially want my wine to be handy. What is worse, the heat from the fridge exhaust ensures that every sip is tepid. And like anything else, the warmth also speeds the rate of spoilage of wine. If you are buying a house or renovating, don't fall for this one.

That said, wines are a lot more forgiving than most people think—you do not need 60 percent humidity and a 55-degree temperature to keep from ruining wine. When you're keeping wine for the short-to-medium term (up to a few years), your basic requirements are darkness and a steady temperature. Darkness is necessary because ultraviolet light can contribute to quicker wine spoilage (watch out for wine shops with a lot of stock in the display window). The steady temperature shouldn't be too high. For example, a steady room temperature is fine, but putting your bottles someplace where the temperature can spike may cause their contents to expand, push against the cork and compromise the seal. If oxygen can get in, the wine will then spoil quickly. A basement is of course the natural spot if you have one; if not, try storing wine under the bed, or in a closet or cabinet, ideally near the floor, since heat rises.

Cellaring Wine

"Cellaring" is the trade term for keeping wine for medium- or long-term storage, to give it time to develop and improve in the bottle. And as I have mentioned, it's not for everyone, or every wine. Most of the wine sold in this country is meant to be consumed within two years (for whites) to three years (for reds) of the vintage year listed on the label. And if the wine isn't going to get better, why wait? Enjoy the wine while its fruit and flavor are fresh and vibrant.

The wine categories that actually improve with bottle age in proper storage conditions are: vintage Port from Portugal, classic French red Bordeaux and Burgundy, the top California Cabernet Sauvignons, top Italian red wines (chiefly the Killer B's—Brunello, Barbaresco, and Barolo—and the best super-Tuscans), and classic dessert wines like Sauternes from France. The rest of the world's wines are generally made for early consumption while the fruit is fresh and vibrant.

But you don't have to stop there. The collectible categories that I have listed are those acknowledged by most wine professionals as appropriate for aging. But I like to age some dry white wines, too. I think French Chablis and Côte de Beaune white Burgundies (see Chapter 6) taste better after a few years' bottle age, and the very top estates in the best years develop mind-bending complexity after seven years and longer. I also love to age classic German Riesling Kabinett and Spätlese wines for at least five years, and have tasted some Austrian Rieslings and Loire Valley Chenin Blancs that were absolutely extraordinary with bottle age. Finally, there is Champagne. Although it generally comes to the customer aged and ready to drink, Champagne's high acidity gives it real stamina in the bottle. With age, the taste becomes quite different but is still remarkable—subtler and less effervescent, more like a world-class still wine than a bubbly. If you are looking for something a little different in your cellar, give some of these a try.

CELLARING OPTIONS The collectible wine categories mentioned above share something else in common besides an ability to grow old gracefully: They are expensive. Without a doubt, buying wines like these justifies an investment in proper storage so that your expenditure, and your patience to wait until the wines are in peak drinking condition, will pay off in pleasure.

If you have a cool basement, then your cellar is ready-made except for the racking system. If not, your options include a plug-in storage unit that maintains temperature and humidity, or outfitting a room or part of a room for wine storage, a more expensive and complex choice that makes sense if you have a large collection and can sacrifice an appropriate space in your home. A third option is to rent a home away from home for your wine.

I am often asked if *I* have a wine cellar, and the anwer is finally yes, because the man I married had a beautiful one lovingly built for his wines (by carpenter-artist and friend, Brother Dan). But for years I just used my basement for wine storage. My "racking system" consisted of the cardboard boxes and wooden cases that my little collection came in. My wine cellar budget all went to the wine part.

Regardless of whether your budget supports serviceable or sumptuous, there are two major factors to consider for cellaring wine:

Racks or bins These are a good idea, because they allow you to store the wine on its side (label up), so that the cork is kept moist. Remember that a dry cork can dry out and contract or shrivel, allowing air into the bottle and prematurely oxidizing the wine. The options are many, from budget do-it-yourself component kits made of wood, plastic, or metal to custom redwood bin cubes and racking systems that must be installed by a carpenter unless you are a very handy do-it-yourselfer. In either case, you can buy as much or as little bottle capacity as you need to accommodate your collection.

Temperature and humidity Fifty-five degrees Fahrenheit is considered ideal cellar temperature to preserve wine for very long term storage, but do you really want to wait that long? I think that most of the collectible categories, in great vintages, begin to taste delicious after ten years or so (exceptions include top California Cabernet and top red Burgundy, which is ready after seven years or so; and vintage Port, which needs at least fifteen years). Unless your cellaring time horizon is very long, up to 65 degrees is a fine cellar temperature, as long as it is pretty consistent. As for humidity, about 60 percent is considered ideal, again to prevent the corks from drying out. In very humid cellars, the bottle labels sometimes mildew a bit–not a problem, except from an aesthetic point of view. But then again, an age-worn label has character, too.

WINE STORAGE UNITS These are refrigerators that maintain a constant cellar temperature, which is warmer than your kitchen fridge, for your wines. They range in size from countertop units that hold a dozen bottles (there's no point in these for your home, but they're great for boats or vacation homes) to cabinets that hold several hundred bottles (here's a tip: clear this with your spouse or partner first). Don't bother with the small units sold in appliance super-stores–they are usually just refrigerators with no humidity control, so your corks can dry out. True wine units have humidity-control capability similar to that in cigar humidors. I have successfully used the Eurocave and Vinotheque brands in several restaurants and several friends have them at home, but there are many others available by mail order from the wine accessory companies mentioned earlier.

Check the electrical requirements and measurements of the space where you plan to put the unit, and make sure to check the clearance needed around the unit for the compressor exhaust to vent adequately. The options you'll have to consider are:

- **The look** You can go industrial plain or, if the unit will be a visible focal point in your house, get fancy with wood finish, glass doors, interior low-temperature lighting, and so on, at a cost

- **The racking** You usually have to pay extra for racks that slide in and out, but I recommend them for easy visibility and access to the wines

- **A keyed door lock** This makes sense in most circumstances

- **Temperature zones** The standard unit has one zone whose level you can program, but you can get units that maintain one compartment at refrigerator temperature (for Champagnes, maybe), or two cellar temperatures to have whites at ready-to-serve temperature (around 48 degrees) and reds at cellar temperature (55 to 58 degrees).

BUILDING A WINE CELLAR If you have several thousand bottles, or think you eventually will, you might consider this option. You need a space that you can both insulate and vent without disrupting whatever it is adjacent to. The major components are a temperature and humidity control unit, and these vary in size according to the square footage of your cellar (and the number of bottles, with more needing greater refrigeration capacity); electrical upgrades as needed to accommodate your unit; a lockable door and/or security system; and the aesthetic aspects—racking, lighting, and other interior features such as furniture, art, and so on.

Most such wine cellars are of necessity custom designs, which need to be executed by qualified installers. There's electrical and insulation work to be done, at a minimum, and possibly much more—millwork and carpentry, lighting design and engineering, interior design, and so on. The point is, you can really go hog wild (again, check first with your partner or spouse), and if you do, treat it like any serious renovation and enlist someone qualified to function as a general contractor (preferably with wine cellar experience). Fine wine stores and architecture firms can often provide referrals.

Unless you are a professional builder, beware of "cellar design services" offered by mail-order companies. They can provide you with ideas and basic specifications, but measuring and assessing electrical, venting, and insulation needs should be done on site by a pro, as several collectors I know discovered firsthand. I have worked on several restaurant design projects where the coordination between our general contractor and the equipment company proved crucial—to correct problems with electrical specifications, dimensions, and so on before a custom-built unit was assembled and shipped. And once a custom order is signed off on, you own it unless there are manufacturing defects covered by the warranty (check it carefully!).

For large collections, a computerized inventory management system can be helpful, too. There are custom wine-inventory software systems available on disk or CD-ROM that include critics' scores for collectible wines, regional sorting tools, and other features. I, and many of the professional sommeliers I know, use standard spreadsheet or database software, because it works with the rest of our PC software. This way, we can print out an elegant wine list or menu, and still have the capability to do inventory cost spreadsheets, and so on.

RENT-A-CELLAR Some collectors put their wine in rented temperature-controlled wine lockers. This is a good option if your home doesn't accommodate a cellar or storage unit, or your collection has grown to exceed its capacity. The prices are usually charged per case, and such spaces are often part of larger storage facilities. Retail stores sometimes provide this service, as do some private membership clubs, such as country clubs. The disadvantage, of course, is that you have to plan your wine needs in advance so that you have time to retrieve what you want to drink from the locker. That puts a cramp on the "what do you feel like drinking?" spontaneity that wine lovers are known for—considering and deciding is for many of us an important part of the overall experience because it builds the anticipation and excitement (okay, the longing).

Investing in Wine

If you plan to purchase wine and hold it, with the hope that the price appreciates so that you can sell it for a profit, a cellar investment is definitely worthwhile, because provenance of a wine (what storage conditions it came from) factors hugely into the resale price. Supply and demand of the particular wine is the other major factor in price appreciation potential, because collectors particularly covet certain famous, historical, or critically acclaimed wines. Another factor in a wine's price potential is bottle size, with large bottles commanding a premium because they are rarer, and their aging potential is longer (this is due to the greater volume of wine relative to the air exposure from the space between the liquid and the cork). Age of the wine is yet another factor in a wine's valuation, with prices appreciating as the wine ages, reflecting its increasing rarity as bottles are consumed. Commercial auctions are where most such wines are resold, and of course like other traded items, from stocks to baseball cards, prices have up and down cycles. Given that, a good buying policy is never to choose wines that you wouldn't appreciate in liquid terms—meaning in your glass rather than in cash. This means don't buy wines that aren't to your taste, or pay prices so high you couldn't justify popping the cork.

For me, buying wine is an investment in pleasure. I buy wines to cellar because I look forward to the joy that they will bring to me and my friends and family when they are at peak, and ready to reward my patience. In the English tradition, I bought a case of vintage Port from my son's birth year that we look forward to sharing on his twenty-first birthday. My 1990 Château Palmer will one day be just reward for my *vendangeur*'s blood, sweat, and tears (trust me when I tell you that picking grapes is *really* hard work). And my little cache of Krug vintage Champagne will be a delicious reminder of the liquid that lured me off Wall Street and into the world of wine.

Every day I think how lucky I am to be here. In the wine world, I can never know everything, or even close to it, so I know that I will never be bored. It is a world full of breathtaking natural and sensory beauty that has been enhanced, for a change, by man through the artistry of skilled winemaking, and of beautiful bottles, labels, and glasses.

Through wine, I feel an intimate connection with every moment and every person in history, from ancient times until today—their customs, love affairs, daily meals, celebrations, momentous occasions, and minor moments—and now with my restaurant guests and with you.

For me, wine is a little daily celebration that I don't have to work hard to pull off, and that always delivers what I'd hoped, or more. I hope that I have shown you how very easy it is for you to take part in that, too. Welcome to the fete!

Bordeaux Wine Classifications

According to the Bordeaux Wine Bureau, there is no single comprehensive classification system that ranks Bordeaux's fifty-seven appellations and thousands of wines. But Médoc (the left bank), Graves, Sauternes and Barsac (the sweet wine appellations near Graves), and Saint-Émilion do have their own official classification systems.

The Official Classification of 1855

In the more than one hundred years since the 1855 classification, which was originally ordered by Napoleon III, there has been only one change. Following tireless lobbying by the Baron Philippe de Rothschild, owner of Château Mouton-Rothschild, Mouton was elevated from a second growth to a first growth in 1973.

(The appellation name for each château is in parentheses)

FIRST GROWTHS (PREMIERS CRUS)
Château Lafite-Rothschild (Pauillac)
Château Margaux (Margaux)
Château Latour (Pauillac)
Château Haut-Brion (Pessac-Léognan)
Château Mouton-Rothschild (Pauillac)

SECOND GROWTHS (DEUXIÈMES CRUS)
Château Rausan-Ségla (Margaux)
Château Rauzan-Gassies (Margaux)
Château Léoville-Las-Cases (Saint-Julien)
Château Léoville-Poyferré (Saint-Julien)
Château Léoville-Barton (Saint-Julien)
Château Durfort-Vivens (Margaux)
Château Gruaud-Larose (Saint-Julien)
Château Lascombes (Margaux)
Château Brane-Cantenac (Margaux)
Château Pichon-Longueville-Baron (Pauillac)
Château Pichon-Longueville, Comtesse de
  Lalande (Pauillac)
Château Ducru-Beaucaillou (Saint-Julien)
Château Cos d'Estournel (Saint-Estèphe)
Château Montrose (Saint-Estèphe)

THIRD GROWTHS (TROISIÈMES CRUS)
Château Kirwan (Margaux)
Château d'Issan (Margaux)
Château Lagrange (Saint-Julien)
Château Langoa-Barton (Saint-Julien)
Château Giscours (Margaux)
Château Malescot Saint-Exupéry (Margaux)
Château Boyd-Cantenac (Margaux)
Château Cantenac-Brown (Margaux)
Château Palmer (Margaux)
Château La Lagune (Haut-Médoc)
Château Desmirail (Margaux)
Château Calon-Ségur (Saint-Estèphe)
Château Ferrière (Margaux)
Château Marquis d'Alesme-Becker
  (Margaux)

FOURTH GROWTHS (QUATRIÈMES CRUS)
Château Saint-Pierre (Saint-Julien)
Château Talbot (Saint-Julien)
Château Branaire-Ducru (Saint-Julien)
Château Duhart-Milon-Rothschild (Pauillac)
Château Pouget (Margaux)
Château La Tour-Carnet (Haut Médoc)
Château Lafon-Rochet (Saint-Estèphe)
Château Beychevelle (Saint-Julien)
Château Prieuré-Lichine (Margaux)
Château Marquis-de-Terme (Margaux)

FIFTH GROWTHS (CINQUIÈMES CRUS)
Château Pontet-Canet (Pauillac)
Château Batailley (Pauillac)
Château Haut-Batailley (Pauillac)
Château Grand-Puy-Lacoste (Pauillac)
Château Grand-Puy-Ducasse (Pauillac)
Château Lynch-Bages (Pauillac)
Château Lynch-Moussas (Pauillac)
Château Dauzac (Margaux)
Château Mouton-Baronne-Philippe (Pauillac)
Château du Tertre (Margaux)
Château Haut-Bages-Libéral (Pauillac)
Château Pédesclaux (Pauillac)
Château Belgrave (Haut-Médoc)
Château de Camensac (Haut-Médoc)
Château Cos-Labory (Saint-Estèphe)
Château Clerc-Milon (Pauillac)
Château Croizet-Bages (Pauillac)
Château Cantemerle (Haut-Médoc)

(The commune name for each château is in parentheses)

FIRST GREAT GROWTH
 (PREMIER CRU SUPÉRIEUR)
Château d'Yquem (Sauternes)

FIRST GROWTHS (PREMIERS CRUS)
Château La Tour-Blanche (Bommes)
Château Lafaurie-Peyraguey (Bommes)
Château Clos Haut-Peyraguey (Bommes)
Château de Rayne-Vigneau (Bommes)
Château Suduiraut (Preignac)
Château Coutet (Barsac)
Château Climens (Barsac)
Château Guiraud (Sauternes)
Château Rieussec (Fargues)
Château Rabaud-Promis (Bommes)
Château Sigalas-Rabaud (Bommes)

SECOND GROWTHS (DEUXIÈMES CRUS)
Château de Myrat (Barsac)
Château Doisy-Daëne (Barsac)
Château Doisy-Dubroca (Barsac)
Château Doisy-Védrines (Barsac)
Château d'Arche (Sauternes)
Château Filhot (Sauternes)
Château Broustet (Barsac)
Château Nairac (Barsac)
Château Caillou (Barsac)
Château Suau (Barsac)
Château de Malle (Preignac)
Château Romer-du-Hayot (Fargues)
Château Lamothe-Despujols (Sauternes)
Château Lamothe-Guignard (Sauternes)

The red and white wines of the Graves region were first classified in 1953, but the classification only became official with the 1959 ranking. Within each category, the châteaus are not ranked by quality.

(The commune name for each château is in parentheses)

CLASSIFIED RED WINES OF GRAVES
Château Bouscaut (Cadaujac)
Château Haut-Bailly (Léognan)
Château Carbonnieux (Léognan)
Domaine de Chevalier (Léognan)
Château de Fieuzal (Léognan)
Château d'Olivier (Léognan)
Château Malartic-Lagravière (Léognan)
Château La Tour-Martillac (Martillac)
Château Smith-Haut-Lafitte (Martillac)
Château Haut-Brion (Pessac)
Château La Mission-Haut-Brion (Talence)
Château Pape-Clément (Pessac)
Château Latour-Haut-Brion (Talence)

CLASSIFIED WHITE WINES OF GRAVES
Château Bouscaut (Cadaujac)
Château Carbonnieux (Léognan)
Château Domaine de Chevalier (Léognan)
Château d'Olivier (Léognan)
Château Malartic-Lagravière (Léognan)
Château La Tour-Martillac (Martillac)
Château Laville-Haut-Brion (Talence)
Château Couhins-Lurton (Villenave d'Ornan)
Château Couhins (Villenave d'Ornan)
Château Haut-Brion (Pessac) (added in 1960)

Bordeaux Wine Classifications

THE SAINT-ÉMILION CLASSIFICATION

In 1954, at the the request of the Syndicat de Defense des Vins de Saint-Émilion, the INAO (Institute National des Appellations d'Origine) established a classification of wines from the Saint-Émilion appellation. The classification is updated every ten years, to reflect changes in quality. The two top ranks are Grand Cru Classé and Premier Grand Cru Classé. Only châteaus from the Saint-Émilion Grand Cru appellation are eligible for these top two classes. Following the original classification, revisions in 1969, 1979, 1984, and 1996 resulted in slight changes to the rankings. The current classification includes thirteen Premier Grand Cru Classés and fifty-five Grand Cru Classés.

FIRST GREAT GROWTH CATEGORY A
   (PREMIER GRAND CRU CLASSÉ)
Château Ausone
Château Cheval Blanc

FIRST GREAT GROWTH CATEGORY B
Château Angélus
Château Beau-Séjour Bécot
Château Beauséjour (Duffau-LaGarosse)
Château Belair
Château Canon
Château Figeac
Château La Gaffeliere
Château Magdelaine
Château Pavie
Château Trottevieille
Clos Fourtet

GREAT GROWTHS (GRAND CRU CLASSÉS)
Château Balestard la Tonnelle
Château Bellevue
Château Bergat
Château Berliquet
Château Cadet-Bon
Château Cadet-Piola
Château Canon la Gaffelière
Château Cap de Mourlin
Château Chauvin
Château Clos des Jacobins
Château Corbin
Château Corbin-Michotte
Château Curé Bon
Château Dassault
Château Faurie-de-Souchard
Château Fonplégade
Château Fonroque
Château Franc Mayne
Château Grand Mayne
Château Grand Pontet

Château Guadet Saint-Julien
Château Haut Corbin
Château Haut Sarpe Saint-Christophe
   des Bardes
Château L'Arrosée
Château La Clotte
Château La Clusière
Château La Couspaude
Château La Dominique
Château La Serre
Château La Tour du Pin-Figeac
   (Giraud-Belivier)
Château La Tour du Pin-Figeac (J.M. Moueix)
Château La Tour Figeac
Château Lamarzelle
Château Laniote
Château Larcis Ducasse Saint-Laurent
   des Combes
Château Larmande
Château Laroque Saint-Christophe des Bardes
Château Laroze
Château Le Prieuré
Château Les Grandes Murailles
Château Matras
Château Moulin du Cadet
Château Pavie Decesse
Château Pavie Macquin
Château Petite Faurie de Soutard
Château Ripeau
Château Saint-George Côte Pavie
Château Soutard
Château Tertre Daugay
Château Troplong-Mondot
Château Villemaurine
Château Yon-Figeac
Clos de l'Oratoire
Clos Saint-Martin
Couvent des Jacobins

There is no classification of Pomerol châteaus, which is ironic when you consider that Bordeaux's most expensive and famous wine, which some would call its best, is a Pomerol— Château Petrus. Here is a list of some of the acknowledged greats. Pomerol is a small appellation and demand is high, so most of the wines are quite expensive.

Château Petrus

Château Le Pin

Château Gazin

Château Clinet

Château Trotanoy

Château La Conseillante

Château L'Église-Clinet

Château Le Bon Pasteur

Château L'Évangile

Château Petit-Village

Château De Sales

Château Latour-à-Pomerol

Vieux Château Certan

Château La Fleur Petrus

Château La Croix de Gay

Château Le Gay

Château La Fleur

Champagne House Styles

To help your selection, here is a guide to the light, medium, or full house style of the major Champagne brands.

Light

A. Charbaut et Fils, Ayala, Billecart-Salmon, Deutz, DeVenoge, Lanson, Laurent-Perrier, Perrier-Jouët, Pol Roger, Pommery, Ruinart, Taillevent, Taittinger

Medium

Delamotte, Jacquart, Jacquesson, Moët Chandon, G.H. Mumm, Nicolas Feuillatte, Philipponnat, Piper-Heidsieck

Full

Bollinger, Charles Heidsieck, Drappier, Gosset, Alfred Gratien, Heidsieck Monopole, Henriot, Jacques Selosse, Krug, Salon, Veuve Clicquot